VS 4
1997

Vietnam

Education Financing

The World Bank
Washington, D.C.

World Bank Country Studies are among the many reports originally prepared for internal use as part of the continuing analysis by the Bank of the economic and related conditions of its developing member countries and of its dialogues with the governments. Some of the reports are published in this series with the least possible delay for the use of governments and the academic, business and financial, and development communities. The typescript of this paper therefore has not been prepared in accordance with the procedures appropriate to formal printed texts, and the World Bank accepts no responsibility for errors. Some sources cited in this paper may be informal documents that are not readily available.

The World Bank does not guarantee the accuracy of the data included in this publication and accepts no responsibility whatsoever for any consequence of their use. The boundaries, colors, denominations, and other information shown on any map in this volume do not imply on the part of the World Bank Group any judgment on the legal status of any territory or the endorsement or acceptance of such boundaries.

Cover photo: Vietnamese school children by Christopher Shaw.

ISSN: 0253-2123

Library of Congress Cataloging-in-Publication Data

Vietnam : education financing
     p.   cm. — (A World Bank country study)
    Includes bibliographical references.
    ISBN 0-8213-4023-9
    1. Education—Vietnam—Finance—Statistics. 2. Education—
Economic aspects—Vietnam—Statistics. 3. Education and state—
Vietnam.   I. World Bank.   II. Series.
LB2826.6.V5V54   1997
379.597—dc21

                                      97-30279
                                       CIP

CONTENTS

TABLES

Annex Tables

MAP OF VIETNAM

Map No. IBRD 28250: Map of Vietnam

ACKNOWLEDGMENTS

The VEFSS report was prepared by a team co-managed by the Government of Vietnam and the World Bank and comprising staff and consultants provided by the following funding agencies: Swiss Development Cooperation, the East Asia Multidisciplinary Advisory Team of the International Labour Office, the Australian Department of Employment, Education, Training and Youth Affairs, the Australian Bureau of Statistics and L'Institut Français de Recherche Scientifique pour le Dévelopement en Coopération, as well as the World Bank. The research team was led, on the Vietnamese side, by *Phan Thu Huong* (Chairperson of the Government Steering Committee that guided the VEFSS study) and, on the donors' side, by *Peter R. Moock* (World Bank Task Manager and author of the report). Major contributors to the research and report drafting included *Ta Ngoc Chau, Rapti Goonesekere, Harry Anthony Patrinos* and *Nicholas Prescott*. VEFSS Steering Committee members included *Pham Kim Cung, Do Minh Cuong, Quan Ngoc Duong, Tran Thi Thu Ha, Nguyen Quang Kinh, Nguyen Le Minh, Nguyen Van Phuc, Pham Thanh Tam, Pham Van Thuan, Pham Trung San,* and *Nguyen Van Tien*. Other contributors to the study included *Michel Carton, Paul Glewwe, Jean-Yves Martin, Jean-Luc Maurer, Ivan Neville, Pham Thanh Nghi, Nguyen X. Nguyen, Xavier Oudin, Richard Phillips, Trevor Riordan, Christos Sakellariou, Christopher Shaw, Shobhana Sosale* and *Maureen Woodhall*. Special thanks are given to the Asian Development Bank and James Knowles, ADB consultant, for sharing preliminary information from the Vietnam Social Sector Survey and tailoring special data runs to the needs of VEFSS. Peer reviewers in the World Bank were Elizabeth King, George Psacharopoulos and James Socknat. The document was processed by Emily Mwai and Denise West.

The VEFSS Steering Committee comprised the following members: Mrs. *Phan Thu Huong* (Director, Department of Science, Education and Environment, MPI); Mr. *Pham Kim Cung* (Deputy Director, Department of Science, Education and Environment, MPI); Mr. *Nguyen Van Phuc* (Vice Director, Foreign Economic Relations Department, MPI); Mrs. *Pham Thanh Tam* (Expert, Department of Science, Education and Environment, MPI); Mrs. *Tran Thi Thu Ha* (Deputy Director, Social Cultural Department, MOF); Mr. *Nguyen Van Tien* (Director, Department of Social and Environment Statistics, GSO); Mr. *Nguyen Le Minh* (Vice Director, Managing Board of the National Programme for Employment Promotion, MOLISA); Mr. *Nguyen Quang Kinh* (Director, Department of Planning and Finance, MOET); as well as the chairpersons of the four VEFSS Working Groups, Mr. *Quan Ngoc Duong* (MOET -- Education Statistics); Mr. *Pham Van Thuan* (MOF -- Public Finance); Mr. *Do Minh Cuong* (MOLISA -- Labor Market Linkages); and Mr. *Pham Trung San* (MOET -- Private Sector Development). Mr. *Phan Quang Trung*, Vice Minister in the Office of Government, also lent valuable support to the study from its inception.

ABBREVIATIONS AND ACRONYMS

ABS	Australian Bureau of Statistics
ADB	Asian Development Bank
COV	Coefficient of variation (standard deviation divided by arithmetic mean)
CPHRS	MOLISA Center for Population and Human Resources Studies
DEETYA	Department of Employment, Education, Training and Youth Affairs (Australia)
E&T	Education and training
EASMAT	East Asia Multidisciplinary Advisory Team
FTE	Full-time equivalent (student)
GDP	Gross domestic product
GER	Gross enrollment rate (GPER, GSER and GTER for primary, secondary and tertiary, respectively)
GFS	Government Finance Statistics
GSO	Government Statistics Office
HCEF	Human capital earnings function
HECRP	Higher Education Consolidation and Reform Project
HEGTS	Higher Education Graduate Tracer Study (1995-96 **VEFSS** survey implemented by ILSSA)
HEI	Higher education institution
HEIFS	Higher Education Institutional Finance Survey (1995 VEFSS survey implemented by MOET)
HPAE	High performing Asian economy
IEA	International Association for the Evaluation of Educational Achievement
ILO	International Labor Office
ILSSA	MOLISA Institute of Labor Sciences and Social Affairs
KEDI	Korean Education Development Institute
IMF	International Monetary Fund
MOET	Ministry of Education and Training
MOF	Ministry of Finance
MOLISA	Ministry of Labor, Invalids and Social Affairs
MPI	Ministry of Planning and Investment
NER	Net enrollment ratio (NPER, NSER and NTER for primary, secondary and tertiary, respectively)
NIE	Newly industrializing economy
ODA	Official Development Assistance
OECD	Organization of Economic Cooperation and Development
OLS	Ordinary least squares (regression analysis)
ORSTOM	French Research Institute for Development in Cooperation (*L'Institut Français de Recherche Scientifique pour le Développement en Coopération*)

RLMVTS	Rural Labor Markets and Vocational Training Study (1996 VEFSS survey implemented by CPHRS)
RMSM	Revised Minimum Standards Model
SDC	Swiss Development Cooperation
SDLMS	Skill Development and Labor Market Study (three inter-related 1996 surveys implemented by GSO under VEFSS auspices)
S&T	Science and technology
UNDP	United Nations Development Fund
UNESCO	United Nation Educational, Scientific and Cultural Organization
UPE	Universal Primary Education
VEFSS	Vietnam Education Financing Sector Study
VLSS	Vietnam Living Standards Survey (1992-93 national household survey financed by UNDP and implemented by GSO)
VOTECH	Vocational and technical education and training
VSSS	Vietnam Social Sector Survey (GSO survey financed by ADB)
VTC	Vocational training center

CURRENCY EQUIVALENTS

Currency Unit = Dong
US$1.00 = VND 11,013 (June 1996)

US$1.00 = VND 11,022 (1995)
US$1.00 = VND 10,955 (1994)
US$1.00 = VND 10,640 (1993)
US$1.00 = VND 11,150 (1992)
US$1.00 = VND 9,274 (1991)

GOVERNMENT FISCAL YEAR

January 1 to December 31

GOVERNMENT SCHOOL YEAR

September to June

VIETNAMESE PHRASES

Ban Công	Semi-public (educational institution)
Bo Giáo Duc và Đào Tao	Ministry of Education and Training (MOET)
Đào Tao	Training (includes higher education)
Dân Lâp	People-founded (educational institution)
Đoi Moi	Renovation, new life
Giáo Duc	Education
Pho Tiên Si	Candidate's degree
Thac Si	Master's degree
Tiên Si	Doctorate degree
Trung Tâm Day Nghê	Vocational training center (VTC)
Trung Tâm Đào Tao và Bao Duong Nghê	Vocational center for training and upgrading skills
Trung Tâm Day Nghê Cho Hoc Sinh Phô Thông	VTC for upper secondary students
Trung Tâm Xúc Tiên Viêc Làm	Center for employment promotion
Truong Day Nghê	Secondary vocational school
Truong Trung Hoc Chuyên Nghiêp	Secondary technical school
Truong Trung Hoc Day Nghê	Secondary vocational school
Truong Trung Hoc Phô Thông	General (academic) upper secondary school
Tu Lâp	Private (educational institution)

ABSTRACT

This study looks at the system of education and training in Vietnam and poses the question: What changes in educational policies will ensure that students who pass through the system today will acquire the knowledge, skills and attitudes needed for Vietnam to complete the transition successfully from a planned to a market economy? The report analyzes the present structure of educational costs and estimates the increase in public expenditure implied by enrollment targets set by Government and the Party. As a starting point, the analysis assumes that the relative shares of government and private beneficiaries in financing education's costs will not change, nor will the technology by which education is produced -- in other words, no policies would be introduced to reduce the cost per graduate, and none to enhance the quality of what is learned in Vietnam's schools, training centers, colleges and universities. These assumptions are then relaxed. The report reviews the experience since 1950 of eight "East Asian miracle" countries (Japan, Hong Kong, the Republic of Korea, Singapore, Taipei-China, Indonesia, Malaysia and Thailand) and draws lessons for Vietnam's education and training system. The report then discusses a number of "promising policy options." Some of these address issues of quality, others are intended to reduce unit costs, and still others would shift some of the costs from the State Budget to private beneficiaries. The report considers the trade-offs among conflicting objectives for Vietnam's education and training system -- namely, higher enrollments, improved quality and increased equity.

EXECUTIVE SUMMARY

Although Vietnam is a poor country with only $250 of gross domestic product per person in 1996, its recent economic growth record has been robust, especially since 1986 when the Government launched a macroeconomic program of renovation and reform. With 91 percent of children between the ages of 5 and 10 enrolled in school and 88 percent of the working-age population reported to be literate, Vietnam can also point to an impressive educational record, even in comparison with many economies at higher income levels. However, as the global community bids farewell to the twentieth century and enters a new millennium, emerging market forces within Vietnam, as well as examples and competition from other economies, especially Vietnam's successful East Asian neighbors, raise important new challenges for the country's system of education and training (E&T).

The Government of Vietnam has set ambitious targets for increasing enrollments in E&T institutions. The question is posed: What policies are required to ensure that the outputs of an expanded E&T system will possess the knowledge, skills and attitudes demanded by private sector employers and critical to the smooth functioning of a leaner public sector in the future? This Study, referred to in the text of the report as the Vietnam Education Finincing Sector Study (VEFSS), was undertaken as a collaborative effort of Government, the World Bank and other funding agencies to address this question.

More E&T implies incremental recurrent costs. This report analyzes the present structure of costs so as to estimate the rise in public expenditure implied by an expansion of the E&T system. The report assumes, as a starting point, that the shares of government and private beneficiaries in financing E&T will remain the same as they were when this study was conducted, and also that production technology will not change (that is, no policies will be introduced to reduce either the cost per student-year or cost per graduate, and none to enhance the quality of E&T's outputs). These assumptions are then relaxed, each in turn. Based on VEFSS' review of present financing patterns, the report discusses the possibilities and advantages of shifting the financial burden of meeting E&T's full economic costs, with government's share either rising or falling at different levels of the system in relation to that of private beneficiaries. Finally, the study considers alternative production technologies amenable to policy change and designed to enhance E&T's internal and external efficiency.

Key Policy Instruments.

From the perspective of public policy, the study distinguishes three key policy instruments. The Government of Vietnam has used a mix of all three in recent years in pursuit of its policy objectives for the sector:

(a)   **Subsidies**. Government can finance a higher or lower proportion of the total costs of the nation's E&T activities out of the State Budget. It can also re-direct public subsidies, to finance more at one level and less at another. Finally, government can put its financing into public-sector institutions directly, or it can channel all or some of it to individual students, who can then use the subsidies to attend institutions and programs of their own choosing, whether in the public sector or in the private. The former approach (the norm seen in most countries including Vietnam) is called *supply-side financing*. The latter (which some economists recommend in the interest of enhancing efficiency in the provision of E&T, by making institutions compete for student clients, and also as a way of targeting subsidies more effectively) is called *demand-side financing*.

(b)   **Cost-recovery**. Whatever part of E&T's full costs that government does *not* subsidize must usually be covered by the users themselves, i.e., by the individuals enrolled as students, or by their families.[1] The earnings foregone by those who are studying and not working are high, especially at the upper levels of the E&T system. In Vietnam and elsewhere, most such indirect costs are financed privately, the exception being the indirect costs of students in tertiary education who are given scholarships, or receive student loans at below-market interest rates; these subsidies can be viewed as off-setting a part of the students' foregone earnings. To help finance the direct costs of E&T, government policy in Vietnam now permits public institutions to charge fees at all levels of E&T except at the primary level. In addition, informal charges and incidental costs must be met by individuals enrolled at all levels including primary. The net result is that Vietnam has reached quite a high level of cost-recovery in E&T. Private financing is estimated here to be above 40 percent of the total direct costs of E&T across all levels. It is highest in pre-school and secondary education (around 60 percent), nearly as high in primary (just under 50 percent) but relatively low in tertiary (19 percent) and in vocational and technical education and training (VOTECH -- 12 percent).[2]

(c)   **Private sector development**. The third policy instrument at government's disposal are incentives (including the removal of legal constraints) that may encourage non-government providers to play a larger role in the E&T sector.

---

[1] In some instances, a part of the costs of an E&T program may be subsidized by some other munificent entity -- such as an educational foundation, or by the education institution itself out of private contributions that it receives from those who graduated in the past, but in Vietnam, it would appear that these contributions do not yet play a major role in education finance.

[2] Specifying cost-recovery as a *separate* policy instrument and defining it as the difference between E&T's full costs and government subsidies may seem redundant. Whatever government does not pay, individuals must pay. In this sense, as soon as the one policy is set, the other is set as well. This would indeed be the case if E&T's full costs were a given. At least some of the costs covered by individual households are, however, *optional*. Textbooks, for example, are in Vietnam the responsibility of families to buy. A poor family might decide to send its child to school but lack the income needed to buy all of the recommended textbooks. In this sense, cost-recovery can vary even after the government's policy in regard to subsidies is set. If a family's income rises, or if its perception of the value of discretionary educational outlays rises, then E&T's full costs will also rise, as will the proportion of full costs "recovered."

Private provision relieves the burden on the public administration, which then does not have to carry the full load of provision, and it also relieves the public financial burden to the extent that students in private institutions do not usually receive public subsidies.

Structure of the Report.

Following Chapter 1, which sets the general context for a consideration of E&T costs and financing in Vietnam, Chapter 2 explains how the system is presently organized and managed. Chapter 2 also portrays sectoral achievements in terms of student enrollments, both absolute and in relation to population numbers. The achievements are impressive given Vietnam's present income level and how little time has passed since the war's end and political reunification of the country. Progress is quite uneven, however, with education participation rates in some regions and in some districts of the country much higher than in others. The differences reflect a combination of income differences, geography (it is, for example, logistically difficult for government to deliver and for people to access educational services in the high mountain areas or on remote islands) and factors that would be expected to affect the returns to investment in E&T. Chapter 2 continues by describing those who teach in Vietnam's E&T institutions, and how much they get paid relative to other workers with comparable education and experience. The chapter concludes by describing the extent to which "non-public" institutions have emerged in recent years and helped to increase enrollments, while imposing low or zero costs on the public budget.[3] The role of the non-public sector has been concentrated to date in pre-school and upper secondary education, although by 1996 there were also 11 semi-public and people-founded tertiary institutions, all of them small and located in just three cities (Hanoi, Ho Chi Minh City and Da Nang).

Chapter 3 provides an assessment of the current financing system, distinguishing first the allocations in the central and provincial components of the State Budget. The chapter then looks at off-budget sources of public finance. These, which include Official Development Assistance and spending incurred by the lowest level of local government (Vietnam's 10,320 communes), were not, in the past, included in the budget figures of MOET and MOF. The chapter continues by examining private sources of funding for E&T. Private funding is the backbone of support to the small but growing non-public sector, but it has also become a significant factor in supporting public sector institutions (in which over 90 percent of Vietnam's students are currently enrolled).

Chapter 4 combines the information on enrollments and on flows of funds from public and private sources to calculate unit costs in Vietnamese E&T -- with "unit cost"

---

[3] Vietnam distinguishes three categories of non-public E&T. "Semi-public" institutions are owned by the state and managed by public authorities; "people-founded" institutions are owned and managed by non-government organizations; "private" institutions, which at this time are permitted only in pre-school education and VOTECH, are owned and managed by private individuals. In all three, operating costs are financed largely, if not entirely, out of student fees.

defined first as the economic *cost per student-year* and then as the economic *cost per graduate* at each level. Chapter 4 continues by analyzing some of the anomalies in unit costs across levels and between different regions of the country. Various ways are suggested by which costs could be reduced, flow-through efficiency increased and student learning enhanced.

Chapter 5 turns to issues of external efficiency and equity. To assess E&T's external efficiency, the information on unit costs is merged with information from other sources on the labor market returns to investments in the sector. The study concludes that "social rates of return" to investments in E&T[4] are at or above 10 percent in the case of primary education, but, at this time, lower in the case of VOTECH, general secondary and tertiary education. The study surmises, based on patterns observed in other transition economies and on signs in Vietnam that earnings differentials across education levels are becoming less compressed, that rates of return have increased since the late 1980s and will continue to increase as the market reforms take stronger hold. The study also shows that private rates of return are high in the case of primary education (between 10 and 20 percent depending on who gets the education and in which sector -- public or private -- he or she finds employment), and they are nearly as high in the case of tertiary education. They are lower at this time in the case of VOTECH and general secondary education.

Chapter 5 concludes with a focus on equity issues, examining how much different groups in Vietnam spend to receive whatever E&T they actually get, and assessing the relative burden of this expenditure in light of differences in their incomes. The findings here, and in related analysis presented in Chapter 3, suggest that there is considerable scope to use all three policy instruments outlined above to achieve a more equitable system of E&T in Vietnam.

Finally, in Chapter 6 the perspective of the report shifts from one that is essentially retrospective and inward-looking, focusing on Vietnam itself, to one that looks ahead to the next decade and draws lessons, where possible, from other countries outside Vietnam. The chapter begins with a review of the experience of eight countries in the region identified in a recent study as "high performing Asian economies" (HPAEs) -- Japan, Hong Kong, the Republic of Korea, Singapore, Taipei-China, Indonesia, Malaysia and Thailand (World Bank 1993a). Although the HPAEs are all well ahead of Vietnam in terms of GDP per capita today, some of the HPAEs had income levels comparable to Vietnam's present level as recently as the 1950s (Thailand) or 1960s (Indonesia). Quite reasonably, Vietnam may look to these countries as models to emulate in choosing their own economic and educational policies over this decade and the next. Although the HPAEs did not follow all of the same policies in the same sequence, the development of their E&T systems did have many things in common -- an emphasis on

---

[4] As estimated in this study, and elsewhere in the literature, the "social rate of return" reflects the *full economic costs* of an education investment but reflects the *private returns only* -- because *external benefits*, while easy to think about and discuss, are very difficult if not impossible to measure, given present estimation techniques.

primary education coverage and quality; a system of user charges kept quite low in primary education but increasing with successively higher levels of education; attention given to VOTECH, especially in the early years, but declining over time; and relatively high student-teacher ratios (to keep educational costs under control), and generous remuneration for teachers (to attract and retain qualified and dedicated individuals in the profession).

By comparison with the HPAEs, when they had income levels in the past equal to Vietnam's today, Vietnam has made very good *quantitative progress* in its system of E&T. Enrollment rates are at least as high in Vietnam today as they were in the HPAEs when their incomes measured $250 per capita in today's dollars. Despite this, Vietnam's plan for expansion of the system over the next decade calls for rapid enrollment increases, which exceed the projected growth of the relevant population groups for all levels and types of E&T. The largest increases are planned for lower secondary education and for vocational education and training. Chapter 6 costs the Government's planned enrollment increases and concludes that the Government's targets are affordable from the point of view of the State Budget given the following assumptions: (a) Government-World Bank projections of economic growth and growth of the State Budget are both met; (b) E&T's share of the budget remains at 13.3 percent,[5] its level in 1994; (c) unit costs and the level of cost recovery in E&T do not change (though changes may, in fact, be warranted to address issues of quality and equity).

Promising Policy Options.

Adequate financing, however, is only one of several factors that must be considered in evaluating an education sector strategy and investment plan. The final section of Chapter 6 draws on findings in the first five chapters and addresses the trade-offs involved among conflicting objectives for the sector, namely, higher enrollments, enhanced quality and increased equity. The discussion considers current policies for the sector and suggests alternatives that seem especially promising in light of the report's findings and Vietnam's broad social and economic goals. Certain policies are suggested that would lower the unit costs of E&T. Other policies would shift some of the costs of E&T from the State Budget to private beneficiaries, and still others would be cost-neutral in fiscal terms. All such measures deserve careful consideration.

Several of the policies discussed in Chapter 6, however, especially those directed at enhancing the quality of E&T in Vietnam, will require additional government spending. Costing all of the suggested policies in detail is beyond the scope of this study, although it should be undertaken by Government as a next step. One expensive quality-enhancing option (increasing instructional hours, by extending the school year from 165 days to 185 days and by extending the school day from four hours to five hours) *is* costed in Chapter 6, to demonstrate the considerable expense of this single reform and to draw policymakers' attention to the fact that serious trade-offs will need to be faced in any

---

[5] This is E&T's share of the "discretionary" (i.e., net of interest payments) *recurrent* budget.

major future reform program. Only some of the desirable quality-enhancing measures will be affordable given the study's budget projections for the next decade. To implement more policy options will require the identification and tapping of new sources of revenue, or the reallocation of the State Budget so that a higher share goes to E&T.

Allocation of Subsidies in General Education.

A key finding of VEFSS has been that public expenditure per student in primary education is low -- in two different senses: (a) *relative to other levels/types of E&T* (public expenditure per student is 13 times higher in technical and tertiary education than it is in primary education), and (b) *relative to private spending on E&T*. On average, across all Vietnamese households, for every VND 100 of government spending on primary education, households spend VND 80. In secondary and in vocational E&T, the ratio is as high or even higher than this. However, in technical education, for every VND 100 of government spending, households spend only VND 47, and in tertiary education VND 44. This pattern suggests an inequitable distribution of public subsidies for education, a conclusion that is reinforced when one looks at the consumption levels of households with family members enrolled at different levels.

Net enrollments rates (NERs) are correlated with income at all levels of E&T, but much less so at the primary level. The NPER of Vietnamese households in the poorest consumption quintile was 68 percent in 1992-93, when the Vietnam Living Standards Survey (VLSS) was carried out; it was 86 percent in the richest quintile. In tertiary education, however, the situation is dramatically different. In 1992-93, families in the poorest quintile had virtually no representation in higher education institutions. Participation was marginally higher in the middle three quintiles; the NTER reached 1.9 percent for those in the fourth quintile. The NTER was 7.0 percent, however, for those in the top quintile. These figures suggest that participation in college and university education is a privilege reserved almost exclusively for high income families, a finding that is all too common in many countries.

The high private costs of education certainly contribute to the high dropout rates at the primary level and also explain much of the inter-regional and inter-provincial variation in participation rates. The high participation rates across the board in Grade 1 of primary school reflect government campaigns to encourage enrollment and demonstrate the high value that Vietnamese families place on education, but some poor families soon find that they are unable to afford the "voluntary contributions" and other education-related costs. They are forced as a result to withdraw their children from school. To provide opportunities for poor children to remain in school, Government should consider a program of *targeted subsidies*, directed at poor families who cannot afford the private costs (direct plus indirect) of primary education. Of course, it is difficult to distinguish families who are truly poor from other families who may be less poor but quite happy, nevertheless, to substitute public financing for their own. To minimize the "free-rider" problem, the special subsidies for primary education will need to be targeted, not at individual families, but at communities identified by sample survey methods to have high concentrations of poverty.

Cost Recovery in Tertiary Education.

The shares of public spending allocated to higher and technical education are each about 15 percent of the E&T budget. However, together these two levels account for fewer than 3 percent of all of Vietnam's students. The fact that students at the top end of the E&T system tend to come from wealthier families has already been noted. Not so much for the savings generated, but for reasons of equity, Government is encouraged to consider policies that would increase cost recovery at the upper levels. A VEFSS higher education survey concluded that student fees actually declined between 1993 and 1995 in the 100 higher education institutions (HEIs) included in the survey, from 44 percent to 24 percent of expenditures. This may have been an accident of the particular three years covered in the survey. The percentage could revert to the 1993 level when the fee structure is next revised. Revising it soon and regularly, however, should be a priority of government policy, as there is virtually no justification for private costs to be higher as a percentage of full economic costs at the basic level than at the highest levels.

Another reason to aim for high levels of cost recovery is that the private rate of return to family investments in tertiary education is high (especially in relation to the measured social rate of return, which is low when compared with the social rate of return to investment in primary education). Students who attend colleges and universities should be expected to share significantly in the burden of the costs of their education, *both* because they come from wealthy homes to begin with, *and* because they will earn more in later life as a result of having received tertiary training. A final reason for wanting to see more cost recovery in higher education is to guide the HEIs in deciding which programs to expand and which ones to contract or eliminate. Many higher education administrators at this early stage in Vietnam's transition to a market economy are waiting for instructions to be given by the government ministry which has responsibility for the particular HEI. Such signals should now come from the students themselves and from a much broader range of employers in the marketplace, including private sector employers. In a market economy, HEIs should be given substantial autonomy to set their own programs and also to raise and then retain revenues that can be used to enhance the quality of the programs offered and research produced. Greater cost recovery ensures that the outputs of higher education are demand-driven and socially useful.

Whereas achieving a greater degree of cost recovery should be an objective of government policy, complementary measures will need to be adopted to ensure that students from poor homes are not financially constrained from attending higher education courses for which they are academically qualified. Again, a program of targeted subsidies is a possible solution. At this top level of education, unlike in general education, the special subsidies should be granted based on evidence supplied by the individual family of its inability to bear a full load of the private costs of tertiary education. The cost of verifying this information is probably worthwhile at this level, because of the larger subsidies and fewer families involved. An alternative is to expand the student loan program now being piloted in Hanoi, but this program should be modified so that interest paid on student loans is at the full market rate and not subsidized. A mixed program that provides "social scholarships" for needy students and access to loans at market rates for others who do not qualify for scholarship but want assistance would appear to be the most efficient way of achieving a higher level of cost recovery in higher education while, at the same time, expanding opportunities for the poor.

Vocational Education.

The two programs that will increase substantially given the Government's medium-term targets for the sector are lower secondary education and vocational education and training. To give priority to the expansion of lower secondary education is understandable, given that UPE has already, or nearly, been achieved. There is a big gap between the NER in primary education (91 percent) and that in lower secondary (45 percent), and there is now pressure to expand enrollments at the higher of the two levels. To do so is also consistent with the goals declared by world leaders at the inter-agency UN Conference on Basic Education for All, in Jomtien, Thailand, in 1990 (UNDP, UNESCO, UNICEF and World Bank 1990).

Prudence suggests greater caution, however, in implementing the Government's plans for expanding vocational education and training. Implementation should be on a step-by-step basis only, with continuous monitoring and evaluation along the way. The evidence available when this report was prepared suggests that the labor market returns to investment in VOTECH are not adequate to justify VOTECH's high costs, although the data used to address this issue (VLSS 1992-93) are somewhat dated, and they confound two quite different programs -- technical education, on the one hand, and vocational education and training, on the other, combining the two as VOTECH; the general finding could be masking large differences between some programs that are cost-effective and others that are not at all so. Also, vocational training is an area where the private sector could play a much larger role. Finally, as with other levels and types of education, the labor market returns to VOTECH may improve as the labor market continues to evolve, but it would be wrong to assume that high returns to VOTECH investments are automatic.

Cost Reductions.

Even when budget is not a constraint, Government should always be vigilant in identifying and eliminating wastage in the E&T system. The VEFSS survey of 100 public-sector higher education institutions (HEIs) identified scope for lowering unit costs at the tertiary level in Vietnam through a carefully considered and fully implemented program of institutional consolidation. Consolidation is one way to address, inter alia, the high staff-student ratios now found in Vietnam's HEIs. Also, the system of narrowly focused HEIs, each under the control of a different government ministry or specialized agency, should give way to an integrated system of higher education, with broad coordination coming from a single umbrella "commission" or "council," but with considerable autonomy left to individual HEIs in regard to programs and financing.

At the general education level, the principal source of savings will come, not from raising student-teacher ratios, which are already high on average (although much lower in some sparsely populated parts of Vietnam), but from lowering dropout and repetition, which inflate the cost of producing graduates. Dropout rates, as already noted, are likely to fall in response to a program of targeted subsidies that would provide poor students with the financial means to remain in school. Both dropout and repetition are likely to respond to a different set of measures intended to raise the quality of education, i.e., *to raise student learning*. Improvements in quality will ensure that fewer students are forced out of the system, or back in the system, for reasons of academic failure. Improvements in quality will also result in higher labor market returns to the knowledge, skills and attitudes acquired while studying and, thereby, raise the incentive to continue to the next level of schooling, while also raising the costs of repeating, since to repeat grades in school is to delay labor market entry.

Quality Enhancement.

Several quality enhancing options are reviewed in the report. However, all of the evidence on the scope for quality enhancement in Vietnamese E&T is *indirect evidence* focusing on the inputs that produce educational outcomes rather than on the outcomes themselves. The VEFSS team was unable to locate direct evidence on the learning outcomes of Vietnamese students and, especially, on measures that would allow comparisons to be made with students in other countries according to internationally agreed definitions of quality. There is a need to put in place mechanisms for setting standards in Vietnamese E&T and for monitoring learning outcomes in relation to these standards and in relation to international norms. Such measures can be used, not only to assess the performance of the E&T system, but also, if linked with proper incentives, to drive the system toward higher levels of performance.

On the input side, one policy option judged here to be important is to raise the number of hours in the Vietnamese school year to a level that approximates international standards. This will be expensive, as it involves extending the school year (from 165 days to at least 185 days) and extending the school day (from four hours on average to at least five hours, if not more, especially in the upper grades). The longer school day will make it difficult to maintain the system of double- and triple-shifts that many Vietnamese communities use to achieve fuller utilization of limited physical facilities. This implies civil works, to build new schools and expand/upgrade existing schools. Teachers will also need to be compensated for the additional hours required by reform of the school calendar. If instructional hours in the year go up by 40 percent, annual teachers' salaries should go up by this percentage -- if not by a greater percentage because of other measures taken to upgrade teacher qualifications and teacher effectiveness.

To be fully "qualified," primary school teachers in Vietnam are expected to have graduated from a teacher training college. Only about two-thirds of those now teaching in primary education have actually received this training, and in some regions the proportion is far lower. Government may wish to consider a massive program of teacher upgrading. This should start with primary education where the problem of low qualifications is now the greatest and where the importance of good teaching is arguably the highest. Primary is the entry level of education that reaches the most children and provides the foundation for secondary and tertiary education. Even teachers who are qualified may be in need of refresher courses, to keep their skills and enthusiasm intact. This implies an expanded program of in-service teacher training. Teacher upgrading and regular in-service teacher training will require additional resources to cover the direct costs of the training and to support salary increments granted to teachers who receive training.

Non-salary inputs are also important factors in determining how much students learn at school. Given the critical importance of textbooks and other learning materials in the process of education, Government may wish to target some part of public spending specifically on these inputs -- if not for all school children, then at least for children in impoverished parts of the country. The present system loads most of the responsibility for the purchase of learning materials, and much of the responsibility for primary school construction, on families. This leads to inequitable results, as already discussed, since poor families cannot afford these costs, at least not in the quantities required both to maintain a child in school through to the end of basic education and to ensure the child's mastery of the curriculum.

System of Budget Classifications.

A large percentage of the E&T allocation (16 percent in 1994) as recorded in Ministry of Finance (MOF) budget records is labeled simply as "other" and cannot be assigned to different functional categories. This stands in the way of sound decision-making by government officials, especially in the Ministry of Education and Training (MOET), the Ministry of Planning and Investment (MPI), and provincial and district authorities responsible for E&T. Combined as "other" expenditure are, *inter alia*: (a) allocations to centrally financed "targeted programs," which are not assigned in the budget to one level/type of E&T or another (even though some of these programs do indeed focus on particular levels/types), and (b) general overhead (administrative) expenditure, which is difficult to break down by sub-program.

The difficulty in interpreting the "other" category in the budget highlights a more general problem of the budgeting system and the way that E&T is planned and administered. The system of budget classifications needed at the level of the central ministries is necessarily a general system that can be used across the full range of economic sectors to decide on an overall budget. Officials in the *central* ministries cannot be expected to understand and monitor sector-specific details. However, these details are precisely those that the *sectoral* ministries need to manage effectively the programs for which they are responsible. It is recommended that MOET, working with MOF, develop a second level of budgetary classifications that are sector-specific and designed to help it discharge its responsibilities as coordinator of sectoral activities. MOET officials at both the central and local levels should have ready access to the details that underlie MOF's aggregated budget data. These are of paramount importance to achieve effective sectoral administration.

Conclusion

Vietnam is a country that cares about social justice, and it is a country that wants to complete quickly the transition from central planning to a market economy and enhanced economic efficiency. Education is, in part, a private good, but it is, in part, also a social good, to the extent that education benefits all of society and not just the individual in whom it happens to be embodied. Education is properly seen, therefore, as a partnership between individual households striving to get ahead, and government looking out for the collective benefit of all of society. A balanced system is sought between one extreme that relies too heavily on households and an opposite extreme that relies too heavily on government. This balance requires constant review, and requires adjustment whenever the scales tip too far in either direction. This is the "art" of public finance, and a purpose of this study has been to assist education policymakers in Vietnam to make equitable and efficient choices.

1. INTRODUCTION

Vietnam is a long, thin, S-shaped country, stretching from below the 10th northern latitude at its southern tip nearly to the Tropic of Cancer along its northern border. Across that border are China's Yunnan and Quangxi Provinces. To Vietnam's west lie Laos and Cambodia, and facing it far to the East across the South China Sea lies the Philippine archipelago. Vietnam's land area is 331,000 square kilometers. In 1994, the population was 71.5 million, implying an average population density of nearly 220 inhabitants per square kilometer. In spite of government efforts to reduce fertility, population growth remains high, about 2.6 percent annually.

Vietnam is divided into seven "regions" -- the Northern Uplands, Red River Delta, North Central, Central Coast, Central Highlands, Southeast and Mekong River Delta Regions. The regions are sub-divided into 53 provinces, the provinces into 560 districts, and the districts into 10,320 communes. For some purposes, the regions are grouped into three "zones," North (*Bac Bô*), Central (*Trung Bô*) and South (*Nam Bô*), each fairly cohesive in terms of its traditions and culture. Table 1.1 reports land area, 1994 population and 1994 GDP per capita for Vietnam's seven regions.[1]

DEMOGRAPHIC AND MACRO-ECONOMIC CONTEXT

As can be seen from the table, the distribution of population across regions is quite unequal, ranging from a low of 53 people per square kilometer in the Central Highlands to 1,124 in the Red River Delta, the region that includes Hanoi (*Hà Nôi*). Ho Chi Minh City in the Southeast Region is the most densely populated urban part of the country, with nearly 4,400 people per square kilometer.[2]

Vietnam is one of the poorest countries in the World today, occupying the fifth position (between Sierra Leone and Burundi) in a global list of 132 economies ranked from low to high on income per capita in the latest *World Development Indicators* (World Bank 1995d). Vietnam's GNP in 1996 is estimated to be US $250 per capita. Yet Vietnam's GNP growth rate has been at or above 8 percent throughout the 1990s. It was

---

[1] Annex 1.1 at the end of the report gives this information for the 53 provinces, and the location of regions and provinces is shown on a map of Vietnam at the end of the report.

[2] The more densely populated regions and provinces tend to be wealthier and better developed. The correlation coefficient between population density and GDP per capita across provinces is 0.28.

9.5 percent in 1995. This is quite high even by East Asia's high standards, and astronomical by comparison with many low-income economies.[3]

Table 1.1. Regions of Vietnam

| Zone | Land Area (km²) | Population, 1994 | | GDP per Capita, 1994 | |
Region		People ('000)	Density (per km²)	('000 VND)	(US $)
NORTH ZONE					
Northern Uplands	102,961	12,389	120	1,577	143
Red River Delta	12,510	14,065	1,124	2,297	209
CENTRAL ZONE					
North Central	51,174	9,726	190	1,490	135
Central Coast	45,192	7,558	167	1,753	159
Central Highlands	56,083	2,999	53	1,715	156
SOUTH ZONE					
Southeast	23,467	8,878	378	5,460	496
Mekong River Delta	39,568	15,851	401	2,338	217
VIETNAM	**330,955**	**71,466**	**219**	**2,382**	**217**

Note: Exchange Rate (August 1994), US$1.00 = 11,000 VND.

Source: State Planning Committee and General Statistical Office.

The cessation of hostilities and the reunification of Vietnam's North and South in 1975 marked the end of a long period of turmoil, by which time the Vietnamese economy was on the verge of collapse. Vietnam's recent economic success is attributable to a radical program of economic renovation, referred to as *Đoi Moi* (new life) and announced at the Party Congress of 1986. Launched by Government soon thereafter and implemented in phases ever since, *Đoi Moi* has included elements of macroeconomic stabilization, adjustment to mitigate against the effect of external shocks, and structural reform. Despite clear movement in the direction of market reliance and encouragement of an expanded private sector, the Government of Vietnam has reaffirmed (at the Party Congress of 1991, for example) its commitment to socialism as the core tenet of the nation's civic philosophy and organization.

EDUCATION AND TRAINING IN VIETNAM

Vietnam's adult literacy rate is about 88 percent. Today, virtually all children of primary school age are enrolled in school. These are remarkable educational achievements and reflect a traditional respect for education (see Box 1.1). Also, in recent decades, education has benefited from a government that afforded a high priority to

---

[3] The average growth rate of a group of 43 low-income countries between 1980 and 1993 was 5.7 percent. When China and India are excluded from this group, the average growth rate for the remaining 41 countries was just 2.9 percent (World Bank 1995d). Estimated growth rates of some other East Asian economies, for the latest available year (1994 or 1995), are as follows: Myanmar 6.8 percent, Cambodia 4.0 percent, Hong Kong 5.5 percent, Republic of Korea 8.0 percent, Indonesia 8.5 percent, Malaysia 8.5 percent, Singapore 7.5 percent and Thailand 8.6 percent.

education and subsidized its expansion heavily. The different governments in the North and the South prior to 1975 and the difference in social policies help explain today's higher educational attainments in the North than in the South.[4]

Box 1.1. The Temple of Literature

Virtuous and talented men are State sustaining elements. The strength and the prosperity of a State depend on its stable vitality, and it becomes weaker as such vitality fails. That is why all the Saintly Emperors and clearsighted Kings sought men of talent and the employment of the literati to develop this vitality, for their role is the most important in the government. Thus, our suzerains have always shown honour and consideration to the literati.

Memoir on the Stele of Doctors.
Laureates at Nham Tuat Examination.
Dai Bao Dynastic Title. Third Year (1442)

Vietnam's Temple of Literature (*Van Mieu - Quoc Tu Giam*), a majestic collection of old and reconstructed stone halls and Confucian statues, sits in the middle of the modern city of Hanoi. This was Vietnam's first national university. According to *The Complete History of the Great Viet*, the Temple of Literature dates from "the Autumn of the year *Canh Tuah*, the second year of *Than Vu*, in the 8th lunar month, during the reign of King Ly Thanh Tong." This was about 1070 a.d. in the Western calendar.

A special characteristic of the Temple of Literature is its 82 Doctors' stelae, large stone pillars, each one resting on a sculpted tortoise and inscribed with the names and birth places of some group of the 1,306 graduates who passed their doctoral examinations at the university between 1442 and 1779. Each stele honors the most accomplished graduates of a different Vietnamese dynasty. This public recognition of their achievements was meant to encourage others to serve society in similar fashion.

Vietnam's first national university provided training in more than 700 scholarly areas. The development of intellectual capacity was considered an excellent way to build the State. Engraved in 1466 on one of the stone stelae are the following words, translated here from the Vietnamese: "The academic skills of a nation are its greatest asset. Clear-sighted leadership is needed to see that mankind's natural talents are honed and virtue put to good use."

Source: MOET

---

[4] No straightforward comparison is possible, however, since the North and South had different educational systems until very recently. The evolution of the two systems and their convergence at the end of the 1980s are described in the next chapter.

Prior to Vietnam's partition under the Geneva Agreement in 1954, formal education was constrained during the 20th century. Under French colonial rule, only a relatively small and elite group of Vietnamese attended public educational institutions, most of which were located in the larger urban areas. In response to this exclusionary policy, non-government schools were started in many parts of the country, including many of Vietnam's rural villages. This satisfied some part of the strong household demand for education, but few poor families could, in fact, afford the private school fees. Hence, illiteracy was widespread in Vietnam, at least until 1945 when Ho Chi Minh, the nationalist leader, launched a grassroots literacy campaign in those areas under the control of his revolutionary forces. At the end of French colonial rule, private schools in the North were incorporated into a free public education system. Expansion of this system was a priority goal of the Government over the next thirty years (Rorris et al. 1994).

Despite high overall literacy and high enrollments in Vietnam today, and despite relatively small differences between males and females,[5] wide regional differences do exist. The mountainous northern province of Lai Chau, for example, has a reported literacy rate of only 49 percent, and in this province there are twice as many literate men as women. School participation rates remain low in the mountainous areas of Vietnam's North and Central Zones, and in the Mekong River Delta Region, particularly for girls. Whereas ethnic minorities account for over 13 percent of Vietnam's population, ethnic minority individuals account for only 4 percent of the *student* population.

Since the introduction of *Đoi Moi*, a number of changes have occurred that impact importantly on Vietnam's system of education (*Giáo Duc*) and training (*Đào Tao*).[6] First, government spending on education and training (E&T) has increased both in absolute terms and as a percentage of overall government spending during the 1990s. Particularly large increases occurred in 1993 and 1994 (46 percent and 33 percent real spending growth in these two years, respectively).[7]

A second important change during the 1990s has been the elimination of many regulations restricting or proscribing the private sector's role in E&T. New decrees and resolutions have been passed that encourage the private sector's expansion. "Semi-public" and "people-founded" institutions, although they account for only a tiny

---

[5] Female enrollments in 1988 were 94 percent and 93 percent of male enrollments in primary and secondary education, respectively, and 1989 adult literacy rates were 84 percent for women and 93 percent for men (World Bank 1995e; UNESCO 1992a).

[6] In Vietnamese, *Đào Tao* includes higher education, as well as all vocational and technical education and training.

[7] E&T's share of the discretionary state budget went from 9.3 percent in 1992 to 9.9 percent in 1993, and then to 11.8 percent in 1994. E&T's percentage shares of GDP in these three years were 2.1 percent, 2.9 percent and 3.6 percent.

proportion of total enrollments as of today, are increasing rapidly in number. Non-public provision is especially common in pre-school education, in vocational and technical education and training (VOTECH), and increasingly also at the tertiary level of general education. Non-public institutions cover nearly all of their operating costs from student fees.

A third and related policy change has been to allow public institutions to levy tuition fees, though only within rather strict limits, and to charge for other goods and services sold to the public. Household outlays on E&T at all levels accounted for 43 percent of total (government plus household) spending on E&T in 1994.[8] This proportion varies from as little as 12 percent and 19 percent in VOTECH and tertiary education to as much as 48 percent, 59 percent and 62 percent in primary, lower secondary and upper secondary education. As in many other countries, government spending on education in Vietnam reflects an implicit bias in favor of the rich -- because this spending covers a relatively small share of the costs at the lower levels of education, which are attended by more children from low-income families, and covers a larger share as one moves up the education ladder, where one finds fewer low-income students.[9]

Between 1989 and 1992, education enrollments tended to fall off in Vietnam. Though only temporary, the decline was dramatic in the case of both secondary (upper secondary especially) and pre-school education. The explanation for the decline must lie in changes in those factors that influence household decisions to invest, or not to invest, in human capital. Economic liberalization and rapid economic growth, such as Vietnam was experiencing during this period, often imply expanded opportunities for high paying work and, therefore, *greater* incentive to invest in education and other productivity enhancing activities. The expected future returns must be balanced, however, against the present costs that households face, including the opportunity cost (foregone earnings) of time spent studying, as well as any direct, out-of-pocket expenses.

Clearly some combination of higher fees and other direct costs, as well as higher foregone earnings resulting from new employment opportunities, discouraged school participation for at least some families in some parts of Vietnam during the early 1990s. On the benefit side of the equation, uncertainty in the face of rapid economic change and the recently introduced renovation policy, as well as the Government's announced decision to phase out guaranteed public sector jobs for upper secondary and higher education graduates, undoubtedly also served as deterrents to household investment in education. Other factors may have contributed. The restructuring of the education

---

[8] Included in household outlays are all fees paid to institutions and all other education-related expenditures that families must bear (e.g., for transportation, school uniforms and books), but not foregone earnings, which is, in many cases, the greatest private cost of all.

[9] A survey of public higher education in Vietnam undertaken as part of this study shows that only 16 percent of the revenues received by colleges and universities in 1994 came from student fees, down from 23 percent in 1993; 79 percent of institutional revenues in 1994 came from State Budget subventions, and 5 percent from other sources.

system in 1989, which added an extra year to the lower secondary cycle in the North, probably reinforced the negative trend seen at the upper secondary level.

Some observers distinguish four periods in the recent history of E&T in Vietnam -- war-time dynamism, post-war stagnation, early *Ðoi Moi* decline, and later *Ðoi Moi* adjustment. The war (which, after very many years, eventually ended in 1975) is said to have been a dynamic period in the history of E&T. It was characterized by revolutionary fervor and a willingness of teachers and students to work hard and make sacrifices in support of the war effort. Following the war, there developed a "wait and see" attitude. Some Vietnamese were disappointed, after years of suffering, that employment prospects and living standards did not improve dramatically overnight. Teachers grew discontented with their low salaries. Enrollments barely kept pace with population growth. The Government's announcement of *Ðoi Moi* in the late 1980s ushered in a third period in the recent history of E&T. The transition from a centrally planned to a market economy implied new self-reliance on the part of all Vietnamese. As noted, Government could no longer be relied upon to provide civil service jobs for all who graduated from secondary and tertiary institutions. Private rates of return to investment in education (estimates of which are presented in Chapter 5) appear to be highest for primary education, lower for tertiary, and lowest for secondary. In response, during this period, secondary enrollments fell off sharply, and tertiary enrollments were nearly static.

But this period lasted only a few years. The "shock" of *Ðoi Moi* soon wore off, and individuals began to see opportunities in the newly opened marketplace and believed that education held the key to unlocking these opportunities. The fourth period, which began in 1992, has seen a recovery of enrollments in both lower and upper secondary education. Tertiary enrollments rose sharply beginning in about 1992. They have more than doubled in the years since. Primary enrollments continued their steady rise, about 2.1 percent annually since 1985.

VIETNAM EDUCATION FINANCING SECTOR STUDY

One of the key challenges for Vietnam is to ensure that the system of E&T responds to the emerging demands of a growing market economy. Expansion and modernization of the education and training system are important elements of the Government's strategy to sustain rapid economic growth and alleviate poverty. The Government has set ambitious targets for raising educational participation. Stated government policy objectives include the achievement of universal primary education (UPE) by the year 2000, the attainment of universal lower secondary education by the year 2010, and a 65 percent increase in university enrollments between 1994 and 2004.

Implementation of these plans will entail substantial costs. To understand how large these costs could become, and to decide whether or not meeting them is feasible, and whether desirable, require a detailed financing strategy for the sector, linked to clearly articulated sectoral and macroeconomic goals. Vietnam's strategy for E&T

should set out careful priorities for sectoral expansion and improvement, define the appropriate role of government in the provision and financing of E&T at different levels of the system; and provide a blueprint for mobilizing resources from all sources, including user fees and private sector development as well as increased public spending.

The purpose of the present study, known as the Vietnam Education Financing Sector Study (VEFSS), is to assist Government in this regard, by pulling together an integrated sector-wide analysis of E&T in Vietnam, with a focus on issues of costs and financing. VEFSS is intended to fill a major vacuum left by the otherwise thorough sector study undertaken by UNESCO, UNDP and the Vietnamese Government in 1991-92 (UNESCO 1992c). Surely the gap in that study's coverage reflected the dearth of information that was available to assess the magnitude of costs and the sources of financing for Vietnam's E&T sector.

To address serious information problems, to strengthen inter-agency linkages and institutional capacity and to instill a sense of local ownership of the findings and policy recommendations of VEFSS, the approach used to prepare this study was collaborative and participatory. This is described and key participants are acknowledged in Annex 1.2. To carry out the study, inter-agency working groups were established under the direction of a senior-level steering committee, which also advised the World Bank on the design and purposes of VEFSS and which will coordinate the study's dissemination. Four survey-based sub-studies were completed under the auspices of VEFSS to fill major information gaps. Surveys are costly, and World Bank financing for VEFSS was supplemented by both monetary and in-kind contributions from several international agencies acknowledged in Annex 1.2. A generous grant from Swiss Development Cooperation (SDC) deserves special mention.

Chapter 2 examines in some detail the performance of Vietnam's E&T system and, in particular, trends in student enrollments, teachers and other inputs since the declaration of *Đoi Moi* in 1986. Chapter 3 evaluates the sources and uses of funds that flow into the E&T system, including a systematic analysis of MOF State Budget figures, organized for the first time for this sector in Vietnam according to the IMF's Government Finance Statistics classification format. It also provides estimates of Official Development Assistance (ODA) for E&T in Vietnam, based on UNDP information, and of commune and household expenditure on E&T, based on recent survey data. Chapter 4 estimates unit costs and addresses issues of E&T's internal efficiency. Chapter 5 looks at the system's external efficiency, in terms of the employment and earnings of system graduates, and at its equity, in terms of the benefit incidence of public subsidies and other measures relating to poverty reduction. Chapter 6 concludes the study, assessing alternative scenarios and offering an agenda for the design and implementation of financial reform policies in relation to the E&T sector over the period ahead.

2. THE EDUCATION AND TRAINING SECTOR

Vietnam's education system is a 5-4-3-4 system. In other words, a student who passes through the entire education system from grade 1 through university graduation without dropping out or repeating a grade begins with five years of primary education, followed by four years of lower secondary and three years of upper secondary, and finishes with four years of university education. Children are expected to enter grade 1 at the age of six, but some Grade 1 pupils are older, especially those in rural areas. According to the 1989 census, whereas 91 percent of urban children were already in school by the age of seven, a quarter of rural seven year olds were still at home and not yet in school. By the age of 10, however, 90 percent of rural children and 97 percent of urban children had entered school. A compulsory attendance law for primary education was passed in 1991 (Anh et al. 1995).

Until very recently, the North and South had different education systems. The South has had twelve years of pre-university education since before World War II. The North too had a twelve-year pre-university system prior to 1954, but only in those areas that were under French control. Areas under control of the revolutionary forces had just nine years of pre-university education. When the French left in 1954, the Vietnamese Government introduced ten years of pre-university education in all parts of the North. This continued even after national reunification in 1975. In 1981, the North moved from a ten-year to an eleven-year primary/secondary cycle. Graduation followed "grade 12," but all students skipped grade 9. Only since 1989 has the North had a true 12-year system and has the entire country followed the same 5-4-3-4 system of education (Anh et al, 1995).

The present system comprises the following main levels and types of education and training (E&T):

(a) **Pre-school education**

- *Nursery school* (optional; minimum age, 3 months; duration, up to 3 years), followed by:
- *Kindergarten* (optional; minimum age, 3 years; duration, up to 3 years), followed by:

(b) **General education**

(i) *Basic*
- *Primary education* (compulsory; official entry age, 6 years; duration, 5 years), followed by:
- *Lower secondary education* (4 years), followed by either:

(ii)   *Upper secondary education* (3 years), or by:

(c)   **Vocational and technical education and training (VOTECH)**
- *Vocational training* (0.5 to 2 years), or
- *Secondary vocational education* (3 to 4 years), or
- *Secondary technical education* which in Vietnam is often known as *professional secondary education* (2.5 to 4 years);

(d)   **Higher or tertiary education**
- *College education* (3 years)
- *University education* (4 to 6 years), followed by:
- *Postgraduate education*

Figure 2.1 is a structural chart showing the student flows and interlinkages within the E&T system. The principal source of information for this and all subsequent figures and tables in Chapter 2 is MOET.

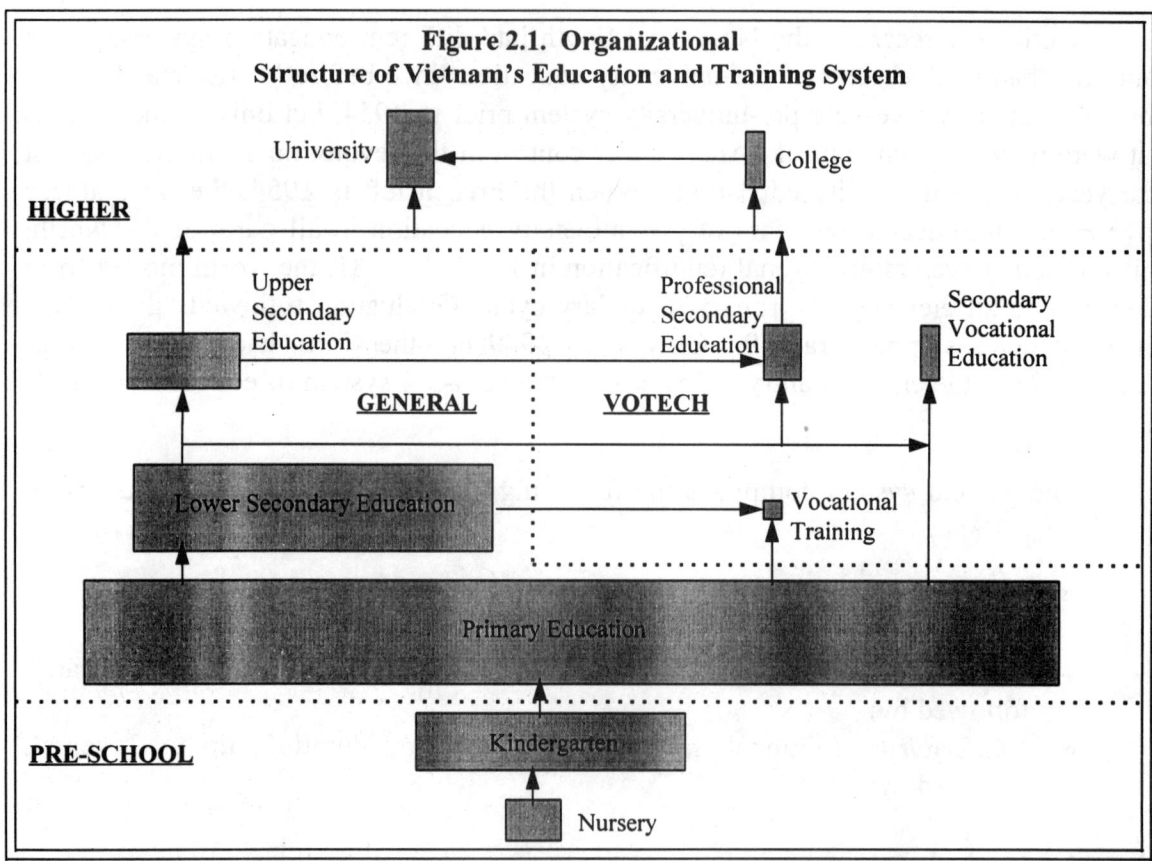

Figure 2.1. Organizational Structure of Vietnam's Education and Training System

Source: MOET and VEFSS Team

MANAGEMENT AND FINANCING

The Ministry of Education and Training (*Bo Giáo Dục và Đào Tao*) has major responsibility for planning and directing Vietnam's system of E&T, as well as for many aspects of curriculum development and materials production. MOET has partial responsibility -- shared with the Office of Government, which is attached to the Prime Minister's Office, with MPI and with MOF -- for broader decisions of policy formulation, target setting, and sectoral financing. The management and financing of E&T are quite decentralized in Vietnam. This can be seen from different perspectives.

Vertical Decentralization

Vertically (in terms of the *functional departments* responsible for E&T) although MOET plays a pre-eminent role, many E&T institutions in Vietnam fall under other line ministries and government agencies. Box 2.1 gives an example of one line ministry's diverse educational responsibilities. The multiplicity of actors can result in duplication, confusion and waste. Well over two dozen line ministries and specialized agencies retain some role in administering public E&T in Vietnam. These are listed in Table 2.1 below.

Box 2.1. Educational Institutions under Ministry of Construction (*Bo Xây Dung*)

- two architecture universities (one each in Hanoi and Ho Chi Minh City)
- six secondary technical schools -- five teaching construction techniques and one training teachers of construction techniques
- nine vocational schools for training specialized building sector workers
- two vocational schools for training workers to repair construction machinery

Source: MOET and VEFSS Team

Horizontal Decentralization

E&T is also decentralized in a horizontal sense, that is, in terms of the different *levels of government* responsible. With respect to the administration of public financing for E&T, it will be shown in Chapter 3 that expenditures of the central government account for only a relatively small share of total budgeted expenditure on E&T programs in Vietnam today -- 24 percent of current and 44 percent of capital (28 percent of total) in FY94. A much larger share (72 percent of budgeted expenditure) is administered by the provinces, which in turn delegate many responsibilities to districts and communes.

In higher education and VOTECH, with the exception of university education, the role of provincial governments in running educational institutions is at least as large as the role of central government. This is shown also in Table 2.1.

Table 2.1. VOTECH and Higher Education Institutions Operated by Central Government Ministries and Specialized Agencies and by Provincial Governments

| | VOTECH | | Higher Education Institutions (HEIs) | | All public VOTECH schools and HEIs |
	Secondary Vocational Schools	Secondary Technical Schools	Colleges	Universities	
Central Government	**92**	**91**	**13**	**64**	**260**
Specialized Agencies[a]	7	15	5	2	29
Ministries	85	76	8	62	231
Agriculture	14	8	-	-	22
Commerce	2	7	-	-	9
Construction	11	6	-	2	19
Culture and Information	-	10	-	6	16
Education and Training	-	4	8	40 [b]	52
Energy	12	5	-	-	17
Finance	-	3	-	2	5
Fisheries	1	3	-	-	4
Foreign Affairs	-	-	-	1	1
Forestry	6	3	-	1	10
Health	1	6	-	5	12
Heavy Industry	7	8	-	-	15
Irrigation	-	4	-	1	5
Justice	-	-	-	2	2
Labor and Social Affairs	2	2	-	-	4
Light Industry	6	4	-	-	10
Transport and Communications	15	3	-	2	20
Water Resources	8	-	-	-	8
Provincial Governments	**85**	**168**	**32** [c]	**1** [d]	**286**
TOTAL (Central Government plus Provinces)	**177**	**255**	**45**	**65**	**542**

[a]The specialized agencies operating VOTECH and tertiary institutions include Government Office, Land Registration, Meteorology, Physical Education and Sports, Planning, Postal and Telecommunications, Price Committee, Radio and TV Broadcasting, Statistics, and Tourism.
[b]Includes two Open Universities operated by MOET.
[c]Of which 29 are provincial teacher training colleges.
[d]The Hai Phong In-Service Training University.
Source: MOET.

Below the tertiary level, central government has no direct role in the running of schools. Thus, the vast majority of Vietnam's students at all levels are enrolled in institutions run by local authorities. Nursery schools, kindergartens and primary schools are the districts' responsibility, with supervision given by MOET's provincial-level departments. The provinces operate all secondary schools and many college-level institutions, which, for the most part, train primary and secondary school teachers. Table 2.2 shows the division of responsibility for different levels and types E&T by level of government.

Table 2.2. **Responsibility for Operating Different Levels and Types of Education and Training Institutions by Three Top Levels of Government**

	District	Provincial	Central
Nursery	X		
Kindergartens	X		
Primary	X		
Lower secondary schools		X	
Upper secondary schools		X	
Vocational training centers		X	
Secondary vocational schools		X	X
Secondary technical schools		X	X
Colleges		X	X
Universities			X

Source: MOET.

Privatization

Vietnam's E&T system has become more decentralized also when one looks at the role of the private sector. "Privatization" can take two forms -- private provision and private financing. In terms of provision, earlier restrictions against private (or "non-public") institutions have been lifted or relaxed during the 1990s, and the number of such institutions is growing at every level. Most of the costs of running non-public institutions are met from student fees. More will be written below about enrollment trends in non-public institutions and the regulations that now govern this sector.

In terms of financing, even when a child enrolls in a public institution, the family must bear a significant share of the full, economic cost of the child's E&T -- in the form of fees paid, which offset some part of the institution's operating expenses, and in the form of other private costs related to the child's education. These costs include earnings foregone by a child who would be working if not in school -- except to the extent that earnings foregone may be offset by scholarships or other transfers from the institution or from government. Such transfers are virtually nonexistent, however, at the system's lower end, which accounts for most students.

ENROLLMENT TRENDS

The school year (SY) in Vietnam lasts about ten months, starting in September and ending in June of the following calendar year.[10] Table 2.2 shows total (public plus private) enrollments at all level of E&T for every year from SY85 to SY95.

---

[10] In this report, a school year, for example, the one beginning in September 1994 and ending in June 1995, will not be referred to as the 1994-95 school year, but rather as SY95. This saves space and is analogous to the convention in the literature for describing fiscal years that span two calendar years. Later in this report, there is discussion of government spending on E&T. The fiscal year in Vietnam follows the calendar year. In other words, FY95 is the same as 1995 or CY95. In these sections of the report, to compute unit fiscal costs (per student government spending), SY enrollments are

The grade-by-grade statistics collected by MOET do not distinguish between male and female enrollments. Other MOET information, however, suggests that gender disparities are smaller than those observed in many other countries. Girls and boys enter the education system almost in equal numbers, and girls drop out of school at rates only marginally higher than boys. In SY95, 49.5 percent of primary, 49.1 percent of lower secondary and 44.8 percent of upper secondary enrollments were female. In higher education, the situation is somewhat poorer, with only 40 percent of those enrolled being women.

Table 2.3. Enrollments in Different Levels and Types of Education and Training, SY85-SY95

School Year	Nursery	Kinder-garten	Primary	Lower Secondary	Upper Secondary	Vocational	Technical	Tertiary
SY85	1,152,626	1,587,338	8,166,372	3,086,414	791,989	171,100	121,069	124,120
SY86	1,157,385	1,636,347	8,254,816	3,253,229	860,226	113,016	135,409	121,195
SY87	1,130,997	1,768,938	8,484,685	3,264,520	917,593	119,783	137,618	127,312
SY88	1,103,989	1,851,597	8,666,281	3,291,344	926,420	102,043	137,112	133,136
SY89	788,454	1,801,806	8,634,819	3,037,775	843,541	118,083	135,648	132,458
SY90	649,578	1,607,888	8,583,052	2,758,871	691,487	92,485	131,246	138,566
SY91	528,012	1,495,403	8,862,295	2,708,067	527,926	105,083	117,506	124,484
SY92	488,948	1,493,583	9,105,904	2,268,192	528,735	77,395	114,038	151,981
SY93	464,052	1,538,882	9,430,527	2,804,543	576,978	78,956	109,560	162,848
SY94	448,692	1,659,247	9,885,083	3,175,318	726,535	46,498	88,276	226,412
SY95	443,737	1,777,032	10,048,564	3,678,804	863,000	62,614	132,502	354,103
SY85-SY95[a]	-9.1%	1.1%	2.1%	1.8%	0.9%	-9.6%	0.9%	11.1%

Note: This table includes both public and private enrollments, and only long-term
　　　regular enrollments in VOTECH and tertiary education.
[a]Average annual rate of increase
Source: MOET.

Pre-school Education

Most pre-school education, which is optional in Vietnam as in many places, occurs in the larger cities. This service is relatively rare in rural areas. Children as young as three months can enter a nursery school (also known as a crèche), where they can stay until they are 2-3 years old. Kindergarten is then available for children from the age of three until they are ready to enter primary school.

In the past, the development of nursery schools was a high priority of government policy. In SY85, more than a million children were enrolled in crèches -- about one out of every four children in the 0-2 year age group. Since SY88, however, nursery school enrollments have dropped sharply. By SY92, they were below 500,000. Private nurseries today account for just over half (52 percent) of the enrollments at this level

---

the report, to compute unit fiscal costs (per student government spending), SY enrollments are converted to fiscal year enrollments. The weighting system used is illustrated by the following equation:

1995 enrollments = 60% of SY95 enrollments + 40% of SY96 enrollments

Kindergarten attendance has fluctuated, but the overall trend since the mid-1980s has been flat, with enrollments hovering around one and a half million children. Here also, private enrollments are important (41 percent in SY96). Figure 2.2 graphs nursery school and kindergarten enrollments from SY85 to SY95 as index numbers with the SY85 enrollment set equal to 100 in each case.

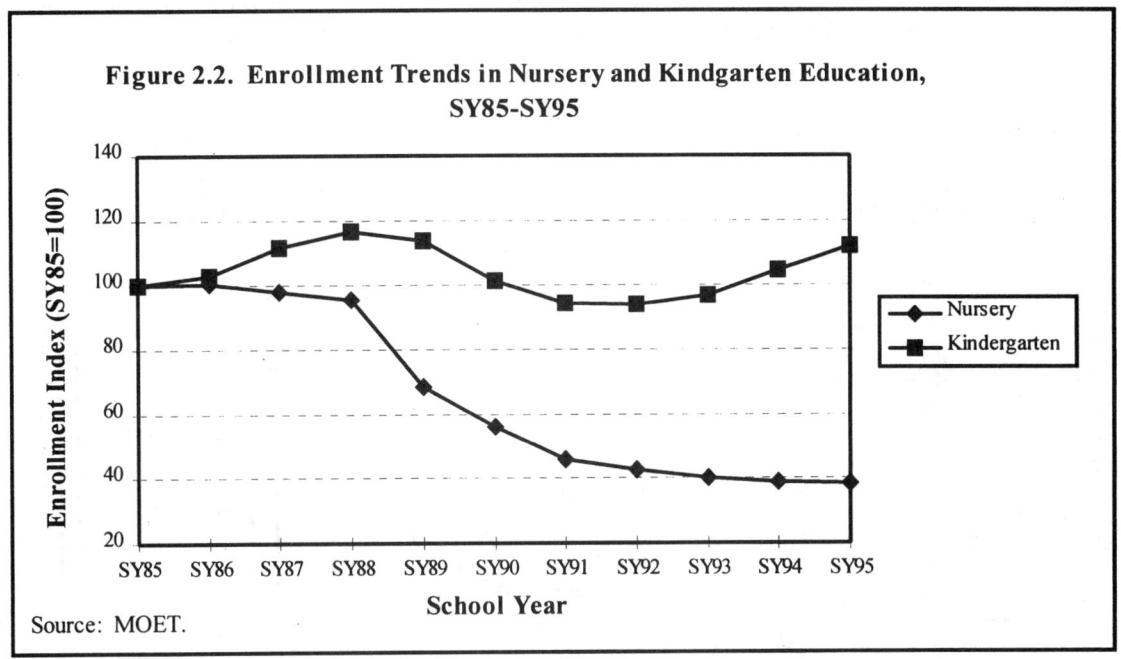

Figure 2.2. Enrollment Trends in Nursery and Kindgarten Education, SY85-SY95

Source: MOET.

Primary and General Secondary Education

Participation in primary education is now universal nearly everywhere in Vietnam, except in the mountainous areas and parts of the Mekong River Delta Region. Basic (primary and lower secondary) is non-diversified in Vietnam. In other words, the curriculum is the same for every child. Diversification occurs after basic education, when a child who continues formal study ends up in one of four different kinds of institutions:

(a)   a vocational training center (*Trung Tâm Day Nghê*), or

(b)   a secondary vocational school (*Truong Trung Hoc Day Nghê),* or

(c)   a secondary technical school (*Truong Trung Hoc Chuyên Nghiêp),* or

(d)   a general, or academic, upper secondary school (*Truong Trung Hoc Phô Thông*), in one of three streams -- the natural sciences (Stream A), natural sciences and technologies (Stream B) and social sciences (Stream C).

In Vietnamese terms, the first three fall under the heading of *Đào Tao* (training), and not *Giáo Duc* (education). They will be discussed in the next section of this chapter.

The enrollment trends in primary and general secondary education over the past decade are illustrated in Figure 2.3. The absolute numbers of students attending lower and upper secondary schools actually declined over the four-year period from SY88 to SY92, an unusual phenomenon that has now reversed itself with upper secondary enrollments nearly the same in SY95 as they were in SY88 and lower secondary enrollments higher than they ever were. Primary education enrollments, on the other hand, increased steadily over the entire period and were 23 percent higher in SY95 than in SY88.

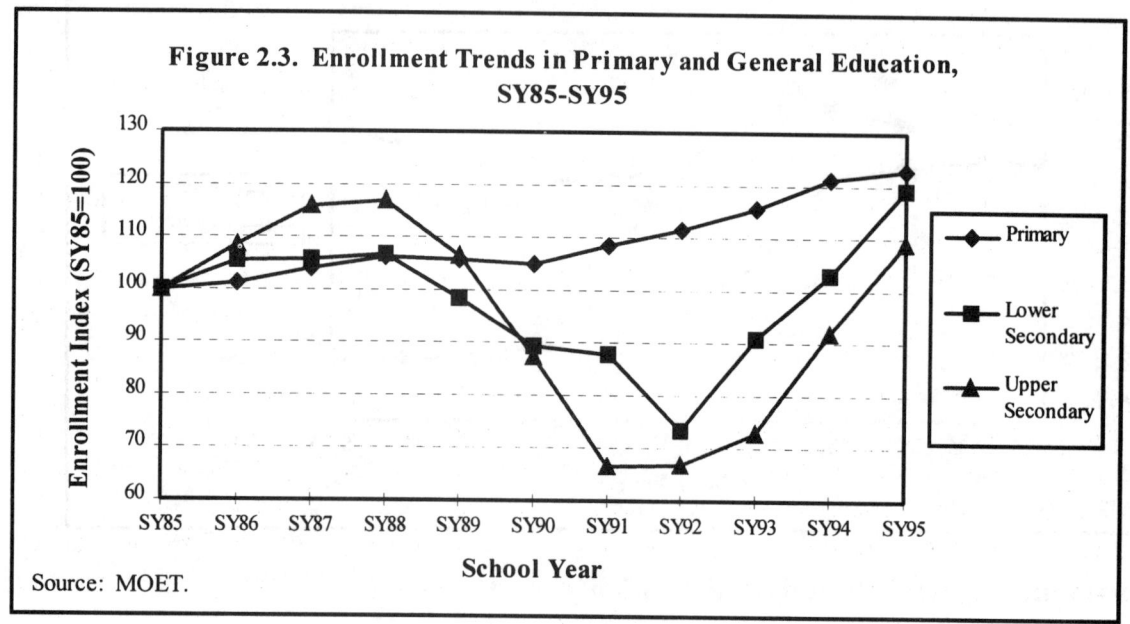

Figure 2.3. Enrollment Trends in Primary and General Education, SY85-SY95

Source: MOET.

Vocational and Technical Education and Training (VOTECH)

VOTECH in Vietnam is intended primarily for those who have attended basic education (primary or lower secondary) but have not been admitted or have chosen not to continue to the next level of general education (lower or upper secondary). Government distinguishes two types of VOTECH programs -- *long-term regular* (by which is meant *school-based*) programs, and *short-term* programs, which are offered in vocational training centers.

Long-Term Regular VOTECH Programs. As seen earlier, many different ministries and central agencies offer school-based VOTECH programs in Vietnam, as do Vietnam's 53 provinces. MOET, which offers no secondary vocational education and runs just four of Vietnam's 91 centrally-managed secondary technical schools, is a small player in terms of provision of VOTECH, although it plays a larger role in terms of pedagogic supervision. The Ministries of Agriculture, Construction, Energy, and Transport and Communications are four big players, each one responsible for a number of centrally-managed vocational schools and technical schools. As a group, the provinces provide the largest number of school-based VOTECH programs.

Secondary vocational schools. These schools admit students at two different levels: those who have completed primary as well as for those who have completed lower secondary education. For the first group, the duration of study is from two to three years, and for the second, from one to two years, depending on the vocation being taught. The objective of secondary vocational education is to train skilled workers. There are many subjects taught in the vocational schools, but these fall into six broad areas: *agriculture, construction, culture and fine arts, industry, trade and services,* and *transportation and communications.*

Secondary technical schools. Like the secondary vocational schools, secondary technical schools (known generally in Vietnam as "professional secondary schools") recruit at two levels, in this case, after both lower and upper secondary education. The course of study varies from three to three-and-a-half years for the lower cycle and from two to two-and-a-half years for the upper cycle. Those who complete the upper cycle are eligible to enter a university, where they can complete a degree in three years as compared with the four-year course for those who enter following upper secondary school. The secondary technical schools are designed to train middle-level technicians. The technical education taught in Vietnam's secondary technical schools comprises six broad areas: *finance and services, agriculture and forestry, culture and information, health and sports, industry,* and *pre-school teacher training.* Secondary technical education is also conducted in provincial level teacher training colleges and medical colleges. Vietnam classifies the lowest level of professional training in these colleges as secondary technical education, rather than higher education, even though it takes place in colleges rather than schools. Responsibility for teacher training at this level is shared between MOET and the provinces. Except for teacher training, all of secondary technical education is organized by line ministries other than MOET.

Enrollment trends in Long-Term Regular VOTECH Programs. Figures 2.4 and 2.5 show what happened to enrollments in different vocational subjects and different areas of technical education between SY91 and SY95. In vocational training, there were fewer trainees in all six broad training areas at the end of the period, except in one area -- trade and services, which grew substantially but from a relatively small base. Enrollments in agricultural training programs, construction, transportation and communications, and culture and fine arts all fell by more than 50 percent over the four-year period. In technical education, enrollments in the six different subject areas did not change significantly between SY91 and SY95, except for pre-school teacher training, where enrollments went up by about 70 percent, and the training of agriculture technicians and sports/health technicians, where enrollments went down by about 20 percent.

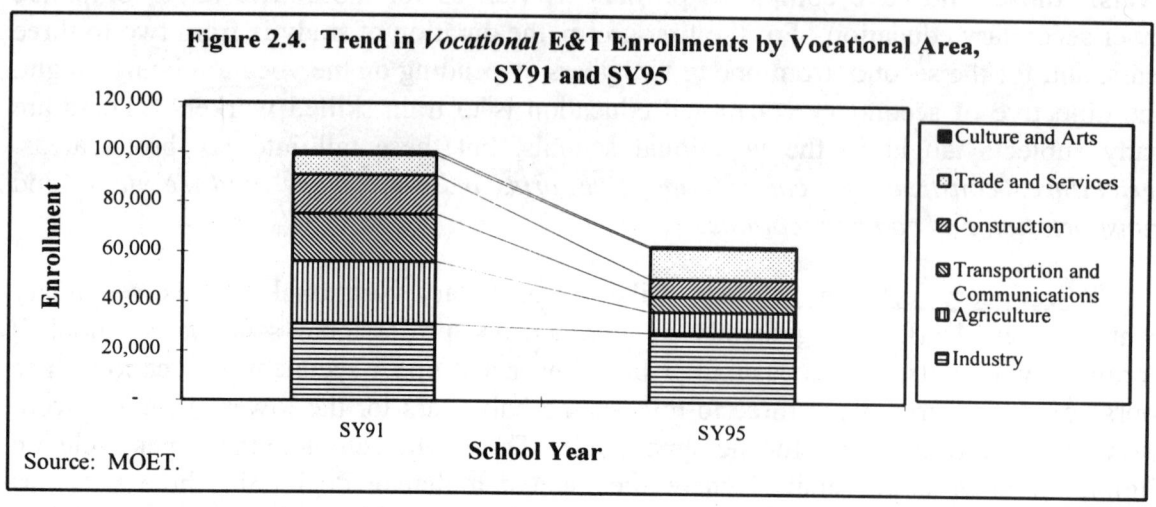

Figure 2.4. Trend in *Vocational* E&T Enrollments by Vocational Area, SY91 and SY95

Source: MOET.

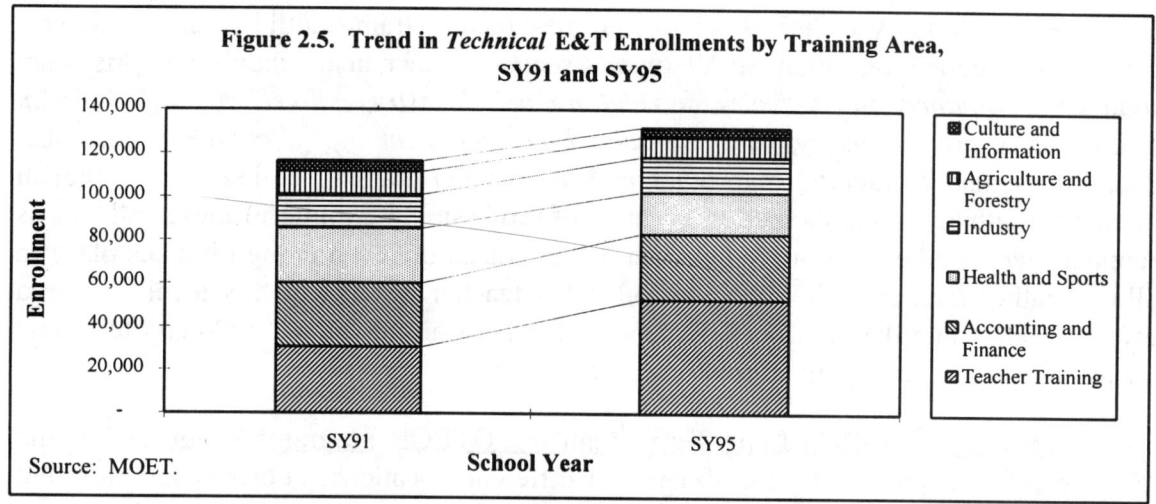

Figure 2.5. Trend in *Technical* E&T Enrollments by Training Area, SY91 and SY95

Source: MOET.

Although there are many types of school-based VOTECH programs in Vietnam, the students and trainees enrolled in them comprise only a tiny proportion (about 1.2 percent) of all the numbers enrolled in formal E&T institutions. School-based VOTECH students and trainees numbered fewer than 200,000 individuals in SY95. This represents about half of one percent of the estimated 38 million working-age labor force participants in Vietnam (Agrawal, Lindauer and Walton 1996). Moreover, the trends in regular VOTECH enrollments over the past ten years have been distinctly downward (Figure 2.6). Regular VOTECH -- the kind that occurs in self-standing school-based programs -- is remarkable in Vietnam today *by its absence*. Most socialist economiesrely heavily on pre-employment, occupation-specific E&T. Vietnam relies heavily on general education, and on the efficacy of on-the-job training and the workers' ability to learn from work experience. This would appear to be one of the clear strengths of Vietnam's education system, given the lessons of international experience, which have shown a pattern of high costs and tenuous labor market linkages for school-based training programs in many countries.

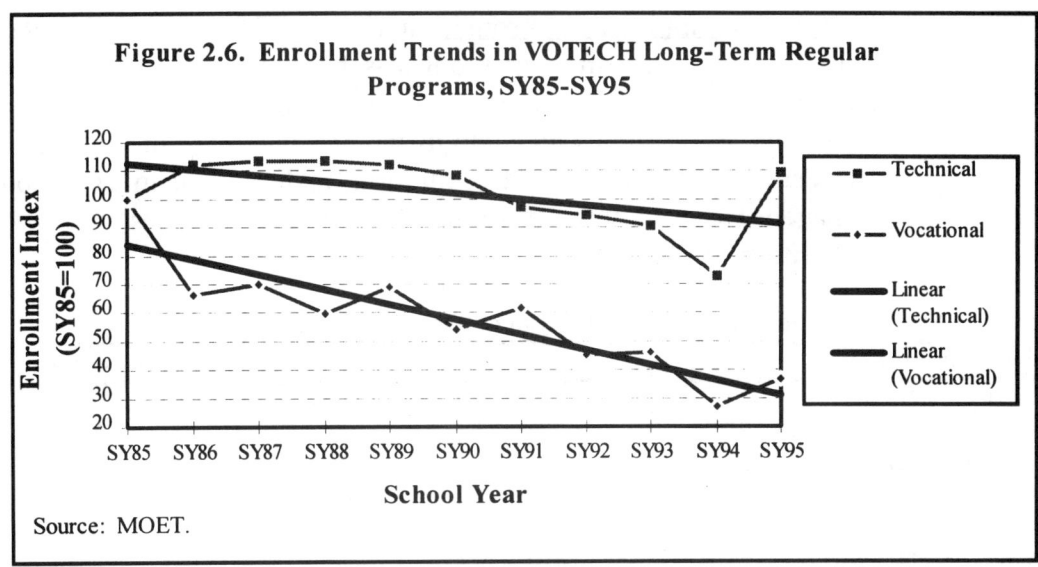

Figure 2.6. Enrollment Trends in VOTECH Long-Term Regular Programs, SY85-SY95

Source: MOET.

Short-Term VOTECH Program. Most of Vietnam's VOTECH occurs, not in school-based programs, but in short-term in-service programs offered by vocational training centers (VTCs) managed at the provincial level by various government ministries. Because of the short-term nature of this kind of training, the numbers of those receiving training can only be approximated. Estimates suggest that the ratio of short-term trainees to long-term regular VOTECH students is currently about 4 to 1 nationwide.

Strictly speaking, there is no formal education requirement for acceptance into a VTC course. Trainees in the VTCs include individuals who have dropped out of primary and lower secondary education, and even some who have never been to school. There are several types of VTC training, with some VTCs offering more than one type. For simplicity, this study groups the various types of training under three headings:

(a) Vocational training centers for upper secondary students (*Trung Tâm Day Nghê Cho Hoc Sinh Phô Thông*). Vietnam's upper secondary general education curriculum requires that students be introduced to manual skills and the world of work. In some upper secondary schools, this practical training is provided by the schools themselves, but more often students are sent out to a nearby VTC. This training can be offered during vacation periods, during shorter periods of time scattered throughout the year, or on a regular basis of a few hours each week during the school year.

(b) Vocational centers for training and upgrading skills (*Trung Tâm Đào Tao và Bao Duong Nghê*). This training is intended for young adults and school age children who have dropped out of school and prepares them to work in specific vocations. Courses last from three to six months depending on the subject.

(c)   <u>Centers for employment promotion</u> (*Trung Tâm Xúc Tiên Viêc Làm*). These VTCs target the same out-of-school groups, but in addition to training, they provide other services, such as credit and marketing assistance, to facilitate entry into different vocations. In 1994, there were 126 centers for employment promotion, at least one in every province, managed by a variety of ministries, central agencies and provincial authorities (Table 2.4).

Table 2.4. Management of Centers for Employment Promotion

Responsible Authority	Number of Centers
Ministry of Defense	9
Ministry of Fisheries	3
Ministry of Interior	8
Ministry of Labor, Invalids and Social Affairs	7
Provincial Authorities	61
Farmer Associations	6
Trade Unions	12
Women's Associations	9
Youth Associations	11
TOTAL	**126**

Source: MOET.

Tertiary Education

Figure 2.7 shows a very rapid increase after SY93 in tertiary or higher education enrollments, which more than doubled in two years, far out-stripping the modest increase in primary education, and even the quite rapid increase of secondary education, on the rebound after the four year decline between SY88 and SY92. Over the entire ten year period from SY85 to SY95, enrollments in higher education increased at an annual average rate of 11.1 percent, as compared with 2.1 percent for primary and 1.6 percent for secondary education.

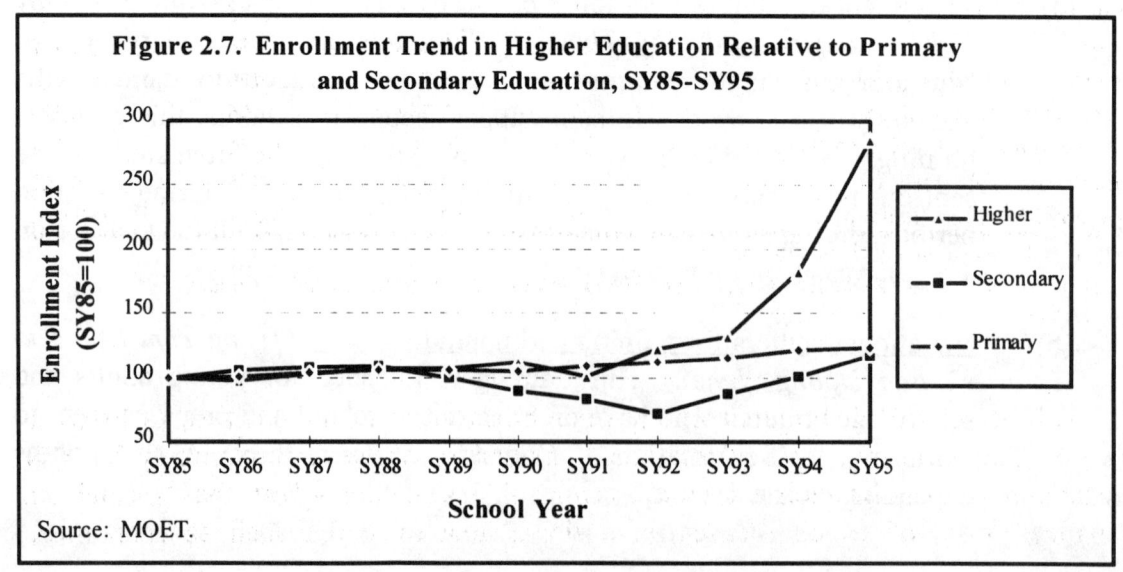

Figure 2.7. Enrollment Trend in Higher Education Relative to Primary and Secondary Education, SY85-SY95

Source: MOET.

As described earlier, higher education in Vietnam takes place both in *colleges* and in *universities*. Most of Vietnam's 45 college-level institutions are managed by the provincial governments. Colleges normally offer three-year courses and grant diplomas to those who graduate. About two-thirds of Vietnam's colleges specialize in training teachers for lower levels of the education system.

Whereas colleges account for four out of each ten higher education institutions (HEIs) in Vietnam, the colleges tend to be small, and the students enrolled in them make up only a relatively small part of the total enrolled in public higher education, about 11 percent in SY95. Most higher education students are enrolled in Vietnam's 65 universities, all but one of which are run by line ministries or specialized agencies of central government (Table 2.5).

Table 2.5. Higher Education Institutions and Enrollments by Agency of Government Responsible, SY95

University or College Level Management Responsibility	Number of Institutions	Number of Students	Average Enrollment	Share of Total Enrollments
Universities	**65**	**315,694**	**4,857**	**89.2%**
Ministry of Transportation and Communications	2	3,295	1,648	0.9%
Ministry of Construction	2	6,792	3,396	1.9%
Ministry of Culture and Information	6	3,955	659	1.1%
Ministry of Education and Training	40	239,591	5,990	67.7%
Regular Universities	*38*	*187,008*	*4,921*	*52.8%*
Open Universities	*2*	*52,583*	*26,292*	*14.8%*
Ministry of Finance	2	26,000	13,000	7.3%
Ministry of Foreign Affairs	1	305	305	0.1%
Ministry of Forestry	1	1,692	1,692	0.5%
Ministry of Health	5	8,776	1,755	2.5%
Ministry of Irrigation	1	2,240	2,240	0.6%
Ministry of Justice	2	20,142	10,071	5.7%
Dept. of Sport and Physical Education	2	1,671	836	0.5%
Province of Hai Phong[a]	1	1,235	1,235	0.3%
Colleges	**45**	**38,409**	**854**	**10.8%**
Central teacher training colleges	8	3,727	466	1.1%
Other central level colleges	5	2,781	556	0.8%
Provincial teacher training colleges	29	29,307	1,011	8.3%
Other provincial colleges[b]	3	2,594	865	0.7%
All Higher Education Institutions	**110**	**354,103**	**3,219**	**100.0%**

[a] Hai Phong In-Service Training University.
[b] Thanh Hoa Medical College, Thanh Hoa Technical and Economic College and Ha Tay Technical College.
Source: MOET.

This study will distinguish among three broad types of universities, as listed in Table 2.6. There are two types of traditional universities, meaning universities that rely on classroom lectures as their principal medium of instruction -- *first*, the "specialized universities," each of which focuses on a single area of study, such as economics, engineering, fine arts or law;[11] and *second*, the "multi-disciplinary universities," including five newly established national and regional universities in some of Vietnam's largest cities.[12]   In addition, there is now a *third* category of university education in Vietnam. Two "open universities" were established in SY94, one each in Hanoi and in Ho Chi Minh City. Already by SY95 these two accounted for 52,583 students, or approximately one out of every seven higher education students in the country.

Table 2.6. Growth of Higher Education Enrollments by Type of Institution, SY91-SY95

University or College Level Type of Institution Name of Institution	SY91	SY92	SY93	SY94	SY95	Growth Rate SY91-95	Share of SY95 Enrollments
Universities	**101,360**	**130,865**	**140,695**	**199,007**	**315,694**	**32.8%**	**89.2%**
Multi-disciplinary universities	*51,042*	*68,997*	*68,728*	*94,492*	*132,339*	*26.9%*	*37.4%*
National University of Hanoi	7,035	8,682	6,557	15,060	20,159	30.1%	5.7%
National University of HCM City	22,686	36,835	40,516	50,812	70,280	32.7%	19.8%
Da Nang Regional University	4,267	3,605	908	4,424	8,166	17.6%	2.3%
Hue Regional University	5,689	5,890	4,879	8,130	10,288	16.0%	2.9%
Thai Nguyen Regional University	4,453	4,804	5,656	5,630	7,086	12.3%	2.0%
Other multi-disciplinary	6,912	9,181	10,212	10,436	16,360	24.0%	4.6%
Specialized universities	*50,318*	*61,868*	*71,967*	*102,570*	*130,772*	*27.0%*	*36.9%*
Agro-forestry	4,803	5,619	6,378	7,044	7,659	12.4%	2.2%
Culture and art	1,856	1,922	1,620	3,016	4,526	25.0%	1.3%
Economics and law	15,345	26,229	33,863	50,455	61,648	41.6%	17.4%
Health and sports	10,283	8,637	9,164	9,856	10,447	0.4%	3.0%
Industry	13,876	15,872	16,618	26,434	39,031	29.5%	11.0%
Pedagogy	4,155	3,589	4,324	5,765	7,461	15.8%	2.1%
Open universities				*1,945*	*52,583*	*..*	*14.8%*
Colleges	**23,124**	**21,116**	**22,153**	**27,405**	**38,409**	**13.5%**	**10.8%**
Central teacher training colleges	3,086	2,269	1,909	2,367	3,727	4.8%	1.1%
Other central level colleges	1,121	1,736	1,955	2,051	2,781	25.5%	0.8%
Provincial teacher training colleges	17,626	15,977	15,926	20,510	29,307	13.6%	8.3%
Other provincial colleges	1,291	1,134	2,363	2,477	2,594	19.1%	0.7%
All Institutions	**124,484**	**151,981**	**162,848**	**226,412**	**354,103**	**29.9%**	**100.0%**

Source: MOET.

Anyone who completes upper secondary education is eligible to be admitted into an open university course after achieving at least minimum grades in an entrance examination; the minimum grades are below the standard required for traditional universities. As might be expected, however, many of those enrolled in the open universities study only part-time. To compare enrollments in higher education across years and between different institutions in the same year, it is necessary to assign fractional weights to students enrolled in part-time programs and then compute the

---

[11] For purposes of this study's analysis, the various specializations of the specialized universities have been collapsed into six larger groups. For example, the economics universities are grouped with the law universities, sports with health, and culture with fine arts.

[12] The two national universities (in Hanoi and Ho Chi Minh City) and three regional universities (in Da Nang, Hue and Thai Nguyen) have all been set up over the last few years, each one by merging some previously existing HEIs into one larger multidisciplinary university. For analytic purposes, to ensure comparability over time, this study treats each of these amalgamated universities as having existed as a single entity even in those years before the merger actually took place.

number of "full-time equivalent" (FTE) students -- a number that is less than the total (unweighted) number of individual students, if the HEI enrolls any part-time students.

Vietnam distinguishes five categories of higher education students:

(a) *Regular full-time students (sinh viên chính quy dài han)* are admitted to colleges and universities according to clearly defined and selective criteria. This group is still the largest of the five higher education groups but has declined in recent years as a percentage of the total number of individuals attending colleges and universities.

(b) Students who have completed two or three years of secondary technical education or vocational training and have a diploma or certificate can undertake upgrading courses and obtain a degree after three years rather than the four or five years required by regular students entering directly from upper secondary school. Such courses are known as *short-term training (ngán han chuyên tu)*.

(c) Another group of students receiving "upgrading" are those who graduated from higher education institutions in the past and are pursuing training or re-training, often in subjects that were not available previously, in order to deal more effectively with their current jobs or to prepare themselves for new jobs. These courses are sometimes called *specialized* or *retraining courses (bòi duong và dào tao lai)*.

(d) Students pursuing *in-service training (tai chúc)* in higher education institutions are, for the most part, civil servants, sponsored by their government offices and studying on a part-time basis. They are studying to upgrade their skills and to prepare for more difficult or more responsible positions upon completion of their training programs. In-service training and short-term training are similar in nature, but the former is usually part-time whereas the latter is more often full-time.

(e) The last group is a residual category simply called in Vietnamese *other (khác)*. This category includes most of those studying at the open universities and is, therefore, a rapidly growing group at this time.

Between 1989 and 1994 there was an additional category of students known as *extra plan students*. During this period, institutions were permitted to take in, on a cost-recovery basis, more students than the number officially approved by the relevant line ministries responsible for particular institutions. These students, who did not qualify for "regular" admission, paid higher fees than regular students and were variously described as "open study mode," "irregular" or "extra plan" students. Because of excess demand for "regular" places in higher education, some HEIs were able to enroll substantial numbers in this category, but MOET reports that this system of admission to HEIs has now been abolished, at least officially. However, the "open study mode" and "extra plan" labels may still be used to refer to students admitted under the old system, some of whom have not yet completed their degrees.

There remains another important distinction, for funding purposes, between "quota" and "non-quota" students. Government grants to HEIs are based on the "quota" of students approved by MPI and MOET, and on the financial norms for different programs and subject specializations set jointly by MPI and MOF. This process is discussed in more detail in Chapter 3. There is no difference between "quota" and "non-quota" students in terms of the content and organization of their courses, and both categories are classified as full-time regular students.

To express enrollments in terms of full-time equivalents (FTEs), the study used differential weights for different categories of students. The weights adopted, which are based on MOET estimates of the relative study load of different courses, were as follows: categories (a) and (b) comprise full-time students and were given full (i.e., 100 percent) weighting; category (c), which refers to part-time students undertaking short periods of upgrading or retraining (not leading to a degree), was given a weight of 25 percent; category (d), which consists of part-time in-service students taking degree-level courses, was given a weight of 55 percent; and (e) which is a heterogeneous category including some students taking non-degree level courses at the professional secondary level in provincial colleges as well as part-time students in open universities, was given a weight of 0.66. These weights result in an estimate of 280,281 FTE students in SY95, which is 79 percent of the total (unweighted) enrollment in both full-time and part-time programs. Figure 2.8 expresses FTEs as a proportion of the total full-time and part-time enrollment of students in higher education from SY91 to SY95. This shows that colleges have a higher proportion of full-time students than universities, but both colleges and universities have enrolled increasing numbers of part-time students in recent years, causing FTE student numbers to decline as a proportion of total enrollment.

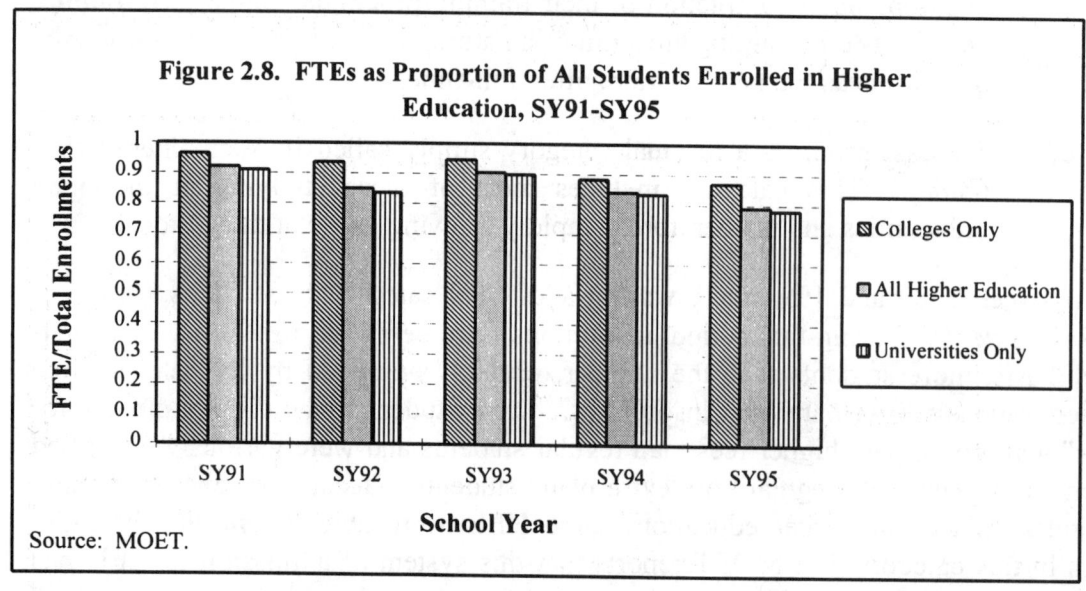

Figure 2.8. FTEs as Proportion of All Students Enrolled in Higher Education, SY91-SY95

Source: MOET.

Figure 2.9 shows the growth of FTEs from SY91 to SY95 in Vietnam's multi-disciplinary universities. Increasing at an average combined annual rate of 24 percent, the multi-disciplinary universities were the fastest growing sub-sector of higher education (with the exception of the open universities, whose FTEs went from about 1,000 to 34,000 in just one year -- between SY94, the year in which the open universities began to operate, and SY95). The National Universities of Ho Chi Minh City and Hanoi grew at a combined annual rate of 29 percent. By SY95 they accounted for 21 percent of Vietnam's FTEs.

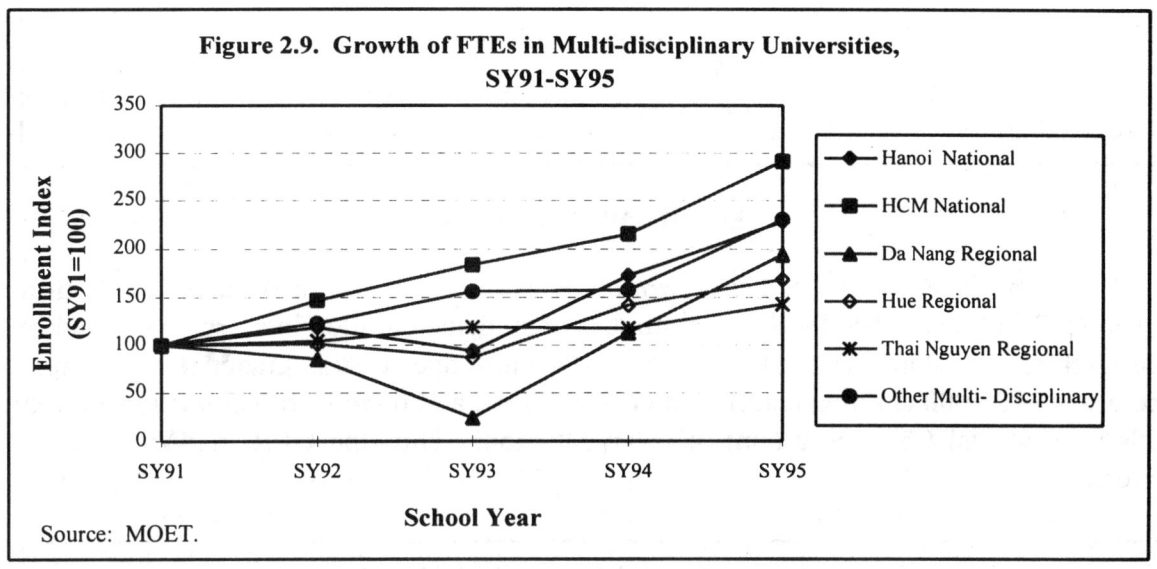

Figure 2.9. Growth of FTEs in Multi-disciplinary Universities, SY91-SY95

Source: MOET.

The specialized universities also grew rapidly during this period -- 22 percent annually (Figure 2.10). The fastest growing categories of such universities were those specializing in economics/law, industry, and culture/arts, whereas FTE enrollments in the health/sports sector were flat over this period. College FTEs grew at 11 percent annually between SY91 and SY94, with teacher training institutions growing more slowly than colleges specializing in other subjects (Figure 2.11).

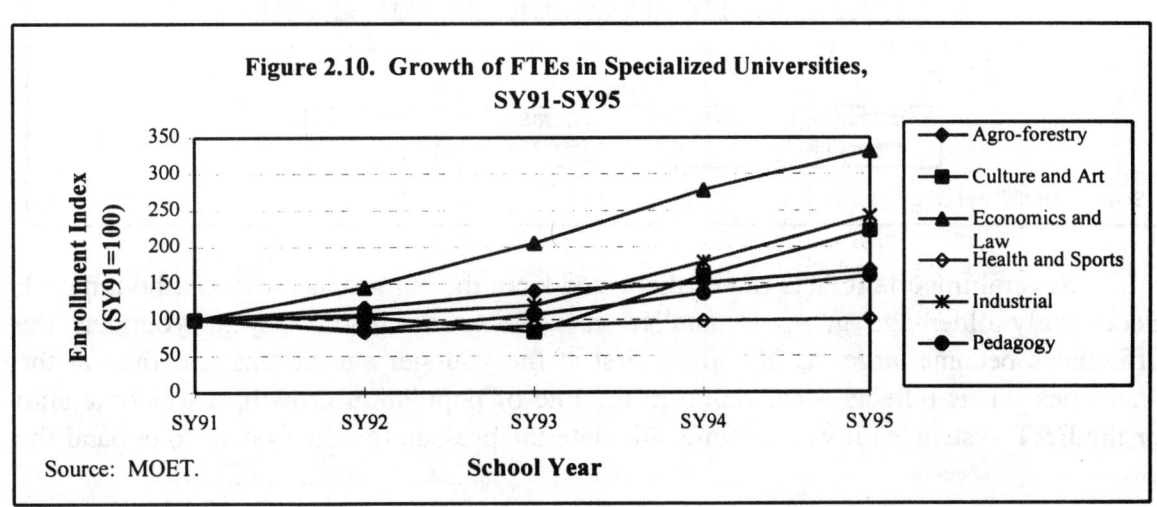

Figure 2.10. Growth of FTEs in Specialized Universities, SY91-SY95

Source: MOET.

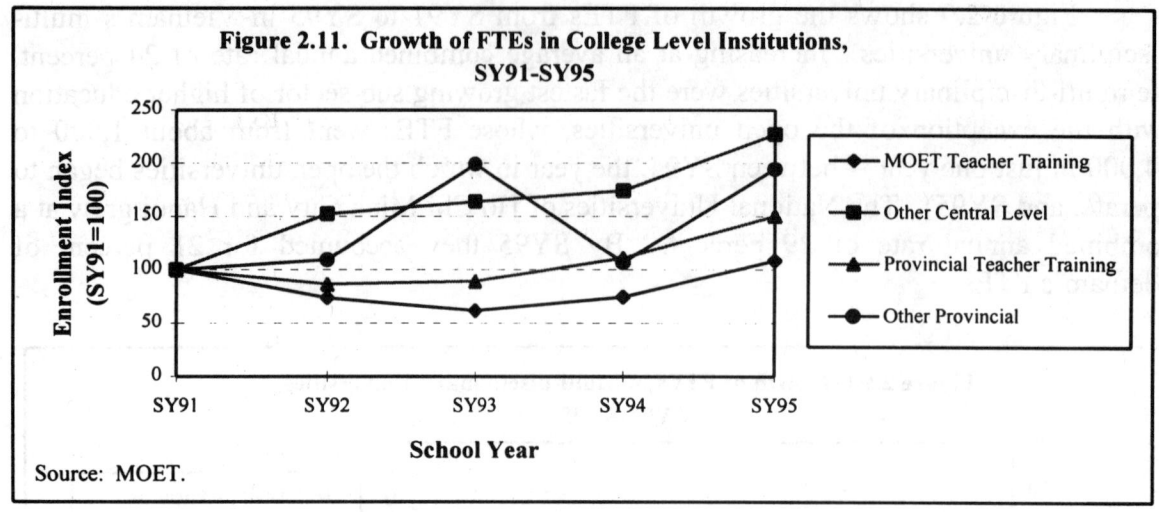

Figure 2.11. Growth of FTEs in College Level Institutions, SY91-SY95

Source: MOET.

ENROLLMENT RATIOS

Figure 2.12 reports the *gross enrollment ratio* (GER) for each school grade from G1 to G12 in SY95. The GER is the number of students enrolled in a grade, divided by the number of children in the population of the right age for this grade. For example, there were 225,000 children enrolled in G12 in SY95, and there were 1.5 million 17 year olds (the official G12 age group) in the population. Thus the GER in SY95 was 15 percent.

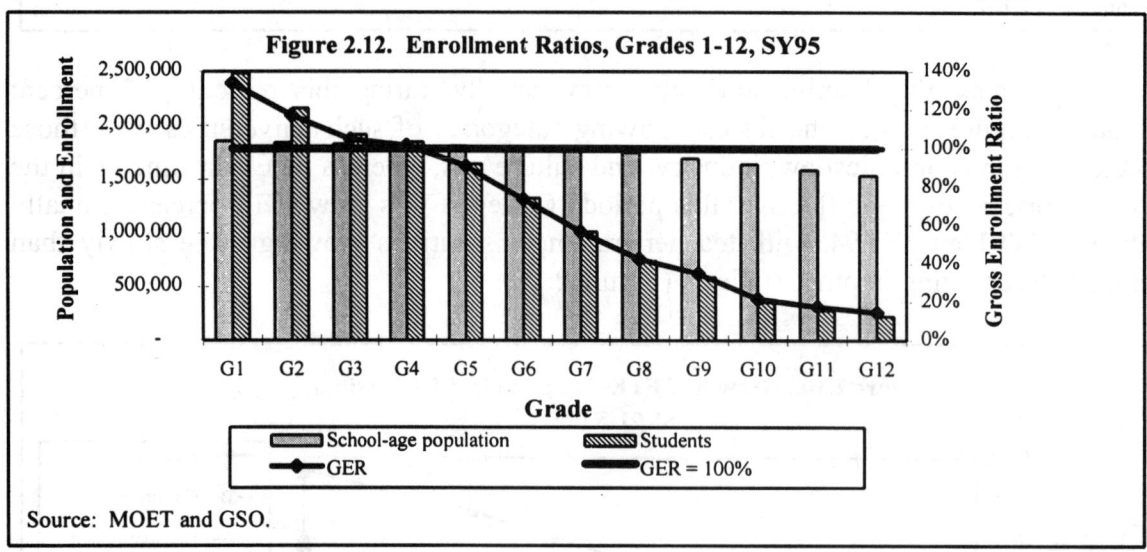

Figure 2.12. Enrollment Ratios, Grades 1-12, SY95

Source: MOET and GSO.

Several important facts can be discerned from the bar graphs. First, although each successively older age group is smaller than the group just one year younger, the differences become larger as one looks first at the younger age groups and then at the older ones. This reflects deceleration in the rate of population growth, a welcome sign for the E&T system, as it will, in time, alleviate the pressure on the system to expand the number of places and allow attention to shift to important issues of consolidation and quality improvement.

Next, one should note that the gross enrollment ratios in G1 to G4 are all above 100 percent. Thus, there are more children actually enrolled in these grades than there are children in the population who fall within the officially sanctioned age ranges for these grades. In other words, children are enrolled in the lowest grades of primary education who are "over-age" (and perhaps a few who are "under-age"). This is quite common in developing countries, especially in rural areas, where long distances to the nearest school and other factors result in children entering school, not at the officially designated entry age, which in Vietnam is six, but at the age of seven, eight or even nine.

Finally, there is a constant and quite rapid decline in GERs moving from left to right -- from G1 to G12. The drop-off in enrollment ratios seen in the data for SY95 reflects a rapid increase in new admissions that occurred between the early 1980s, when those now in G12 were just entering school, and today. It reflects also a high rate of school drop out at each rung of the educational ladder.

The *net enrollment ratio* (NER) is more meaningful than the GER as a measure of an education system's coverage, because it nets out from the numerator both over-age and under-age children. Figure 2.13 presents GERs and NERs for different levels of Vietnam's education system.[13] The difference between GER and NER is largest at the primary level, which most Vietnamese children enter eventually but far fewer children complete. More detail on student flow-through efficiency (enrollment, repetition, drop-out and completion rates) is presented in Chapter 4.

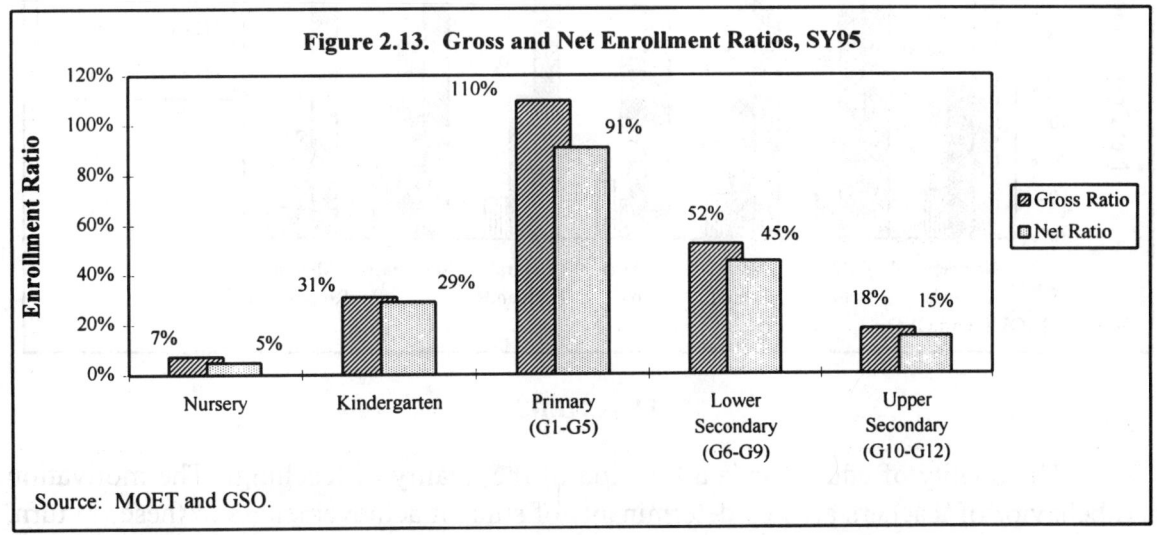

Figure 2.13. Gross and Net Enrollment Ratios, SY95

Source: MOET and GSO.

---

[13] Enrollment ratios are not presented for tertiary education or VOTECH, because of the large age flexibility of students and trainees who participate at these levels.

REGIONAL ENROLLMENTS

Figure 2.14 presents *net enrollment ratios* for primary, lower secondary and upper secondary education in each of Vietnam's seven regions, and it gives the region's ranking on each of the three variables. The Red River Delta and Southeast Regions (those that include Hanoi and Ho Chi Minh City) rank high on all three levels of education. The Mekong River Delta Region (in the South) and North Central Region rank low on all three. Interestingly, the Central Highlands Region, one of the least developed areas of Vietnam, ranks second to last in lower and upper secondary but first in primary education.

Figure 2.15 shows the *growth of enrollments* in primary and general secondary education between SY91 and SY95, region by region. The Central Highlands, which already has high primary enrollments, tops the list on all three growth variables, suggesting that its enrollment ratios for lower and upper secondary education could, in time, match those in Red River Delta and Southeast, the regions with the highest secondary ratios at present. The relatively low growth rates in Northern Uplands, Mekong River Delta and North Central are problematic, since enrollments in these three regions rank low today.

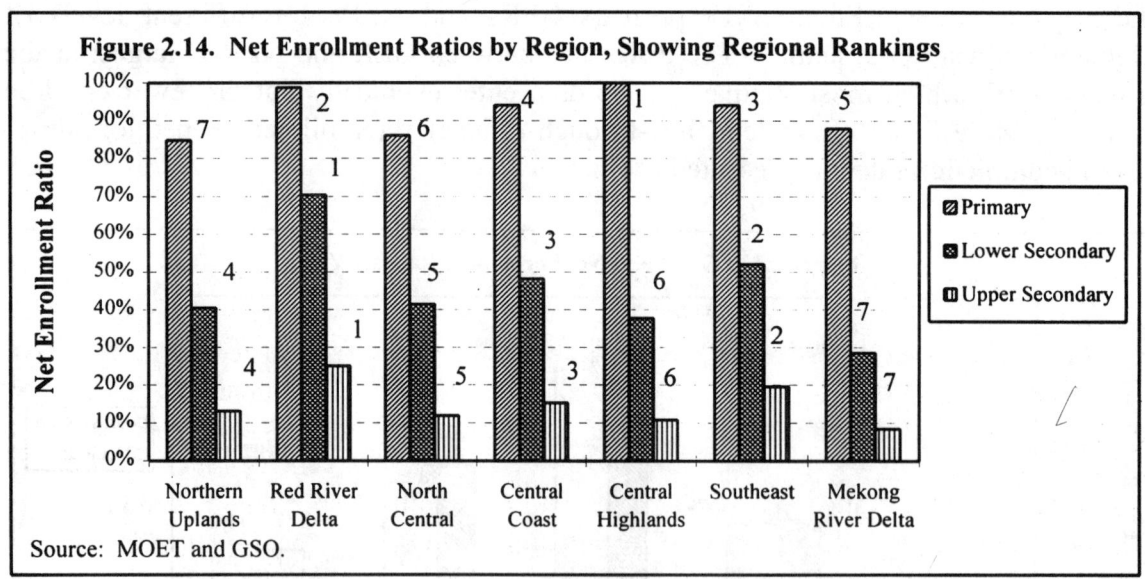

Figure 2.14. Net Enrollment Ratios by Region, Showing Regional Rankings

Source: MOET and GSO.

TEACHERS

The quality of education is a function of the quality of teaching. The motivation and behavior of teachers are key determinants of student achievement, and these, in turn, depend on teachers' qualifications and other characteristics. The importance of good teaching as an input into education tends to be especially true in developing countries, where non-salary inputs, such as teaching aids and textbooks, are in short supply. By the same token, the salaries of teachers account for a very high proportion of current expenditure on education in developing countries, and using teachers efficiently,

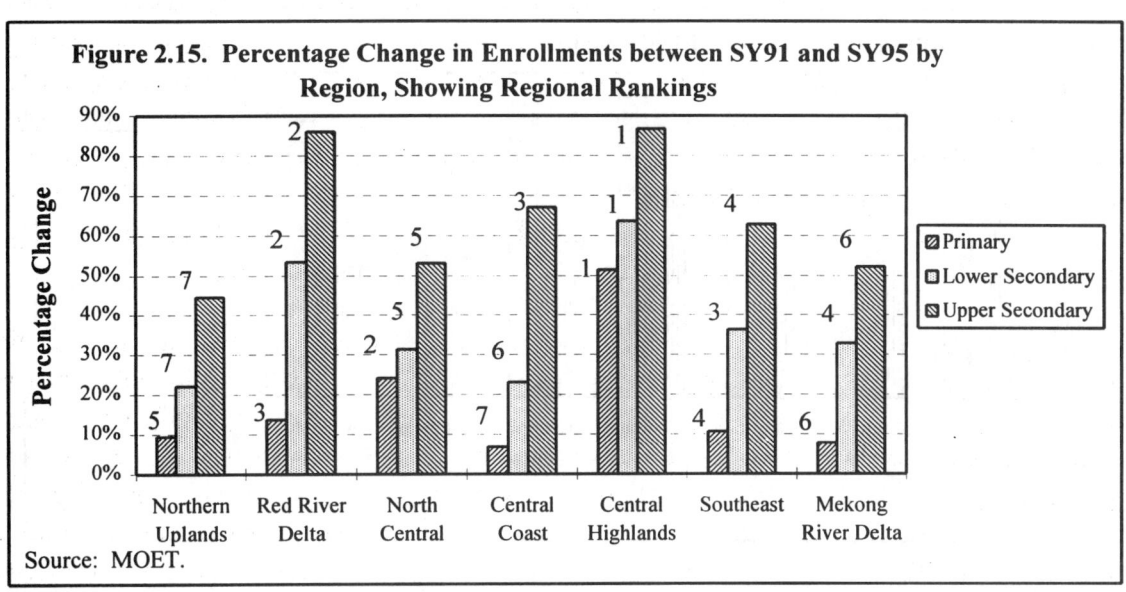

Figure 2.15. Percentage Change in Enrollments between SY91 and SY95 by Region, Showing Regional Rankings

Source: MOET.

therefore, is often the single most important aspect of educational management. This section of the report describes the qualifications and key characteristics of Vietnamese teachers. The utilization of teachers is discussed below (Chapter 4) in the context of education's internal efficiency.

Teacher Qualifications

The definition of what is a "qualified" teacher is specific to every nation and time. In Vietnam today, a teacher in primary and lower secondary education is expected to have graduated from a college-level teacher training institution, and in the case of an upper secondary school teacher, to have graduated from a university. There are, however, teachers at all levels who do not meet these qualifications. It is in primary education that the proportion of qualified teachers is the lowest, about two-thirds, as compared with just under 80 percent and 90 percent in lower and upper secondary education, respectively. The proportion of qualified teachers tends to be lower in the South than in the rest of the country (Figure 2.16). An objective of government policy is to increase the proportion of fully qualified teachers in all regions.

In tertiary education, surprisingly few teaching staff hold the rank of professor or assistant professor, only 5.9 percent in SY95 (as compared with 2.8 percent in SY91). The percentage of professors and assistant professors is marginally higher in the specialized universities (8.5 percent) than in the multi-disciplinary and open universities (6.1 and 7.7 percent), and it is virtually zero (0.3) in Vietnam's college-level institutions.

Academic rank depends on both length of service and academic qualifications. Table 2.7 presents percentages of teaching staff in higher education who hold some post-graduate degree -- Master's (*Thac Si*), Candidate's (*Pho Tiên Si*) or Doctorate (*Tiên Si*)

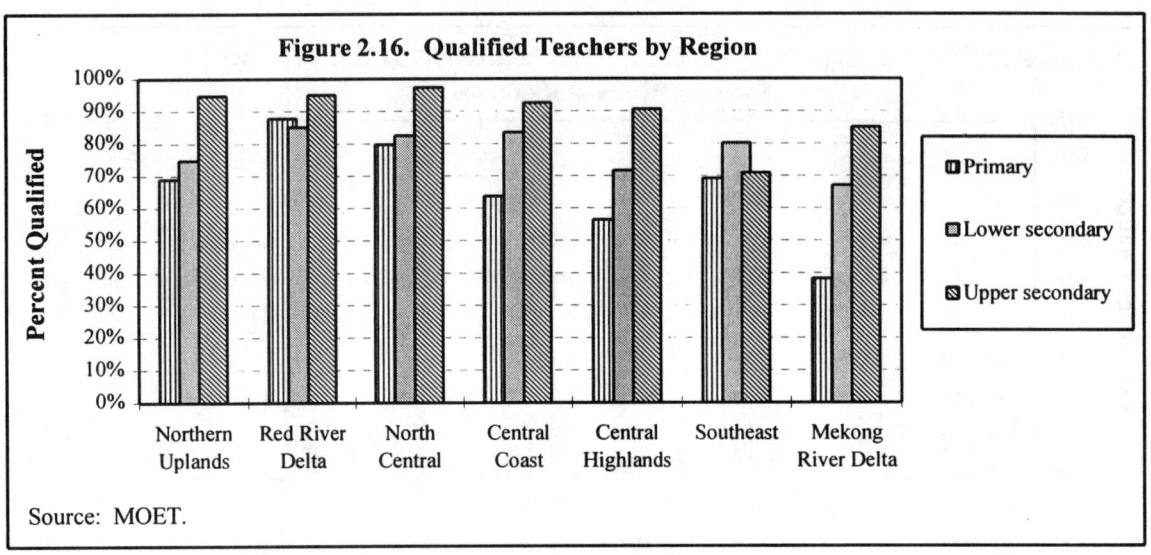

Figure 2.16. Qualified Teachers by Region

Source: MOET.

degree. The percentage increased rapidly between SY91 and SY95 in all types of institutions, reaching 18 percent on average by the end of this period. This percentage is highest in the National Universities of Hanoi and Ho Chi Minh City, and in some types of specialized universities. The percentage can be expected to increase further as many Vietnamese now studying abroad return home and take up academic positions.

Teachers' Salaries

Salaries are low in Vietnam, and people feel poor and, by objective standards, are poor. Many teachers end up "moon-lighting," i.e., taking on second jobs to supplement their teachers' salaries and to help make ends meet. Table 2.8 presents rough estimates of teachers' earnings, calculated by dividing the fiscal salary bill for teachers in 1994 by the number of staff (headmasters, teachers, and nonteaching staff) in 1994.[14] The average annual payroll remuneration of staff in primary education in 1994 was approximately VND 2.8 million ($254). Staff in lower secondary education earn 21 percent more and those in upper secondary 92 percent more than those in primary education.

Comparing the earnings of education workers to the average income of everyone in the population, Table 2.8 shows that the average remuneration of a staff person in primary education was 17 percent above GDP per capita in 1994. The average remunerations of workers in lower and upper secondary education, respectively, were 41 percent and 124 percent above GDP per capita. Are these differentials large or small in international terms? By comparison with 12 high-income OECD countries and, even more so, by comparison with 14 other countries in the Asia Region, the relative earnings

---

[14] The number of staff in 1994 is a weighted average of the numbers in SY94 and SY95.

Table 2.7. Teachers in Higher Education Institutions with Post-Graduate Degrees

Type of HEI	SY91	SY92	SY93	SY94	SY95
Universities	**14.2%**	**15.0%**	**15.4%**	**16.7%**	**20.8%**
Multi-disciplinary universities	*13.2%*	*13.3%*	*14.1%*	*15.4%*	*21.2%*
National University of Hanoi	27.0%	27.0%	28.1%	30.4%	31.2%
National University of HCM City	11.9%	12.8%	14.8%	16.0%	22.7%
Da Nang Regional University	6.2%	7.9%	6.9%	5.6%	9.6%
Hue Regional University	4.9%	5.2%	5.5%	6.2%	18.8%
Thai Nguyen Regional University	8.7%	7.3%	7.7%	8.1%	18.3%
Other multi-disciplinary	4.0%	4.3%	4.2%	7.3%	12.3%
Specialized universities	*14.9%*	*16.6%*	*16.6%*	*18.1%*	*20.1%*
Agro-forestry	12.6%	16.2%	17.3%	21.0%	20.7%
Culture and art	3.7%	2.4%	5.1%	4.0%	8.1%
Economics and law	9.6%	11.0%	10.8%	13.2%	16.6%
Health and sports	9.2%	9.8%	11.0%	11.1%	18.3%
Industry	26.8%	27.4%	26.6%	27.9%	26.3%
Pedagogy	9.8%	10.8%	8.7%	10.3%	10.8%
Open universities	...	...	...	n.a.	23.2%
Colleges	**1.0%**	**0.7%**	**1.0%**	**3.1%**	**6.7%**
Central teacher training colleges	4.6%	0.7%	0.7%	3.8%	9.1%
Other central level colleges	1.5%	3.0%	2.5%	11.2%	1.8%
Provincial teacher training colleges	0.3%	0.5%	0.9%	2.8%	7.5%
Other provincial colleges	0.9%	0.8%	1.0%	0.7%	0.0%
All Institutions	**11.8%**	**12.2%**	**12.6%**	**14.1%**	**18.0%**

... = not applicable (open universities not yet established); n.a. = information not available

Source: MOET

Table 2.8. Annual Earnings of Staff in Education, 1994

Level	Average earnings of teachers in Vietnam			Average earnings of teachers as compared to GDP per capita in:		
	VND ('000)	US$[a]	Index (primary=1)	Vietnam[b]	14 Asian countries	12 OECD countries
Primary	2,778	253	1.00	1.17	2.4	1.6
Secondary	--	--	--	--	2.7	1.7
Lower Secondary	3,356	305	1.21	1.41	--	--
Upper Secondary	5,334	485	1.92	2.24	--	--

[a] Exchange Rate (August 1994): US$1.00 = VND 11,000.
[b] 1994 per capita GDP: US$217.

Sources: For Vietnam, MOF and MOET data; for Asian and OECD comparators, Mingat 1996.

of education staff in Vietnam, especially those working in basic education (primary and lower secondary) are rather low. This finding is consistent with the fact, to be discussed in Chapter 5, that wages in Vietnam are compressed -- in other words, the differences in earnings of individuals who have more and less education are smaller than the differences observed in most market economies. An outcome of the current economic transition in Vietnam is likely to be a more differentiated wage structure. In the meantime, however, many education workers in Vietnam are likely to continue to "moon-light." The impact of this behavior on the quality of education is problematic.

Male and Female Teachers

The proportion of teachers who are women is high in Vietnam in pre-tertiary education. It is highest at the primary level (77 percent) and gets smaller as one moves up the education ladder. But even in upper secondary education, about half of the teachers in SY95 were female. The proportion tends to be highest in the North, lower in the South and Central Zones (Figure 2.17). The proportion becomes quite small in tertiary education (32 percent).

PRIVATE (NON-PUBLIC) EDUCATION AND TRAINING

Government's objectives for E&T include increasing educational coverage and changing educational content so as to prepare workers to perform effectively in the labor market. A major reform designed to further these objectives is the development of a "non-public" system of education and training to parallel the public system. The Fourth Plenum of the Central Committee of the Communist Party in 1992 reached several important decisions for the future development of E&T in Vietnam, including plans for the consolidation of public education, encouragement of people-founded institutions at all levels, and legalization of private institutions in pre-school education and VOTECH.

Vietnam's history of free education and centralized planning made this a politically sensitive direction in which to move. This may explain the reliance on

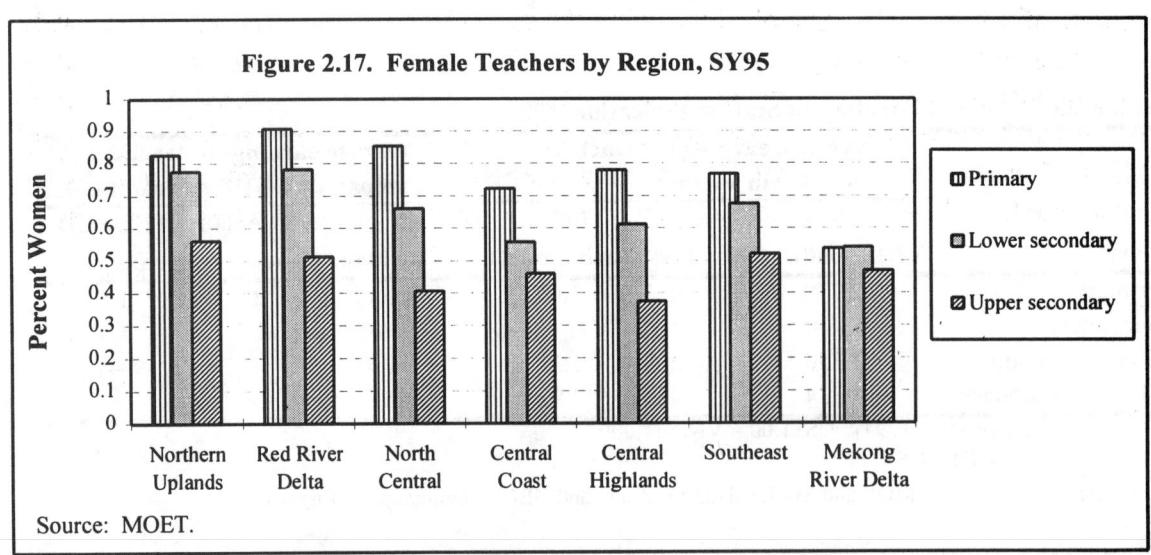

Figure 2.17. Female Teachers by Region, SY95

Source: MOET.

euphemisms such as "non-public" in most contexts instead of clear reference to "privatization" of education. Nevertheless, the policy changes introduced over a relatively short period of time are quite profound and will affect future developments in the sector.

Definitions of Non-Public

Three categories of non-public educational institutions can be distinguished:

- Semi-public (*Ban Công*). The facility is owned by the state and managed by a public authority at the central, provincial, district or commune level, but all operating costs are covered by student fees.

- People-founded (*Dân Lập*). People-founded institutions are owned and managed by non-government organizations or private associations such as trade unions, cooperatives, youth organizations and women's' associations. As with semi-public institutions, there is close to full cost recovery.

- Private (*Tu Lập*). These are private institutions in the usual sense of the word, owned and managed by private individuals. Fully private institutions are not allowed in general education (primary and secondary), but only in pre-school, VOTECH and tertiary education. A regulation permitting the establishment of private higher education institutions (HEIs) in 1993, based on Decision 240/TT of the Prime Minister, was suspended soon thereafter, but a new such regulation appears imminent. For the time being, the non-public HEIs in Vietnam (ten or so at this time, concentrated in just three cities, Hanoi, Ho Chi Minh City and Da Nang) are all semi-public or people-founded.

The best of the people-founded and private institutions in the country offer an attractive alternative form of education for some families. Box 2.2 describes a successful example of a non-public school. Increasing the number of such institutions nation-wide, under guidelines from the state, can provide high-quality education for those families who can afford to pay "full price." This strategy should help Government to meet its medium- to long-term enrollment targets and reduce what must be covered from the state budget. For the foreseeable future, however, the public system will continue to be the source of educational access for most families in Vietnam, especially in basic education.

Box 2.2. Luong The Vinh Secondary School

Founded in 1989, Luong The Vinh in Hanoi was the first people-founded secondary school in Vietnam. The directors and staff of Luong The Vinh are justifiably proud of the school's success in meeting its original objectives, which were to provide a high quality education, with an emphasis on discipline and ethics, and to prepare students to enter universities. By SY94, Luong The Vinh had produced its first graduates, and in that year 90 percent of the graduating students were admitted into tertiary institutions. This gives the school one of the highest admission rates in the country. The average for public schools in Vietnam is between 15 and 20 percent. The school's 130 teachers are, for the most part, experienced and successful teachers teaching in public universities and schools, who teach only part-time at Luong The Vinh.

The school's administrators have considerable autonomy in financial management, but they are clearly accountable to students and their parents, who pay a monthly tuition fee equivalent to about $10 per student. Not counting the other costs of sending a child to school, this high fee, which represents about half of the average per capita income in Vietnam, obviously rules out Luong The Vinh attendance by most children from poor homes, even though the school does have a scholarship fund set up to attract some poor but deserving students. Merit awards and commendations are given to the school's highest achieving students.

Luong The Vinh provides instruction at both the lower and upper secondary education levels. Although the school offers all of the subjects stipulated by MOET for public schools, its curriculum emphasis is different. For instance, in grades 6-8, students concentrate on mathematics, Vietnamese language and foreign languages. From G10 onwards, students are divided into four groups according to their choice of subjects. Study of each group is geared to success in one of the entrance examinations for universities: (a) mathematics, physics and chemistry; (b) mathematics, chemistry and biology; (c) literature, history and geography; (d) mathematics, literature and foreign languages.

The student body has increased rapidly at Luong The Vinh -- 6 percent on average annually since 1989. In SY95, there were 1,670 students enrolled. All that holds back further expansion is a lack of facilities necessary to cope with additional students. Of 2,300 who applied for admission in SY95, only 500 were admitted. At present, the school rents its classroom space and other facilities. This provides little long-term security in Hanoi's high-rent environment. The school's directors are exploring the possibility of a major capital campaign to provide the school with a more stable future. Clearly, there is adequate economic demand at this time for the kind of education that Luong The Vinh and schools like this can provide.

Source: VEFSS Team

Non-Public Enrollments.   Figure 2.18 shows the growth of non-public enrollments as a percentage of total enrollments between SY94 and SY96. In pre-school and upper secondary education, non-public enrollments now comprise a significant proportion of the total, but total (public plus non-public) enrollments at these two levels comprise only a small part of all students in the system -- less than 15 percent in the case of pre-school and 4-5 percent in the case of upper secondary (see Table 2.3 above). Basic education (primary and lower secondary), which accounts for about 80 percent of all students, is still almost entirely publicly provided.

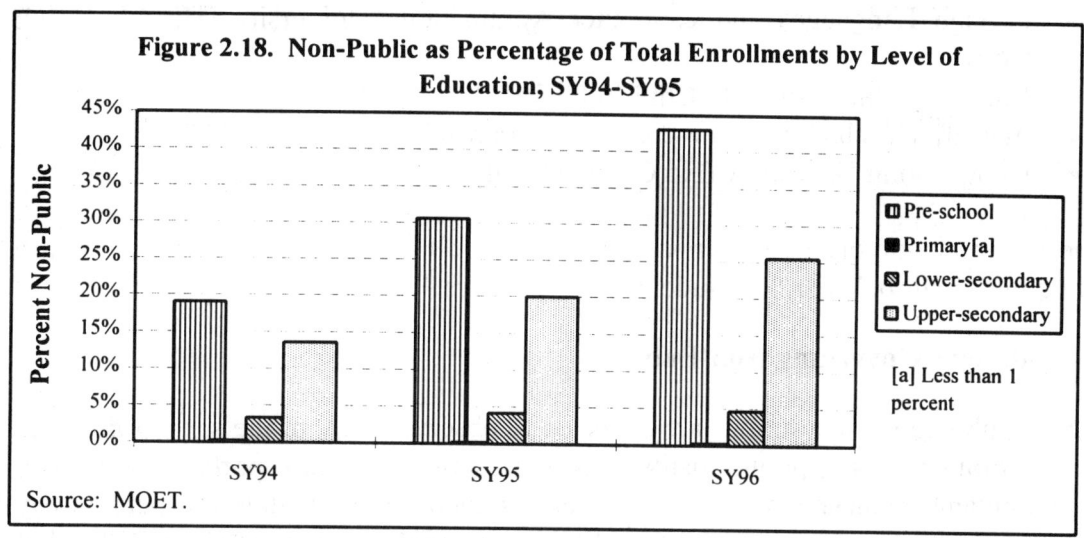

Figure 2.18. Non-Public as Percentage of Total Enrollments by Level of Education, SY94-SY95

VOTECH includes large numbers of semi-public (i.e., fee-paying) trainees, but it is difficult to assign a precise percentage because of the difficulty in getting an accurate count of trainees enrolled in short-term VTC courses (see above). The number of people-founded and private vocational schools and training centers is also growing. Most of these serve industrial areas in Vietnam's larger towns and cities.

Non-public tertiary education was not permitted under the law until 1993, but Thang Long, Vietnam's first private university, opened its doors on an experimental basis several years before this (see Box 2.3). Non-public enrollments make up a small part of enrollments in those traditional tertiary institutions that rely on face-to-face instruction. Vietnam's two open universities, however, which started offering courses only in SY94 but which already account for 15 percent of students in higher education, enroll students on a semi-public basis. Thus, taking the open universities into account, non-public enrollments have increased rapidly recently as a proportion of total tertiary enrollments.

In SY96, there were 11 non-public HEIs in Vietnam, four of them semi-public and the rest people-founded. All but one are located in Ho Chi Minh City or Hanoi:

(a)   *Semi-public HEIs*

- Ho Chi Minh City Open University
- Hanoi Open University
- Ho Chi Minh City Marketing College

(b)   *People-founded HEIs*

- Thang Long University (Hanoi)
- Phuong Dong University (Hanoi)
- Dong Do University (Hanoi)
- Duy Tan University (Da Nang)

- Foreign Languages and Computer Applications University (Ho Chi Minh City)
- Van Lang University (Ho Chi Minh City)
- Industrial Technology University (Ho Chi Minh City)
- Hung Vuong University (Ho Chi Minh City)

With the exception of the two open universities, enrollments in these institutions are currently quite small, below 1,000 students in most cases.

Legal Regulations Governing Non-Public

Non-public E&T institutions are expected to observe many of the same guidelines as public institutions. Non-public institutions must submit annual reports to MOET on their academic and financial status. They are also subject to unscheduled inspections by provincial or district representatives of the Ministry. MOET can shut down an institution if any of the following has been demonstrated: (a) inadequate revenues to cover current expenditures; (b) instruction that does not meet MOET's quality standards; (c) violation of any regulation or law of the State.

Fees charged by non-public institutions are only loosely monitored by MOET. How much an institution can charge is controlled largely by the unwillingness of families to pay fees that are out of line with those charged by public institutions or competing non-public institutions. Monthly fees are typically about VND 15,000 (slightly more than $1) at the pre-school level, and 10 to 20 times higher than this at the upper secondary and tertiary levels.

Many teachers in non-public institutions also teach in the public system. Public system teachers are allowed to work in second jobs so long as they satisfy the minimum number of hours required in their main jobs. The minimums are quite low, only 20 hours a week (or the hours set in the teaching plan) for a primary or lower secondary teacher, and 18 hours for an upper secondary teacher.

Box 2.3. Thang Long University

Thang Long University was founded in 1988 on the outskirts of Hanoi as the Thang Long "University Center." Thang Long started on an experimental basis, to test the viability and desirability of a new model of higher education. As the first non-public tertiary institution in modern-day Vietnam, it received careful scrutiny. The pilot stage actually lasted longer than it took the first of Thang Long's students to graduate. Only in August 1994 did Thang Long itself graduate to full legal status, since which time it has been called a "University."

When Thang Long first opened, there were just 100 students enrolled. In SY96, the number was 450, although MOET had actually approved an enrollment of 700. Approximately 90 percent of the students come from Hanoi itself, and 80 percent are children of civil servants. Access from neighboring provinces is difficult owing to the high cost of living in the city. The university intends to conduct external classes outside Hanoi starting in SY97 in order to increase the number of students from other provinces.

When Thang Long opened, students were asked to pay the equivalent of 10 kilograms of rice per month as their tuition fee. In 1996, the annual fee was set at two million VND, about $180, which yields enough to meet the institution's recurrent expenditures. About 5-10 percent of students receive merit-based awards that may cover up to 50 percent of their fee. Although Thang Long does not receive financial support from the Government, it does receive modest assistance from Vietnamese living abroad and from several non-governmental organizations.

Unlike public universities, Thang Long has considerable autonomy to decide what is taught and how it is taught. The university's stated mission is to provide students with a high standard of academic training so as to impart skills geared to the labor market in Vietnam's transitional economy. Thang Long's first department taught mathematics and information science only. A management department was added in 1992, and two more departments (law and English language) in 1996. The graduates of Thang Long (more than 100 by 1996) are reported to be employed in a wide range of jobs, including private sector work, in Vietnam's large urban centers.

A student at Thang Long completes four years (eight semesters) to obtain a Bachelor of Science or Bachelor of Management degree awarded by MOET. Instruction during the first two years is general, with courses offered in fields such as philosophy, languages and computer science. Students who leave after two years receive a Diploma in General University Studies awarded by the University itself. In the third and fourth years, students specialize in one of the four departments of study. Although the medium of instruction is Vietnamese, two foreign languages, one of them English, are compulsory requirements for all students.

Source: VEFSS Team

The procedures to be followed to get permission to open a non-public institution are outlined in Box 2.4. By the standards of some countries, where suspicion of private education remains much stronger, the regulations in Vietnam are not particularly onerous. The willingness of individuals, organizations and associations in Vietnam to set up non-public institutions in response to the recent relaxation of official restrictions that limited such institutions previously has been remarkably quick and wide-spread. Government has not only lifted restrictions, but has provided a number of positive incentives as well. For example, private vocational schools and training centers are exempt from paying business and income taxes (Socialist Republic of Vietnam, Government Instruction No. 347/KTTH, January 21, 1995).

Box 2.4. Procedures for Registering Non-public Education Institutions

<u>Lower levels of education</u>. To establish a non-public institution below the level of a university requires that a proposal be submitted to either the provincial or district education department and the people's committee. The level of government whose approval is required depends on the level of the proposed institution and whether it would operate on a semi-public, people-founded, or fully private basis. The proposal for any new institution also needs to have the prior endorsement of the authorities of the commune in which the institution would be opened.

<u>Higher education</u>. To establish a non-public HEI currently requires the approval of the Prime Minister's Office. Some non-public universities are started as new institutions. Others are converted from public to semi-public or people-founded status. In either case, the first step is to convene a council of founders or initiators who accept responsibility to govern the new institution if opened. The council prepares and submits a preliminary proposal to MOET, which reviews it and, if acceptable to MOET, transmits it to the Prime Minister's Office via the Office of Government. In the case of a people-founded university, the application must include a draft corporate charter. If and when the application receives the Prime Minister's approval, a decision is announced by MOET recognizing the new university. This process can take several years to complete. Typically, between the time an application is submitted and approval is given, MOET will send at least one supervision mission from the relevant provincial department of education to meet with the council of initiators, discuss with them the proposed academic program, review the financial plan and inspect the facilities.

The government regulations pertaining to these legal steps are spelled out in a series of legal decisions of the Socialist Government of Vietnam, indicated by asterisks in this report's bibliography.

Source: MOET

The private education movement is a subject of intense interest to policymakers in Vietnam at this time. The jury is still out, as it were, on whether or not this is a movement fully consistent with the ideals of Vietnamese society. Whatever information this study and future investigations can provide policymakers as to the efficiency and equity consequences of the private education movement in Vietnam will be a vital input into the Government's final verdict.

3. EDUCATION EXPENDITURE AND FINANCE

Redefining the role of government has been a central feature of Vietnam's transition from central planning to a market economy. In the social sectors this transition has been reflected in major changes in the provision and financing of social services. As part of Vietnam's program of structural reform, user fees were introduced for publicly-provided education services, and private sector provision was liberalized in 1989. This diversification of resource mobilization presents new challenges to policymakers in education. Instead of allocating resources for education subject to the public budget constraint alone, policymakers can now choose between three alternative financing instruments in meeting education policy objectives: (1) public subsidies, (2) cost recovery for public schooling, and (3) private sector provision of education, which usually implies high levels of private financing. In order to meet this challenge, policymakers need reliable and up-to-date information on the structure of education expenditure and finance: How much is spent on education? Who spends it? What is it spent on?

This chapter assesses the present pattern of education finance as Vietnam emerges from the ongoing process of economic transition. Section A begins by analyzing the structure of government spending, including the State Budget and off-budget expenditures in the form of disbursements of Official Development Assistance (ODA) and outlays by communes. This analysis draws on new data compiled by the Ministry of Finance for VEFSS using the IMF's Government Finance Statistics (GFS) classification format. Section B examines the role of cost recovery in publicly provided E&T, using evidence on the structure and affordability of prices and assessing the complementary roles of scholarships and student loan schemes in promoting equity. Section C then reviews briefly the emerging but still limited role, described more fully in Chapter 2, of the private sector in the provision and financing of education today in Vietnam. Finally, Section D assembles the flow of funds for the E&T sector in a matrix that shows aggregate sources and uses of funds. This matrix summarizes the current structure of education finance, and it sets the baseline for assessing alternative scenarios for education sector development in Chapter 6.

PUBLIC EXPENDITURE ON EDUCATION

Intergovernmental Expenditure Assignments

The assignment of government expenditure responsibilities for E&T spans not only the official State Budget, comprising two components (central and local government), but also off-budget expenditures funded by ODA and communes. Taken together, the on-budget and off-budget sources of government expenditure on E&T added up to about VND 6,035 billion in 1994, which was about 3.6 percent of GDP (see Table 3.1). About 85 percent of public outlays on E&T are on-budget, i.e., spent through the

State Budget. These State Budget expenditures are allocated broadly according to the distribution of administrative responsibilities across the two main tiers of government.

Table 3.1:   Expenditure Assignments for Education and Training by Level of Government, 1991-1994
(in VND millions at current prices)

	1991		1992		1993		1994	
	Amount	Share	Amount	Share	Amount	Share	Amount	Share
CURRENT EXPENDITURE	997,976	67%	1,544,686	65%	2,635,511	67%	4,058,743	67%
State Budget	957,357	96%	1,496,954	97%	2,572,329	98%	3,977,673	98%
Central	224,877	23%	356,640	24%	478,196	19%	937,634	24%
Local	732,480	77%	1,140,314	76%	2,094,133	81%	3,040,039	76%
Off-Budget	40,619	4%	47,732	3%	63,182	2%	81,070	2%
Commune	40,619	100%	47,732	100%	63,182	100%	81,070	100%
ODA	-	0%	-	0%	-	0%	-	0%
CAPITAL EXPENDITURE	483,971	33%	825,563	35%	1,325,920	33%	1,976,558	33%
State Budget	298,839	62%	541,293	66%	934,167	70%	1,033,430	52%
Central	142,269	48%	246,720	46%	395,314	42%	455,208	44%
Local	156,570	52%	294,573	54%	538,853	58%	578,222	56%
Off-Budget	185,132	38%	284,270	34%	391,753	30%	943,128	48%
Commune	121,512	66%	147,772	52%	189,827	48%	314,015	33%
ODA	63,620	34%	136,498	48%	201,926	52%	629,113	67%
TOTAL EXPENDITURE	1,481,946	100%	2,370,249	100%	3,961,431	100%	6,035,301	100%
State Budget	1,256,196	85%	2,038,247	86%	3,506,496	89%	5,011,103	83%
Central	367,146	29%	603,360	30%	873,510	25%	1,392,842	28%
Local	889,050	71%	1,434,887	70%	2,632,986	75%	3,618,261	72%
Off-Budget	225,750	15%	332,002	14%	454,935	11%	1,024,198	17%
Commune	162,131	72%	195,504	59%	253,009	56%	395,085	39%
ODA	63,620	28%	136,498	41%	201,926	44%	629,113	61%

Source: MOF.

Central Government. The central component of the State Budget finances most university education and some VOTECH and college education (cf. Tables 2.2, 2.3 and 2.6 above). About two-thirds of the central budget for E&T is allocated to the Ministry of Education and Training. MOET administers nearly half of Vietnam's universities and pedagogical colleges training teachers for upper secondary and post-secondary education. Other central agencies with substantial involvement in higher education are Culture and Information (six universities), Health (five), Communication and Transport, Finance, Justice, Construction and Sport and Physical Education (two each). Several other ministries administer one university each and are allocated budget for this purpose. The central government budget also finances a variety of "targeted" education programs (a subset of Vietnam's 28 national priority programs). These are financed through the central budget but implemented by local governments on behalf of the center.

Local Government. Local budgets subsidize the lower levels of schooling. The provincial tier of local government is responsible for secondary schools, and for colleges that train primary and lower secondary school teachers, as well as for post-secondary VOTECH. District governments are responsible for allocating State Budget subsidies going to primary and pre-school education (cf. Table 2.2). Given the administrative responsibilities of these three tiers of government, the central budget plays a relatively minor role in the overall allocation of State Budget expenditures for education, accounting for only about a quarter, while the remaining three-quarters is spent by local governments.

Off-Budget. About 15 percent of public sector outlays on education are off-budget. Most of these off-budget expenditures comprise ODA disbursements for E&T, which should be, but most of which are not, recorded as part of the official State Budget. ODA grew rapidly in the early 1990s, rising from US$ 8 million in 1991 to US$ 57 million in 1994 (see Table 3.2). This amounts to VND 629 billion, or more than 10 percent of recorded public sector outlays for the sector in that year. Commune level governments provide additional financing for education, but the magnitude and allocation of these outlays nation-wide is not known with precision, since commune budgets were not integrated into the official State Budget in the past.[15] Results from the recent Vietnam Social Sector Survey (VSSS), carried out by GSO with ADB assistance, of a small sample of 60 urban and rural communes indicate that commune expenditures on education averaged about VND 5,500 per capita in 1994. This suggests that commune level financing contributes a relatively small additional amount to off-budget government expenditure -- in the range of VND 400 billion per year. Most of this amount finances capital spending on primary schools.[16]

Table 3.2:   Official Development Assistance by Level and Type of Education and Training, 1991-1995
             (in US$ thousands at current prices)

	1991		1992		1993		1994		1995 (planned)	
	Amount	Share	Amount	Share	Amount	Share	Amount	Share	Amount	Share
Sector Policy and Planning	299	3%	177	1%	769	4%	1,169	2%	1,338	4%
Primary Schooling	517	6%	1,188	10%	2,170	11%	21,248	37%	4,682	12%
Secondary Schooling	2,135	24%	3,636	30%	2,489	13%	4,530	8%	465	1%
Tertiary Education	1,778	20%	2,501	20%	3,784	20%	14,519	25%	19,770	52%
Technical/managerial	3,648	41%	3,810	31%	7,957	42%	14,293	25%	9,894	26%
Non-Formal Education	483	5%	930	8%	1,809	10%	1,668	3%	1,647	4%
TOTAL	8,860	100%	12,242	100%	18,978	100%	57,427	100%	37,796	100%

Source: UNDP 1995.

Trends in Public Expenditure. Government spending on education grew rapidly during the early 1990s, more than doubling in real terms between 1991 and 1994 (see Table 3.3). Since this increase exceeded the growth of population, expenditure rose also in per capita terms. The strong fiscal performance in the E&T sector was made possible by the financial recovery that began in 1992 in response to the government's macroeconomic stabilization program implemented during 1990-91. The strength of the overall government expenditure effort allowed public spending on E&T to rise in absolute terms even though the sector share of the State Budget experienced some setbacks during the early 1990s. E&T's share of the overall discretionary State Budget (i.e., net of interest payments) fell from nearly 12 percent in 1991 to 9 percent in 1992, before recovering to around 12 percent in 1994. Over the same period, current spending

---

[15] They will be included in the future, under the new Budget Law passed on March 20, 1996.

[16] A recent World Bank Report provides an additional source of data on expenditure by Vietnam's communes on E&T and other services (World Bank 1996).

on E&T as a share of the discretionary budget increased slightly (from 8.8 to 9.3 percent), while capital expenditure's share declined (from 2.8 to 2.4 percent). The end result of these trends has been that the E&T sector achieved a remarkable increase in its share of GDP during the early 1990s, nearly doubling from 1.9 percent in 1991 to 3.6 percent in 1994.

Table 3.3. Trends in Government Expenditure on Education, 1991-1994

		1991	1992	1993	1994
EXPENDITURE AT CONSTANT 1991 PRICES (in VND millions)					
State Budget	Current	957,357	1,128,700	1,696,436	2,290,572
	Capital	298,839	408,134	616,078	595,108
Government Expenditure[a]	Current	997,976	1,164,689	1,738,105	2,337,257
	Capital	483,971	622,473	874,437	1,138,215
	Total	1,481,946	1,787,162	2,612,541	3,475,472
GROWTH OF EXPENDITURE (Annual Percent)					
State Budget	Current		18%	50%	35%
	Capital		37%	51%	-3%
Government Expenditure[a]	Current		17%	49%	34%
	Capital		29%	40%	30%
	Total		21%	46%	33%
PER CAPITA EXPENDITURE AT CONSTANT 1991 PRICES (in VND)					
Government Expenditure[a]	Current	14,725	16,781	24,471	32,234
	Capital	7,141	8,969	12,312	15,697
	Total	21,866	25,750	36,783	47,931
PERCENTAGE SHARE OF DISCRETIONARY STATE BUDGET					
Government Expenditure[a]	Current	8.8%	6.8%	7.3%	9.3%
	Capital	2.8%	2.5%	2.6%	2.4%
	Total	11.6%	9.3%	9.9%	11.8%
PERCENTAGE SHARE OF GDP					
Government Expenditure[a]	Current	1.3%	1.4%	1.9%	2.4%
	Capital	0.6%	0.7%	1.0%	1.2%
	Total	1.9%	2.1%	2.9%	3.5%
Memorandum Items:					
GDP deflator (1991=100)		100	133	152	174
Population (in millions)		68	69	71	73
State current excl. interest (in VND billions)		21,401	37,888	63,016	76,309
State capital expenditure (in VND billions)		5,235	15,815	23,539	28,198
Discretionary state budget (in VND billions)		26,636	53,704	86,556	104,507
Discretionary at constant 1991 prices		10,863	16,514	23,280	24,544
GDP at constant 1991 prices		76,713	83,346	90,077	98,036

[a] State Budget plus off-budget.
Source: MOF.

Allocation by Level/Type of Education and by Economic Purpose

Assessing the allocation of public expenditures by level and type of education and by economic purpose (capital versus current, salary versus non-salary, and so on) is the key to understanding the government's true expenditure priorities and their coherence with stated policy objectives. It is important to note that the comprehensive information base needed to make this assessment on an aggregated State Budget basis (aggregating central and local government budgets) has not been previously available to policymakers in Vietnam. The present analysis uses a new database on E&T expenditure created by the Ministry of Finance using the standardized GFS classification system (see Table 3.4).

Table 3.4. State Budget Allocations by Level of Education and Economic Purpose, 1991-1994
(in VND millions at current prices)

	1991		1992		1993		1994	
	VND millions	%	VND millions	%	VND millions	%	VND millions	%
STATE BUDGET EXPENDITURE	**1,256,196**	**100%**	**2,038,247**	**100%**	**3,509,769**	**100%**	**5,011,103**	**100%**
BY LEVEL/TYPE OF EDUCATION								
Pre-primary	61,398	5%	65,223	3%	128,277	4%	227,258	5%
Primary	475,273	38%	815,830	40%	1,145,412	33%	1,484,030	30%
Lower secondary	191,999	15%	300,648	15%	616,115	18%	885,540	18%
Upper secondary	45,478	4%	121,387	6%	241,175	7%	432,339	9%
Vocational training	88,772	7%	123,087	6%	190,189	5%	249,968	5%
Secondary technical	107,495	9%	160,325	8%	226,948	6%	309,617	6%
University/college	210,492	17%	312,649	15%	494,836	14%	591,180	12%
Postgraduate	1,251	0%	14,318	1%	19,045	1%	35,295	1%
Other	74,038	6%	124,780	6%	447,772	13%	795,876	16%
BY ECONOMIC PURPOSE								
Current	*842,448*	*67%*	*1,496,962*	*73%*	*2,572,329*	*73%*	*3,977,673*	*79%*
Wages and salaries	559,194	45%	465,416	31%	1,652,635	64%	2,488,130	63%
Goods and services	274,902	22%	396,860	27%	640,435	25%	848,714	21%
Subsidies and transfers	421,500	34%	627,799	42%	275,976	11%	494,504	12%
(of which, scholarships)	(290,740)	-23%	(88,709)	-14%	(115,306)	-42%	(150,595)	-30%
Other current	600	0%	6,887	0%	3,283	0%	146,325	4%
Capital	*413,748*	*33%*	*541,293*	*27%*	*937,440*	*27%*	*1,033,430*	*21%*
Construction	798,410	64%	168,146	31%	254,880	27%	412,701	40%
Equipment and repair	457,786	36%	373,147	69%	682,560	73%	620,729	60%

Source: MOF.

Classification by Level and Type of Education and Training. In 1994, the largest identifiable share of State Budget expenditure on E&T, including both capital and current expenditure went to primary education (30 percent), followed closely by secondary education (27 percent -- 18 to lower and 9 to upper secondary). Higher education, including universities, colleges and postgraduate education, received 13 percent and VOTECH 11 percent of total State Budget outlays on education.

The situation in 1994 represents the outcome of a gradual shift in expenditure priorities over the three-year period from 1991. Primary education's share declined by 8-10 percentage points, while secondary's share increased by about the same amount. VOTECH's and higher education's shares both declined over the period, and the main beneficiary of these changes was "other" expenditure. This category of unidentified expenditure, which increased steadily, from 6 percent of the budget in 1991 to 16 percent in 1994, is made up of two sub-categories of expenditure: (1) allocations to the targeted E&T programs, some of which could be (but have not been) assigned to one level or another in MOF's classification system for E&T; and (2) general overhead (administrative) expenditure, which is difficult to assign by level of E&T. At the very least, especially given the recent growth in "other" expenditure, the classification system should distinguish between sub-categories (1) and (2), to be sure that the present allocation and future changes are truly consistent with Vietnam's priorities.

Classification by Economic Purpose. The allocation of government expenditure by economic purpose exhibits two prominent features. First, at the broadest level, the bigger share (79 percent in 1994) of overall government spending pays for current, operational expenditures on E&T. The biggest share of this (nearly two-thirds in 1994) pays for wages and salaries. This high ratio reflects the labor intensive input mix that characterizes E&T in most countries.

Second, the smaller share spent on "capital" emphasizes equipment purchase and maintenance of existing capital stock (60 percent), over new construction.[17] This breakdown is unusual by comparison with what one finds in other developing countries -- which is *not* to say that Vietnam's allocation needs necessarily to be adjusted. A relatively low allocation to new construction promises a sustainable situation over time, as does a high allocation for capital stock repairs.

Regional and Provincial Distribution of Public Expenditure

The distribution of government spending matters for equity reasons. Targeting public subsidies for education to favor poorer areas is advocated as a policy instrument in situations where a key objective of the government is poverty alleviation. Given the wide disparities in income levels and in the incidence of poverty across Vietnam's 53 provinces, and given the high priority attached to poverty alleviation in the policy statements of the Government, it is important to determine whether the distribution of public expenditure on education effectively serves re-distributional goals.

A partial answer can be given using information on the distribution of per capita government expenditure across Vietnam's 53 provinces. In Section A of Table 3.5, this information is aggregated up to the level of Vietnam's seven regions. The first fact that one observes is that the distribution of per capita government expenditure on E&T across regions is quite unequal. Current general government (central plus local) expenditure varies from a low of VND 36,617 (about $3.50) per capita in the Mekong River Delta to a high of VND 100,668 in the Red River Delta. Of course, these differences in regional distribution occur in no small measure because of the geographical distribution of educational facilities, especially the concentration in Hanoi and Ho Chi Minh city (Red River Delta and Southeast) of higher education institutions, which serve students not just from these two regions but from all over Vietnam.

Second, the pattern of interregional and interprovincial variation differs with different categories of expenditure. The inter-provincial variation in expenditure on E&T

---

[17] The GFS format classifies the purchase of small equipment and major repairs as "capital expenditure," and not as "current expenditure," which is how Vietnam has classified these two items in the past. This reassignment of equipment purchases and maintenance outlays raises capital's share from 8 percent (for construction only) to 21 percent of the total of State Budget expenditure in 1994.

is measured in Section B of the table by the coefficient of variation (cv). Disaggregation of the main expenditure components shows that variation at the local government level is smaller for current spending (cv = 0.25) than for capital spending (cv = 0.60) and, within current spending, greater for "training," which in Vietnam's classification system includes higher education as well as VOTECH (cv = 0.46), than for "education" (cv = 0.24).

Table 3.5. Distribution of Per Capita Government Expenditure, 1994

	Per capita Government Expenditure (VND)										
	Local Government						Capital + Current	Central Gov't Current	General Gov't Current (ranking)	GDP/capita ('000 VND) (ranking)	
	Current			Capital							
	Education	Training	Total	Education	Training	Total					
A. Distribution by Region											
Northern Uplands	42,141	4,849	46,990	5,097	1,669	6,767	53,757	6,651	53,641 (4)	1,577	(6)
Red River Delta	37,723	5,330	43,053	4,397	1,400	5,796	48,849	57,616	100,668 (1)	2,297	(3)
North Central	36,773	3,657	40,431	4,055	1,190	5,245	45,675	4,160	44,591 (5)	1,490	(7)
Central Coast	34,142	4,275	38,417	6,140	1,930	8,070	46,487	5,455	43,872 (6)	1,753	(4)
Central Highlands	47,948	6,977	54,925	9,117	2,890	12,007	66,933	4,307	59,232 (3)	1,715	(5)
Southeast	43,697	6,293	49,991	15,885	2,666	18,551	68,541	16,244	66,235 (2)	5,460	(1)
Mekong River Delta	30,841	4,506	35,347	5,073	1,246	6,320	41,666	1,270	36,617 (7)	2,338	(2)
Vietnam	**37,626**	**4,913**	**42,539**	**6,431**	**1,660**	**8,091**	**50,630**	**16,116**	**58,655**		
B. Coefficient of Variation by Province[a]											
Coefficient of Variation (cv)	0.24	0.46	0.24	0.69	0.68	0.60	0.25	2.66		0.93	
C. Double-log Regressions (t-statistics in parentheses)[b]											
Intercept	9.283	3.758	8.947	-1.004	4.698	0.951	7.938		-0.791		
(t-statistic)	(9.906)	(2.702)	(10.204)	(-0.445)	(2.154)	(0.505)	(9.556)		(-0.476)		
Regression coefficient[c]	0.094	0.357	0.129	0.729	0.197	0.602	0.219		0.359		
(t-statistic)	(1.308)	(3.358)	(1.923)	(4.222)	(1.177)	(4.175)	(3.448)		(2.822)		
Correlation coefficent (r)	0.117	0.413	0.224	0.498	0.088	0.494	0.419		0.347		

[a] Coefficient of variation (cv) = ratio of standard deviation to population-weighted mean.

[b] Population-weighted regression of log government expenditure per capita on log GDP per capita (Vung Tau Province excluded).

[c] Regression coefficient measure elasticity of government expenditure per capita with respect to GDP per capita.

Source: MOF.

Third, local government expenditure is more equal across regions than central government expenditure. Current spending undertaken by local governments on E&T in 1994 ranged from a low of VND 35,347 per capita in the Mekong River Delta to a high of only VND 54,925 per capita in the Central Highlands. Per capita current expenditure undertaken by the central government (which, it should be remembered, is responsible for about 90 percent of higher education in Vietnam) is quite unequal by comparison, ranging from a low of VND 1,270 in the Mekong River Delta to a high of 57,616 in the Red River Delta, the region that includes Hanoi.[18] Looking at the coefficients of variation and at inter-provincial variation, one sees again that central government per capita spending varies much more than does local per capita spending (cv's = 2.66 and 0.24, respectively), and it varies even more than GDP per capita (cv = 0.93). Again, much of this variation is because of the differences in financing responsibilities between the local government and central government. The central government provides the majority of

---

[18] More than half of all central government current expenditure on the education sector in 1994 was spent in Hanoi alone, while 21 provinces received nothing from this source. Current central budget expenditure per capita in Hanoi was about VND 310,300, some 20 times higher than the average for all of Vietnam. Of course, higher education that is provided in Hanoi serves students not just from the Red River Delta but from all of Vietnam.

funding for higher education, which recruits students nationally, while the local government finances general schooling, which recruits only locally.

Finally, spending variation is systematically related to variation in income per capita, but in a direction that is pro-rich rather than pro-poor. Looking first at inter-regional variation, the regions that rank first and third on the measure of GDP per capita (Southeast and Red River Delta), which might be expected to receive less from government than poorer regions, actually rank first and second on subsidies per capita going to E&T. Again, this reflects the geographical concentration in these two regions of higher education, which serves the whole country. The same thing can be seen at the provincial level when one looks at the regression coefficients on GDP per capita in Section C of Table 3.5. These coefficients are estimates of the elasticity of government expenditure with respect to GDP per capita.[19] The Pearson correlation coefficient between per capita income and E&T subsidies from the general government budget was 0.347.

The information presented in Table 3.5 suggests that, in spite of intentions probably to the contrary, the pattern of government spending going to E&T does not necessarily benefit those parts of Vietnam with the lowest incomes and the highest concentrations of poverty. Instead, government spending follows the present skewed distribution of educational facilities, especially at post-school levels. The issue of equity, or the lack thereof, will be revisited in Chapter 5 below.

Planning and Budgeting Criteria: Expenditure Norms

The way in which government expenditure is allocated to E&T institutions plays a critical role in determining the effectiveness and efficiency of budgetary resources in meeting the policy objectives for the sector. What are the allocation rules that underlie observed patterns of current public expenditure on E&T in Vietnam? The allocation of expenditure reflects a set of *expenditure norms* decided and reviewed annually by MOF, MPI and MOET. In higher education, the expenditure norms are specified on a per student basis. In general education and VOTECH, the same used to apply, but norms are specified today on a general population per capita basis.

Budget Norms for General Education. In 1993, the funding formula for current expenditure on general education by local government authorities was changed from a per student system to a per capita system. Per capita funding already applied in some other sectors such as health and culture and sport. Now, instead of determining the size of provincial budgets for primary and secondary schooling on the basis of how many students are enrolled in school, the budgets are based on the total number of people living

---

[19] The elasticity measures the percentage change in government spending associated with a one percentage point difference in GDP per capita. In 1994, this was 0.219 for the subsidies received from local government budgets. It was 0.359 for the subsidies received from the general government (local plus central government) budget.

in the province, regardless of what fraction of this number falls within the school-going age range, or what fraction of this group is actually enrolled, or how many are enrolled across the different levels of schooling -- primary, local secondary and upper secondary. This change attempts to move away from the skewed allocation driven by the historical geographical distribution of tertiary facilities mentioned above (para. 3.15 et seq).

Different weights are assigned, however, to populations living in different areas. The budget circular distinguishes five residential categories: (a) cities, (b) plains and delta, (c) midlands and coastal, (d) low mountains and remote, and (e) high mountains and islands. In principle, this categorization takes account of differences in needs (reflecting income differences) as well as differences in the cost of providing educational services. The assumption is that as one moves from the plains and delta areas at one end of the spectrum, to the high mountain areas and islands at the other, one finds lower family incomes and higher unit costs of education. The standardized norms for education thus vary widely, from VND 26,700 to 42,800 per capita (Table 3.6) Since provinces may contain more than one type of area, each province is required to project its education expenditures on the basis of its composition of population in terms of the five categories. In practice, after provincial budgets are formulated based on the cost of providing services (via norms for each line item), provincial budgets are negotiated to fit within the budget constraint.

Table 3.6.   Budget Norms for General Education
(VND per person in the population)

	1993	1994 and 1995
Plains and delta areas	16,900	26,700
Midlands and coastal areas	20,900	29,400
Cities	24,000	37,500
Low Mountains and remote areas	32,000	33,500
High mountains and islands	32,000	42,800

Source: MPI and MOET.

If properly designed, a system of expenditure norms could be a useful component of a general purpose transfer program. Ideally, such norms would reflect a combination of factors, including an index of educational need (based on achievement test scores) and economic need (based on income levels). Such norms might also take into account differences in the cost of providing a "standard" level of services in different regions, reflecting population density, the terrain and other factors. In Vietnam, the norms are differentiated to take some account of cost differences, but it is not clear that the central government has adequate cost information on which to base the norms written into the budget circular.

Budget Norms for Higher Education. In principle, the recurrent budget grant-in-aid allocated to a higher education institution (HEI) is determined by its student enrollment target or "quota," which is set by MPI and MOET (or other relevant line ministry for the particular HEI) and by a series of financial norms which determine the per student subsidy. There are different norms fixed for seven broad fields of study and for different programs. For example the norms for "in-service" students, who study on a part-time basis, are lower than for regular full-time students, and the norms for students taking secondary level professional education in colleges are lower than for degree-level students. Grants are calculated on the basis of the formula:

$$(3.1) \quad G_i \quad = \quad \sum_{ij} (S_{ij} * N_j)$$

where G_i is the budget allocated to institution i, S_{ij} is the number of "quota" students in HEI i in field of study j, and N_j is the budget norm per student in field of study j. The grant may be supplemented by earmarked funding for specific purposes, but the main determinants of the government's grant to each HEI are the number of "quota" students and the budget norms, which are fixed by MOF, in consultation with MOET or other line ministries. The funding formula is based on the HEI's quota and not on the actual number of students enrolled, nor on the total FTEs.

Institutions are permitted to take additional students, above their quota, but they do not receive government funding for these "non-quota" students. If the cost of running the institution exceeds its grant-in-aid, the difference must be covered from other sources, including fees. Since SY93 institutions have been permitted to collect fees from both quota and non-quota students. The fees for quota and non-quota students are now the same, although in the past institutions were permitted to enroll "extra plan" or "open study mode" students, who paid higher fees than "quota" students. This is no longer allowed, and the current policy is that both "quota" and "non-quota" students are "regular" students paying the same fees and following the same programs, although quota students, who usually have higher grades in the entrance examination, are probably more likely than non-quota students to be awarded merit scholarships or fee reductions on the basis of good or excellent grades. Merit scholarships are awarded annually, so that a student on scholarship in a given year may be denied a scholarship in the subsequent year on the basis of falling performance.

Table 3.7 presents the standard budget norms for regular full-time higher education students, by field of study, over the period 1993-1995. These norms represent government funding per quota student. The basis for the setting of the allocation norms is unclear. It would appear that the allocation norm is driven more by the availability of budgetary resources than by the actual or even historical distribution of costs. This is illustrated in Table 3.7, which shows the average grant per quota FTE student received in each year, and the average unit cost (recurrent expenditure per FTE), calculated from the institutional finance survey (HEIFS) data, taking account of actual student numbers, including both quota and non-quota and both full-time and part-time students.

The current system of higher education budget norms raises some questions. First, the norms change, often quite significantly and inexplicably, from one year to the next (see Figure 3.1). Expressing the norm for each field of study as a ratio of the "basic norm" (the average norm for all fields of study), the most dramatic change is seen for students in teacher training institutions between 1994 and 1995. The norm for this

Table 3.7. Budget Norms, Average Grants and Unit Costs per FTE Student in Higher Education, 1993-1995 (VND '000)

Field of Study	Budget Norm per Quota Student			Unit Cost per FTE			Average Grant per Quota FTE		
	1993	1994	1995	1993	1994	1995	1993	1994	1995
General	3,200	4,000	5,500	997	1,466	1,765	4,363	5,546	5,114
Agro-Forestry	3,100	3,900	4,900	2,191	3,095	5,201	4,664	5,562	5,116
Medicine	3,100	3,900	5,000	1,959	2,792	2,860	6,154	7,934	7,476
Economics and Law	2,600	3,300	4,300	783	1,008	901	3,462	4,060	3,613
Art, Culture and Sport	3,600	4,200	6,000	1,632	2,469	2,993	6,345	7,177	6,181
Teacher Training	2,200	2,700	5,500	1,431	1,891	1,866	3,359	4,985	4,656
Science and Technology	3,000	3,800	5,200	1,272	2,078	1,577	4,257	5,902	5,356
All Higher Education	3,000	3,800	5,000	1,289	1,818	1,812	4,112	5,490	5,039

Sources: MPI and MOET.

category shifted from well below to well above the basic norm in that year. The norm for art, culture and sport dropped from 20 percent above the basic norm in 1993 to 10 percent above it in 1994, and returned to 20 percent above it in 1995. Other shifts, while less extreme, are no easier to understand.

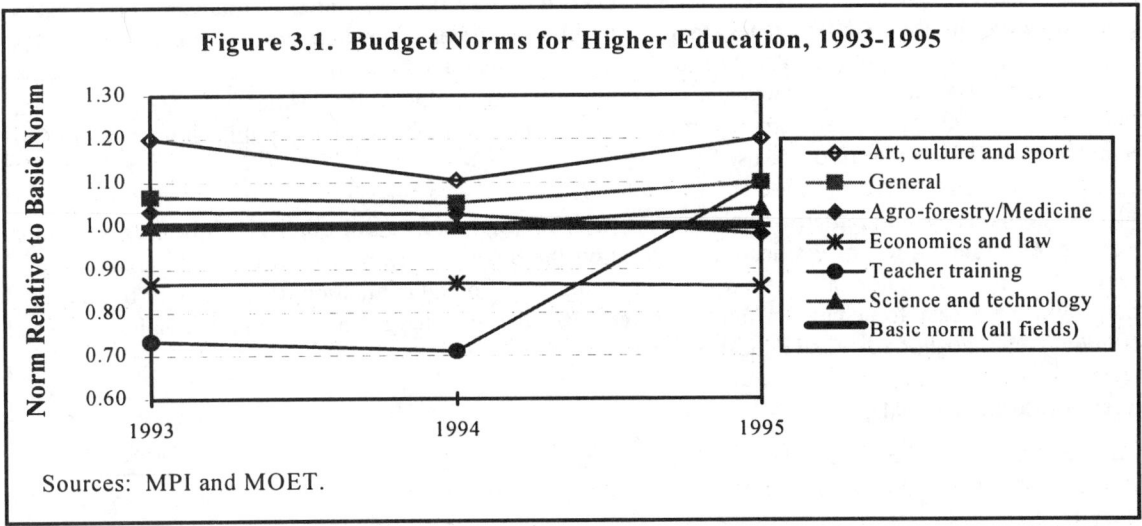

Figure 3.1. Budget Norms for Higher Education, 1993-1995

Sources: MPI and MOET.

Second, the norms are not consistent with international patterns of higher education funding allocations (see Box 3.1). Most systems that use differential weights for different fields of study (for example, the Higher Education Funding Councils in the United Kingdom) give a greater weighting to fields such as science and technology (S&T) and medicine, on the grounds that these subjects require more specialized equipment and are more expensive to teach than other subjects such as law, economics and education. In Vietnam, however, the highest norms are for reserved for art, culture and sport, while those for science and technology and for medicine were close to the basic norm during 1993-1995.

Box 3.1. Funding Formulas For Higher Education

A recent World Bank study of higher education policies and practice identifies four types of funding formulas used in different countries to allocate public resources to universities. A common but least desirable approach, seen in many developing countries, is to rely on "negotiated" budgets, which "fail to provide incentives for efficient operation and make it difficult to adjust the distribution of financial resources to changing circumstances."

In other countries, including Vietnam, funding is allocated using "input-based" funding formulas. This approach combines enrollment figures and unit costs and may use coefficients or weights to provide incentives for internal distribution of resources. The World Bank report notes that these formulas "differentiate institutions on the basis of the numbers of students enrolled in different fields of study and levels of education, and the weights reflect the differential costs faced by different institutions -- for example for engineering students compared with arts students." The World Bank concludes that input based formulas, while preferable to negotiated budgets, fail to provide sufficient incentives for efficiency. While they usually do reflect cost differences, they do not motivate institutions either to lower costs or to raise quality, relative to the input norm.

A third and better approach is to link funding with performance by using an "output-based" formula. Performance indicators used to determine funding levels may include the number of graduates produced, a truer measure of educational effectiveness than the number of students enrolled, particularly where there is significant wastage or repetition. The World Bank study concludes that "in countries such as Australia, Denmark and the Netherlands, the introduction of output-based funding formulas has been associated with reductions in student wastage and improvement in the overall efficiency of the public higher education system and the efficiency of resource use."

Finally, some countries have tried to link funding with measures of output quality. Chile, for example, allocates public funding to universities today based on the quality of learning (measured by examination scores). The United Kingdom allocates research funding based on an evaluation of the quality of research output. While not easy to achieve, a funding mechanism that encourages higher output quality at lower cost should be the goal of any good education system.

Source: World Bank (1994).

A third question about Vietnam's system of higher education budget allocations is why the norms do not reflect the actual structure of cost differences. Significant unit cost differences have been revealed in the recent VEFSS survey of higher education institutional finance (HEIFS). In general, budget allocation norms in Vietnam are higher than observed unit costs, even taking into account off-budget expenditure. However, this pattern is not uniform across all HEI groups. Agro-forestry universities have higher unit costs than medical colleges, but the budget norms going to the two types of institutions have been nearly the same. In 1995, the norms going to general universities, S&T universities and teacher training colleges were all higher than the basic norm of VND 5 million, whereas HEIFS has shown that their unit costs were at or below the average for all HEIs (see Figure 3.2). One reason for the wide differences is that unit costs reflect institutional size and the effects of economies of scale, whereas the norms used for allocating grants take no account of size nor of the historical costs of different specializations but are based, rather, on resource availability.

Finally, it appears that the norms that apply in theory are not always applied in practice when grants are actually allocated to individual universities. In 1995, the grant per quota student and the basic budget norm were about equal, on average, across all HEIs, but in each of the previous two years, the average grant was significantly higher than the basic norm -- VND 4.1 million versus VND 3.0 million in 1993, and VND 5.5 million versus VND 3.8 million in 1994 (cf. Table 3.7). Moreover, the pattern of grant allocations per quota student does not always reflect the planned relativities as expressed in the structure of budget norms. In 1994, for example, the actual grant per quota student in medical universities (VND 7.9 million) was twice the budget norm (VND 3.9 million) while in economics and law actual grants-in-aid exceeded the budget norm by only 25 percent (VND 4.1 million versus VND 3.3 million).

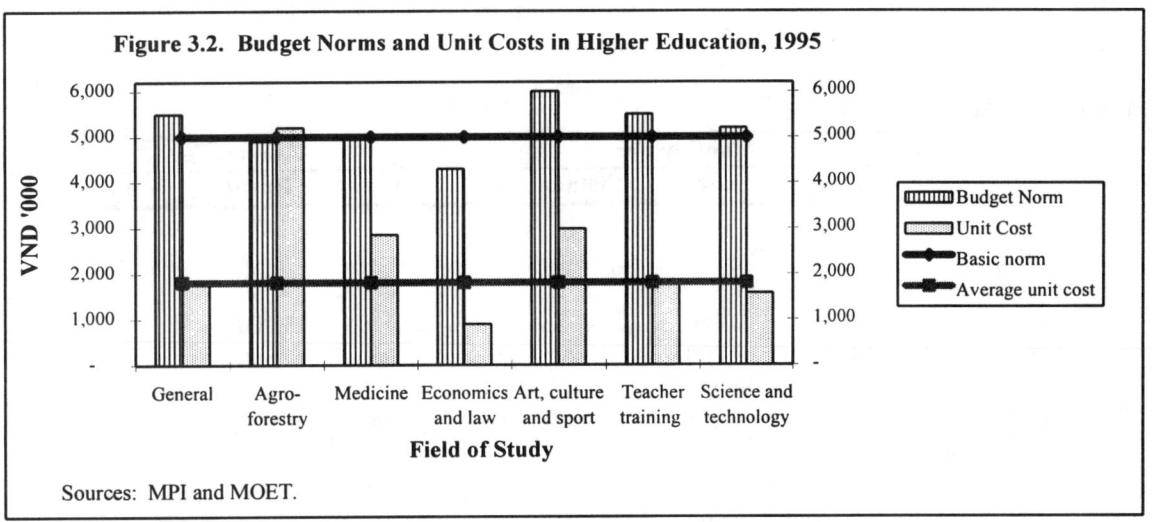

Figure 3.2. Budget Norms and Unit Costs in Higher Education, 1995

Sources: MPI and MOET.

In sum, the present system of input-based budget norms in place for determining the allocation of current grants-in-aid to HEIs does not appear to be effective in providing incentives for improved efficiency and enhanced quality. Nor do the norms reflect cost differences systematically. The present system lacks transparency and consistency, making it difficult for institutions to engage in forward planning. More important, it appears that the system of norms that applies in theory is not really used in practice. A resource allocation system based on clear and consistent criteria is needed to provide institutions with the incentives to improve efficiency and quality. Vietnam should consider moving away from its "input-based" formula and the use of arbitrary weights, to an "output-based" formula that incorporates clear and justifiable performance criteria.

COST RECOVERY IN PUBLIC EDUCATION AND TRAINING

Pricing policy and government subsidies for public E&T are intimately linked. Together they profoundly affect resource mobilization, efficiency and equity in the entire E&T sector, especially in the policy environment of Vietnam where government remains the dominant E&T provider at all levels of the system. Before the economic reforms, prices were not explicitly used as a policy instrument to finance educational services. Now, however, education policymakers must face the challenge of choosing among widely different pricing options -- at one extreme, fully subsidizing education; at the other, charging fees that recover the full provider-borne costs; or choosing some *combination* of prices and subsidies. The complexity of the challenge is exacerbated by the fact that pricing and subsidy policies are determined more or less independently at the present time in Vietnam, instead of being explicitly coordinated as complementary policy instruments.

This section examines the evolving structure of student charges for public E&T since fees were legalized in 1993. The discussion covers the unofficial as well as the official fee structures. Table 3.8 presents the official fee structure authorized by government for public institutions at each level.

Table 3.8.   Official Fee Structure

Level	Monthly Fee			Annual Fee		
	Urban	**Rural**	**Vietnam**	**Urban**	**Rural**	**Vietnam**
General Education						
Primary	0	0	0	0	0	0
Lower-secondary						
G6	3,000	2,000	--	27,000	18,000	--
G7	4,000	3,000	--	36,000	27,000	--
G8	5,000	4,000	--	45,000	36,000	--
G9	6,000	5,000	--	54,000	45,000	--
Upper-secondary						
G10	7,000	5,000	--	63,000	45,000	--
G11	8,000	6,000	--	72,000	54,000	--
G12	9,000	7,000	--	81,000	63,000	--
Tertiary Education and Training	--	--	Between 40,000 and 100,000	--	--	Between 400,000 and 1,000,000

Note   :   VND per student. In general education, the annual fee consists of nine monthly payments, and in tertiary, ten paments.

Source: Joint Ministerial Circular on Guidance for Tuition Fees for Public Basic Education, Ministry of Education and Training and Ministry of Finance, No. 14/TT-LB, September 4, 1993.

Pricing Policy and Affordability

Fees in General Education. The official pricing policy for general education has the following key features:

- fees are not authorized in primary education (G1-G5);

- authorized fees are higher in urban than in rural areas;

- authorized fees increase at each grade, rising to VND 81,000 per student per year in the last grade of upper secondary school in urban areas;

- certain categories of students (e.g., war invalids, orphans, certain ethnic minorities, and the children of public sector workers) are partially or fully exempted from having to pay fees.

In fact, the government's official fee policy plays a minor role in determining the full price that families face in sending a child to public school. Household survey data show that the full cost is much higher than the official price (see Table 3.9). The most recent estimates are from the Vietnam Social Sector Survey (VSSS) carried out in 1996. The average private cost of attending school varies widely between urban and rural areas, and also across different levels of education. In urban areas, each child enrolled in a public primary school pays on average about VND 261,000 per year (about $24), not counting foregone earnings or the cost of meals,[20] despite the fact that official school fees are zero. Outlays rise to VND 488,000 in lower secondary and VND 788,000 in upper secondary schools. In rural areas, out-of-pocket costs are considerably lower -- about VND 105,000 ($9-10) at primary, VND 203,000 at lower secondary and VND 503,000 at upper secondary levels.

But even in rural areas these private costs of public education are high in relation to *authorized* fee levels (zero in primary, between VND 18,000 and VND 45,000 in lower secondary and between VND 45,000 and VND 63,000 in upper secondary education). The affordability and equity implications of a *de facto* price structure that imposes nontrivial out-of-pocket costs for attending public education is an important policy concern, because of the likely adverse effect on the educational participation of poor children. Experience in other countries confirms that higher prices do lower the probability that parents, especially poor parents, will decide to enroll their children in school. A crude measure of the burden of education on a family's consumption expresses the private costs of education as a percentage of the family's total per capita consumption (Table 3.10).

---

[20] The cost of meals consumed while at school should not be treated as a cost of education, since the child must eat whether in school or not. To the extent, however, that food costs are higher when at school and out of the home than they would have been if eating at home, then it is fair to treat the *differential* amount as a cost of education.

Table 3.9. Household Spending per Year per Student Enrolled by Level of Education (VND per student per year)

	Pre-school	Primary	Lower secondary	Upper secondary
URBAN				
Amount paid to school	**126,709**	**50,130**	**85,055**	**146,569**
School fees	81,250	379	33,500	82,823
School improvement fees	35,000	29,370	28,347	37,113
Parent association fees	4,259	10,201	10,244	11,619
Insurance	6,200	10,180	12,964	15,015
Other out-of-pocket payments	**388,291**	**368,642**	**594,436**	**853,461**
Textbooks	360	32,888	54,243	86,352
School supplies/materials	5,566	30,798	46,334	71,521
Uniforms	12,235	46,649	72,163	90,718
Tutoring	5,147	65,339	182,750	356,310
Transportation	1,559	2,777	14,779	12,003
Meals away from home	356,115	157,873	191,971	212,493
Other	7,309	32,320	32,196	24,063
Total including meals	**515,001**	**418,772**	**679,490**	**1,000,030**
Total excluding meals	**158,886**	**260,899**	**487,519**	**787,537**
RURAL				
Amount paid to school	**27,114**	**26,749**	**53,858**	**141,724**
School fees	13,968	291	25,608	91,687
School improvement fees	7,058	16,947	19,093	33,444
Parent association fees	991	3,321	1,840	5,093
Insurance	5,097	6,191	7,317	11,500
Other out-of-pocket payments	**54,491**	**112,868**	**174,883**	**449,519**
Textbooks	1,190	22,500	38,106	73,208
School supplies/materials	2,836	19,421	33,620	53,493
Uniforms	8,985	26,907	43,606	61,732
Tutoring	-	5,825	24,093	120,472
Transportation	-	757	3,604	24,254
Meals away from home	39,737	34,785	26,045	88,014
Other	1,743	2,674	5,809	28,345
Total including meals	**81,605**	**139,618**	**228,741**	**591,242**
Total excluding meals	**41,868**	**104,832**	**202,696**	**503,228**

Source: VSSS 1996.

Table 3.10.   Burden of Public Schooling, 1996

	Income Quintile							
	I	II	III	IV	V	Viet Nam	Urban	Rural
A. Private expenditure on education, excl. meals ('000 VND per year)								
Primary	97	112	132	173	256	149	261	105
Lower secondary	195	215	290	343	441	309	488	203
Upper secondary	392	599	596	660	787	679	788	503
B. Quintile-specific education burden ratio[a]								
Primary	14%	11%	10%	10%	7%	9%	11%	7%
Lower secondary	29%	21%	22%	19%	12%	18%	20%	14%
Upper secondary	58%	57%	44%	37%	21%	40%	32%	36%
C. National average education burden ratio[b]								
Primary	22%	14%	11%	8%	4%	9%	6%	11%
Lower secondary	46%	30%	23%	17%	8%	18%	13%	22%
Upper secondary	100%	65%	50%	38%	18%	40%	28%	48%
Memo:								
Per capita HH consumption ('000 VND/yr)	678	1,046	1,348	1,795	3,726	1,716	2,456	1,403

Note :   Sample = 9,312 enrolled children in 4,087 households in 60 urban and rural communes.

[a]Group-specific private cost per student as percentage of group-specific per capita consumption

[b]National average private cost per student as percentage of group-specific per capita consumption.

Source: VSSS 1996.

The "education burden" rises sharply with the level of education. For families in all of Vietnam, the ratio is 9 percent for primary education, rises to 18 percent for lower secondary and reaches 40 percent for upper secondary. This last figure means that the private cost of sending a family member to upper secondary school is equivalent to four-tenths of a full year's average family member's consumption. But this burden is relatively much greater in poor homes than in rich ones. For an individual in the top income quintile of individuals in the sample, the ratio is only 21 percent, whereas for an individual in the bottom quintile, it is 58 percent, which would explain why so few individuals in the bottom quintile currently attend this level of education and virtually none attend the next level, a phenomenon discussed in the section on "Poverty and Access to Schooling" in Chapter 5.

The actual level of private expenditure on education varies considerably between different income groups, and the quintile-specific education burden ratios in Part B of Table 3.10 do not control for the variation in the quality of schooling across income groups. Looking in Part C at what the burden *would be* in different income groups if they were all spending at the national average level and thereby all purchasing the same quality-adjusted education reveals even more starkly the relative disadvantage of the poor. To pay the average (across all income groups) private cost of upper secondary education would amount to 18 percent of per capita consumption for an individual in the richest quintile. It would amount to just over 100 percent of per capita consumption for an individual in the poorest quintile. Although the education burden gradient is less steep for primary and lower secondary education, it is still significant. Even to attend primary

These education burden ratios suggest that raising enrollment rates among the poor, even at the primary level of education but especially at the secondary levels and above, may be difficult to achieve without pricing reforms designed to lower the private costs of schooling for poor families. A first step could be to eliminate official fees, but since these comprise only a small part of total private costs, further price adjustments may need to be considered. One would be to increase schooling subsidies to reduce the need for parental PTA contributions. Another would be to provide free textbooks for poor children, instead of charging for books as present policy requires. These pricing reforms would not have to be implemented nationwide. Instead they could be targeted to those areas that have a high incidence of poverty.

Higher education institutions. HEIs are permitted to charge fees, subject to government regulations on: (a) fee levels, (b) the categories of students entitled to pay reduced fees or exempted from paying fees altogether, and (c) the institutions' use of the fees they collect.

MOET and MOF issue joint guidelines periodically specifying the range within which fees are permitted in public higher education. The original fee structure introduced in 1993 set a range of VND 20,000-60,000 per month. This range was adjusted upwards to VND 40,000-100,000 per month in 1994. HEIs have discretion to set their own fee levels within this range, taking into account the characteristics of different fields of study and regional and individual ability to pay. In 1994 MOET and MOF indicated that agro-forestry and teacher training institutions should charge lower fees than other HEIs.

Under these regulations, institutions have a measure of discretion regarding the level of tuition fees charged, but they are required to report their revenues each year to the line ministries or provincial governments that oversee their operations. Fees may also be charged for special services, such as matriculation, examinations, boarding and graduation. In addition, institutions may enter into "training contracts" with employers or provincial authorities to provide in-service training. The fees charged under these training contracts are not regulated and may be set at full cost-recovery level. The official regulations also specify categories of student who should be granted 100 percent exemption from paying fees (war invalids, orphans and those with outstanding academic achievements) and 50 percent fee reductions (students from certain ethnic minority groups and the children of public employees and soldiers).

Revenue generated by fees is retained by institutions, but its use is regulated as follows. It can be used to cover some costs of teaching (such as remuneration given to teachers who teach extra classes) and to cover facility maintenance and procurement of teaching equipment. Ten percent is reserved for the collective welfare, health benefits and cultural activities of staff and students.

Looked at from the supply side, the effectiveness of cost-recovery policies for mobilizing additional resources in support of public higher education appears to be only modest. The institutional finance survey (HEIFS) showed that the average level of fees collected from students declined from around VND 560,000 (about $50) per student per year in 1993 to about VND 420,000 in 1994 and 1995. This decline occurred despite the upward adjustment in the official fee range announced in 1994. The average fee charged was close to the bottom of the authorized range (VND 400,000-1,000,000), and the percentage recovery rate declined during this period. The decline in average fees between 1993 and 1995 was probably due to the fact that institutions are no longer permitted to admit "extra plan" or "open study mode" students, who paid higher fees than regular students.

From the demand-side perspective, the affordability and equity implications of the government's official fee policy are more complex to assess because, as in general education, fees are only one component of the total private costs faced by users of public HEIs. Estimates from the Vietnam Living Standards Survey (VLSS) show that average expenditure on fees in post-secondary education accounted for less than half of total out-of-pocket expenditures. Again, one index of "affordability" for different income groups is the total private cost of post-secondary education expressed as a percentage of non-food consumption. The private costs of higher education, including all household expenditures on fees, books, transportation, and room and board while studying, exceeded the per capita household non-food consumption of all Vietnamese households in 1992-93 *except* those in the richest consumption quintile. The remaining 80 percent of Vietnamese would have needed to spend more on higher education for one year than it cost them to live for one year.

To help very poor students who qualify for entry into higher education it will be necessary for Government and institutions to take the level of family income into account when setting fee levels and exemptions. The conclusion is that the effects of fees on affordability and equity are not clear, and this issue needs to be better understood. Government and institutional policies on fees need to be considered in connection with policies on student loans and scholarships. These are examined in the following section.

Scholarships and Student Loans

The current policies on fees and fee exemptions do not take family income into account in determining how much different families or students pay. In higher education, fee levels for different programs are supposed to reflect priority subject areas, while specific categories of students, including war invalids, orphans and ethnic minorities, may be granted fee exemptions. In the interest of equity objectives the government does provide scholarships and has recently established a student loan scheme, on a pilot basis, to assist students whose families cannot afford the fees and other private costs of public education. For now, however, this assistance is available only for students in higher education.

In order to effectively target the poor the government's policies on fees and the supporting structure of higher education student loans and scholarships need to be integrated to form a coherent system of student support. At this stage, some students may be eligible for more than one type of government assistance, while other students are denied access to higher education because of financial hardship. Institutions have considerable discretion both in the determination of fee levels and the allocation of financial aid. In the long term, Vietnam may need to move towards a more coordinated system that is transparent and equitable and that targets assistance effectively on the basis of family income.

Scholarships. There are two types of scholarships provided by government to assist students with direct and indirect costs of higher education (fees and living expenses). The first type, called *merit scholarships* are intended to reward high achievement, and are awarded purely on the basis of academic grades, with no allowance made for levels of family income. The second category, called *social scholarships* are reserved for specific categories of disadvantaged students, including war invalids, orphans, certain ethnic minorities and students from mountainous regions. Disadvantaged students eligible for social scholarships who also achieve high grades can receive both forms of assistance. In 1995 MOET allocated over VND 50 billion, or about 10 percent of the recurrent budget for higher education, for merit and social scholarships, and in addition war invalids and orphans received social scholarships or allowances directly from MOLISA.

Higher education institutions are responsible for the allocation of scholarships, subject to guidelines issued by MOET that determine the proportion of a "full" scholarship that should be allocated for different categories of students. The value of a "full" scholarship is not related to the full costs of tuition or boarding but, rather, is fixed periodically by MOF and MOET. Until 1993-94 the value of a full scholarship was VND 22,000 a month, but since 1994 it has been increased to VND 49,500 a month, for 11 months a year.[21] Students with "excellent" grades, or those from certain ethnic minorities may be awarded up to 150 or even 180 percent of a "full" scholarship, while others may be awarded less than the full amount. Students may receive a scholarship for living expenses even if they are exempt from paying fees.

The government grant allocations to HEIs include a sum for scholarships, to be allocated to students on the basis of the specified criteria for merit and social scholarships. The size of the scholarship fund for each HEI depends on the number of "quota" students and on the subject areas taught. Most HEIs receive scholarship funds equal to 70 percent of their "quota" numbers multiplied by the value of a "full" scholarship. In the case of teacher training, which the government regards as a high priority, an institution's funding for scholarships is based on 100 percent of the quota, rather than 70 percent. Since some students receive more than 100 percent of a "full" scholarship, and others less, there is scope for considerable variations between HEIs in the proportion of students who receive scholarships, and also in the value of scholarships awarded.

---

[21] This compares with a maximum student loan of VND 120,000 a month.

An institution has discretion as to how it allocates its scholarship fund, provided that its allocation satisfies general guidelines issued by MOET and MOF. These stipulate the categories of students eligible for social scholarships and how examination grades should be used to award merit scholarships. The categories of students eligible for social scholarships are broadly similar to those eligible for fee reductions and exemptions at lower levels of the E&T system. War orphans, children of injured soldiers and certain ethnic minorities are all eligible. As in the case of fee reductions, however, need is not defined explicitly in terms of family income. Statistics provided by MOET's Department of Planning and Finance show that the proportion of higher education students awarded scholarships has been about 50 percent of the total enrollment in each year since 1992.

The 1995 HEIFS asked institutions to give details of the range of scholarships awarded. Very few HEIs responded to these questions, but based on the small number that did, it is clear that wide differences exist in the discretionary policies of different HEIs. The smallest scholarships reported were valued at VND 250,000 a year, less than half the "full" scholarship amount, and the largest at VND 1.2 million, more than twice the full amount and equivalent to the maximum student loan. A "typical" scholarship was in the range of VND 450,000-850,000 (about $40-$50) a year. Some institutions try to take account of national priorities by awarding more scholarships to students in higher priority fields of study, but there seems to be little consistency in the criteria used by individual HEIs, by different kinds of HEIs or in different regions of the country.

Student Loans. The student loan scheme was started in November 1994 as a pilot program covering just four universities, all in Hanoi -- the Agricultural University, Polytechnic University, National Economic University and Pedagogic University. The pilot is administered by the Industrial and Commercial Bank of Vietnam (Incombank). After an evaluation of the initial pilot scheme in the four universities in Hanoi, the loan scheme was extended to 20 universities in 1995-96. So far a total of 2,359 students have received loans, totaling VND 2.7 billion.

Loans are provided only to students who have already completed the first year of their university program and who have achieved high grades. The program does not, therefore, address the issue of students who are deterred by fees from entering the first year of higher education. The maximum loan is VND 1.2 million a year (VND 120,000 a month for the 10-month academic year). The maximum loan amount was fixed in 1994, at the start of the program, and has not been increased as yet. Loans are normally expected to be repaid within ten years (15 years in exceptional circumstances) from the date of loan approval, and Incombank charges interest of 1 percent per month (more than 12 percent per annum). Student borrowers do not have to provide collateral, but each is required to give the name of a parent or other sponsor who accepts responsibility for repayment in the event of default. In addition, loan applications must be endorsed by the local People's Committee, which will be expected to assist Incombank to trace borrowers who default.

Since the scheme has been in existence for such a short time, as yet there is no experience with loan repayment. Incombank is examining alternative ways of collecting repayments, but the present regulations simply stipulate that the borrower is responsible for making monthly repayment deposits, either by mail or in person at an Incombank branch, according to a schedule agreed with Incombank at the time of signing the loan agreement. While still too early to know, Incombank officials believe that the scheme will work as planned. This expectation reflects both a high private demand for post-secondary education in Vietnam and a strong social tradition of debt repayment. If correct, this means that the problem of high student loan default rates experienced in many countries will not occur in Vietnam.

The interest rate on student loans represents a significant subsidy. The annual rate of approximately 12 percent, is below market rates of interest, which are currently about 20 percent per annum. International experience suggests that subsidizing student loans is not a cost-effective funding mechanism, since the cost of administering a student loan scheme (over and above any interest subsidy) is already high, and the benefits of nearly all such schemes flow disproportionately to affluent students, who can expect a high private rate of return on their investment in higher education. A more efficient policy may be to target scholarships, rather than loans, to the neediest of low income students and to provide loans only at full market interest rates for those from higher income families.

There are other issues that will need to be addressed before Vietnam's student loan pilot scheme can be brought to scale nationally. Although the program currently targets high achieving students rather than low income students, the program's description does include discussion of equity as well as efficiency objectives. These two objectives may not coincide, and it is not yet clear whether an expanded loan scheme will succeed in reaching those from very poor families (in the interest of equity) or whether priority will continue to be given to the highest achieving students (in the interest of efficiency and a higher anticipated rate of repayment). The fact that the loan scheme was established on a pilot basis and is being evaluated before being implemented, in phases, nationwide is a prudent feature of the program, but care will be needed to ensure that the evaluation is comprehensive and its results used to adjust details of the program as necessary.

PRIVATE SECTOR DEVELOPMENT

Until recently the Government assumed virtually full responsibility for providing E&T in Vietnam. Since 1989, however, as discussed in Chapter 2, non-public institutions have been tolerated, if not actively encouraged. But these institutions still enroll only a very limited number of students. At all education levels except pre-school and upper secondary, the purely public schools account for more than 95 percent of students enrolled. Moreover, non-public E&T in Vietnam is not completely private. Many "semi-public" institutions are mixed-mode, with operating costs still heavily subsidized by government.

AGGREGATE FLOW OF FUNDS

This study takes a broad view of education finance and recommends that policymakers in Vietnam look at the three main financing instruments at their disposal in deciding how best to promote education sector development -- (a) public subsidies, (b) cost recovery in publicly provided E&T institutions, and (c) incentives to encourage the development of the private sector's role. The purpose of the following section, which concludes Chapter 3, is to assemble a consolidated empirical picture of the overall flow of funds for E&T through each of these instruments.

Because VEFSS included a special survey on higher education finance (HEIFS), and this provided institution-level details for the higher education sub-sector not currently available for other levels and types of E&T, this section begins with an in-depth case study of the flow of funds into higher education during the period 1993-95. The results of HEIFS provide, for the first time, an integrated perspective on the relative magnitudes of public subsidies and of non-budgetary revenue sources in financing the operations of Vietnam's publicly-owned HEIs. Unfortunately, HEIFS did not include coverage of the now small but rapidly growing private sector component of the higher education system. Following this higher education case study, the chapter ends by presenting a consolidated picture of the aggregate flow of funds from all major sources of financing into the E&T sector as a whole in 1994.

Financial Operations of Higher Education

The survey collected information on all sources of revenue and all types of expenditure in HEIs. This information is summarized in Table 3.11. In order to avoid double counting, scholarships were deducted from both income and expenditure in compiling this table. Total current *revenues* of the public university system (excluding scholarships) increased sharply between 1993 and 1995, rising by over 50 percent in nominal terms. This impressive change reflects a rapid increase in current grants (not including scholarships) provided by the central and provincial governments -- 67 percent over this period. Meanwhile, the volume of revenues generated from tuition fees and room-and-board charges barely increased, resulting in a deterioration of this category's share of current revenues from 23 percent to 17 percent. These developments increased the dependence of Vietnam's HEIs on government grants to finance their current operations. The share of current grants in total current revenues climbed from 72 percent to 79 percent.

Table 3.11.   Financial Operations of Public Higher Education Institutions

	VND Billions			Percentage Change	
	1993	**1994**	**1995**	**1993-94**	**1993-95**
1. CURRENT REVENUES	**434.7**	**551.6**	**661.4**	**27%**	**52%**
1.1. Student charges	100.7	86.7	111.6	-14%	11%
1.2. Production and contracts	5.7	8.7	7.9	54%	41%
1.3. Other revenue	14.2	18.4	17.9	30%	26%
1.4. Current grants	314.2	437.8	524.0	39%	67%
2. CURRENT EXPENDITURES	**230.0**	**370.4**	**472.2**	**61%**	**105%**
2.1. Salaries & wages	89.9	187.8	215.1	109%	139%
2.2. Goods & services	96.3	127.5	183.9	32%	91%
2.3. Subsidies and transfers	7.4	21.6	26.4	191%	255%
2.4. Other	36.4	33.5	46.8	-8%	29%
3. CURRENT SAVING (1 - 2)	**204.7**	**181.3**	**189.2**	**-11%**	**-8%**
4. OFFICIAL CAPITAL GRANTS	**58.2**	**96.6**	**142.0**	**66%**	**144%**
5. CAPITAL EXPENDITURES	**172.8**	**204.7**	**275.2**	**18%**	**59%**
6. TOTAL REPORTED INCOME	**492.9**	**648.2**	**803.4**	**32%**	**63%**
7. TOTAL REPORTED EXPENDITURES	**402.8**	**575.1**	**747.4**	**43%**	**86%**
8. RESIDUAL	**90.1**	**73.1**	**56.0**	**-19%**	**-38%**
MEMORANDUM ITEMS					
Scholarship expenditures	**37.0**	**50.3**	**63.3**	**36%**	**71%**
Student scholarships	33.2	46.8	55.8	41%	68%
Scholarships for staff training	3.8	3.6	7.5	-7%	97%
Capital expenditures + residual (5+8)	**262.9**	**277.8**	**331.2**	**6%**	**26%**
Total expenditures (2+5+8)	**492.9**	**648.1**	**803.4**	**31%**	**63%**
Total grants (1.4+4)	**372.4**	**534.4**	**666.0**	**44%**	**79%**
RATIOS					
Student charges as % of current revenues	23%	16%	17%		
Student charges as % of current expenditures	44%	23%	24%		
Student scholarships as % of student charges	33%	54%	50%		
Current grants as % of current revenues	72%	79%	79%		
Current grants as % of current expenditures	137%	118%	111%		
Salaries & wages as % of current expenditures	39%	51%	46%		
Current savings as % of current expenditures	89%	49%	40%		
Capital as % of current expenditures	114%	75%	70%		

Source: HEIFS 1995.

Total *expenditures* (again excluding scholarships) incurred by the HEIs nearly doubled in nominal terms, from around VND 490 billion in 1993 to VND 800 billion in 1995.   HEIFS followed the standardized GFS classification system and reclassified the purchase of small equipment and major repairs as capital expenditure, a departure from Vietnam's present practice of classifying these under current expenditure.[22]   *Current* expenditures more than doubled.   The impetus for much of this change came from a reform of civil service wages, as a result of which the share of salaries and wages in current spending rose from 39 percent to 46 percent.   Current expenditures grew much

---

[22] This reclassification of expenditures was not, however, accompanied by a parallel reclassification of the corresponding portion of the government's current grant to the public higher education system, an oversight that should be corrected in any follow-up survey of HEIs.

faster than current revenues, resulting in a decrease in the overall current savings of the higher education system from about VND 200 billion in 1993 to VND 190 billion in 1995. Meanwhile *Capital* expenditures, which include the reclassification of small equipment and repairs as capital expenditure, also recorded a large increase, rising nearly 60 percent over the two-year period. *Unreported* expenditures, derived as a residual from the financing identity and presumed to be mainly capital in nature, diminished as a share but remained a significant part of total expenditures (8 percent in 1995). This increase in capital expenditure was more than matched by the increase in official capital grants, which rose by 144 percent between 1993 and 1995. Without these official capital grants from the State budget or from foreign sources, the financial operations of the HEIs would have been in deficit.

The total reported income (current revenues and capital grants) of all HEIs exceeded their total reported expenditures in each year. International accounting definitions require an identity between total income and expenditures, taking account of net savings and loans, and asset drawdown. In Vietnam public HEIs are not permitted to take out loans, or to carry forward unspent income derived from government grants to the following financial year, although other forms of income may be carried forward. Since the HEIFS data showed that reported income exceeded reported expenditure, Table 3.11 shows a residual of VND 90 billion in 1993, falling to VND 56 billion in 1995. There are several possible explanations for this residual: (a) it could represent unreported expenditure, quite possibly capital in nature; (b) it could represent unreported transfers to financial reserves, and (c) it could be a mixture of both unreported expenditure and transfers. The fact that scholarships were deducted from both income and expenditure may have slightly distorted the picture of total financial flows, since individual HEIs may have received more funds for scholarships than they actually allocated, or vice versa. It is likely that some HEIs under-reported both income and expenditure. Since this was the first comprehensive financial survey of HEIs in Vietnam it is not surprising that there remain some uncertainties and under-reporting. Future surveys of HEIs should try to clarify these issues.

Despite the reclassification of small equipment and repairs as capital expenditure, current expenditures of the HEIs grew much faster than current revenues, resulting in a decrease in the overall current savings of the higher education system from about VND 200 billion in 1993 to VND 190 billion in 1995. The decline in current savings was not matched by corresponding restraint in the growth of capital expenditure, and without official capital grants from the State Budget or from foreign sources, the financial operations of the HEIs would have been in deficit for VND 60 billion in 1993 and VND 142 billion in 1995.

Several conclusions emerge from this analysis of the financial operations of higher education. To begin with, the public HEIs as a group have become more dependent upon state financing during the period under review (75 percent in 1993 and 83 percent in 1995). Second, the financial health of the HEIs merit careful regular monitoring given the very rapid growth in both current and capital expenditures. Third, the reclassification of equipment and repairs to the capital account shows that there is an imbalance, with an excessively high ratio of capital to current expenditures. Taking a broad definition of capital expenditures that includes the "residual" shown in Table 3.11 as unreported capital expenditures would mean that capital spending exceeded current spending in 1993. The ratio of the two would be 1.14 in that year, falling to around 0.70 in 1994 and 1995. Further adjustments will be necessary to put capital expenditures on a sustainable trajectory in relation to current spending. The central concern for policymakers is that the incremental current cost implications of such high rates of capital investment will outstrip the ability of the higher education system to finance them without some major adjustments on the revenue side. Cost recovery from student fees is the most equitable adjustment, given the needs lower down in the system and given the high socio-economic profile of those who attend HEIs, but cost recovery has stagnated over the recent period with declines in the collection rate, thereby threatening the financial health of the higher education system. This reflects a failure in pricing policies, which should be seen as an instrument to strengthen and diversify the resource base for public higher education.

Aggregate Sources and Uses of Funds for Education and Training

Pulling together all of the estimates from the various sources of information identified or created by VEFSS suggests that aggregate expenditures on E&T in 1994 amounted to nearly VND 10.5 trillion (see Table 3.12). This total, which made up approximately six percent of GDP, is a conservative estimate of the costs of E&T. The table, which estimates monetary outlays only, does not include the cost of foregone earnings required to complete the E&T investment. This can easily equal the direct costs, especially at the higher levels of the system.

Nor does the table distinguish between expenditure on public and expenditure on non-public E&T. A rough estimate of this breakdown, based on enrollment information at different levels, suggests that the latter, while growing, still accounts for less than 1 percent of all expenditures on E&T in Vietnam. Private expenditures on E&T, borne largely by households, though to some extent at the higher education level also by private companies, are significant (estimated to be 43 percent of total expenditures in 1994), but nearly all of these private outlays on E&T pay for the users' share of the costs of *public* E&T.

A very important source of financing of E&T in Vietnam is the household (43 percent). Cost recovery in public and non-public E&T now contributes nearly as much as the entire public sector. However, the single most important source of financing for E&T remains public subsidies, including both State Budget (central and local totaling 48 percent) and off-budget (9 percent) subsidy sources.

Table 3.12.   Sources and Uses of Funds Matrix, 1994

	SOURCES OF FUNDS							
	Public Sector				Private Sector			
	State Budget		Off-budget				Total	
USES OF FUNDS	Central	Local	ODA	Communes	Households	Firms	Sources	Percent
IN VND BILLIONS								
Pre-school	2.5	224.7	-	-	335.2	-	562.5	5.4%
Primary	19.3	1,464.7	232.8	314.0	1,870.8	-	3,901.6	37.2%
Lower secondary	-	885.5	49.6	-	1,320.2	-	2,255.4	21.5%
Upper secondary	25.3	407.0	-	-	705.1	-	1,137.4	10.9%
VOTECH	330.3	229.3	156.6	-	99.9	-	816.1	7.8%
Higher education	526.4	100.0	159.1	-	181.2	8.7	975.4	9.3%
Other	489.0	306.9	31.1	-	-	-	827.0	7.9%
Total Uses	**1,392.8**	**3,618.3**	**629.1**	**314.0**	**4,512.5**	**8.7**	**10,475.4**	**100%**
AS % OF FUNDING FOR LEVEL/TYPE								
Pre-school	0.4%	40.0%	-	-	59.6%	-	100%	
Primary	0.5%	37.5%	6.0%	8.0%	47.9%	-	100%	
Lower secondary	-	39.3%	2.2%	-	58.5%	-	100%	
Upper secondary	2.2%	35.8%	-	-	62.0%	-	100%	
VOTECH	40.5%	28.1%	19.2%	-	12.2%	-	100%	
Higher education	54.0%	10.3%	16.3%	-	18.6%	0.9%	100%	
Other	59.1%	37.1%	3.8%	-	-	-	100%	
Total Uses	**13.3%**	**34.5%**	**6.0%**	**3.0%**	**43.1%**	**0.1%**	**100%**	

Source: MOF; VLSS 1992-93; and VSSS 1996.

Turning from *sources* to *uses* of the aggregate funds for E&T, primary education emerges with the largest share (37 percent). This is not surprising given that three out of every five students in 1994 were enrolled at this level. Figure 3.3 shows the shares of each level and type of E&T of total expenditures (with the "other" category allocated on a pro-rated basis) and of total enrollments in 1994. As expected, the pattern reverses as one moves up the education ladder, with relatively high enrollment shares at the bottom and relatively high expenditure shares at the top, indicating that unit costs are lower at the bottom than at the top, a phenomenon observed in all countries and elaborated in the next chapter.

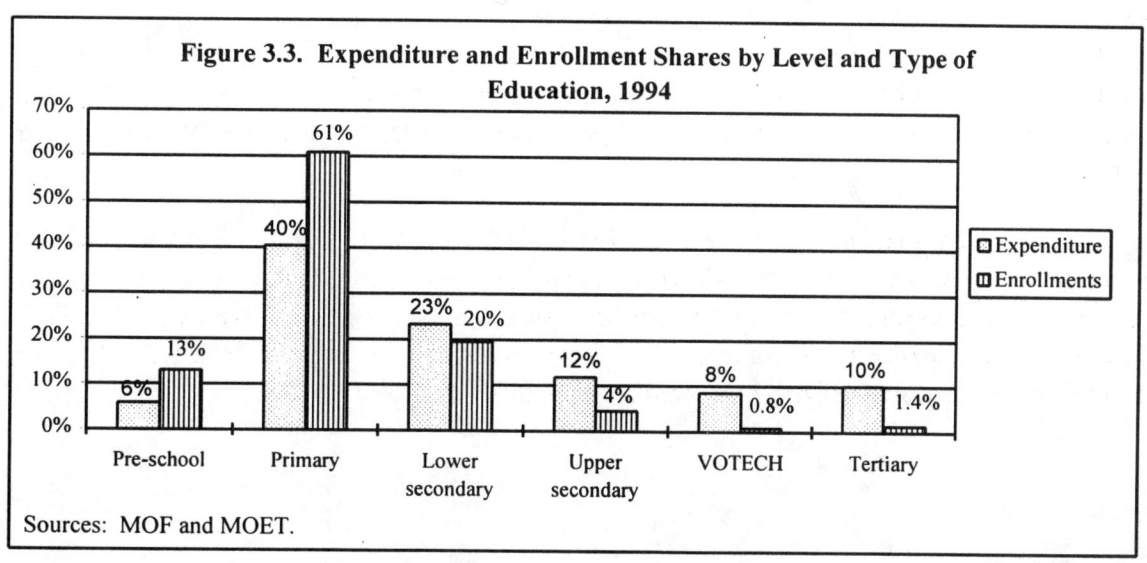

Figure 3.3. Expenditure and Enrollment Shares by Level and Type of Education, 1994

Sources: MOF and MOET.

4.   UNIT COSTS AND INTERNAL EFFICIENCY

The previous chapter focused on macro-financing issues, describing and analyzing the mechanisms and the magnitude of resources flowing into Vietnamese E&T from all sources. This chapter looks inside E&T and analyzes the microeconomic efficiency of resource use. Section A provides estimates of unit costs (i.e., average current cost per student per year) by level and type of E&T -- given the internal efficiency that now prevails, and taking into account both the fiscal expenditures borne by government and the private outlays incurred by those households that have family members enrolled in E&T programs. The unit cost estimates bring together the enrollment information from Chapter 2 and the expenditure information from Chapter 3. They serve as an essential input into the analysis of external efficiency (in terms of rates of return) and equity (in terms of fiscal incidence) presented in Chapter 5, and they provide a benchmark for evaluating levels of cost recovery implied by current pricing policies.

Subsequent sections of the present chapter provide evidence of variation in unit costs and analyses of their determinants. Here the aim is to identify the scope for lowering the average costs of educational production in order to improve internal efficiency and enhance the output attained from given levels of resource use. Section B focuses on student-teacher ratios and two important components, class sizes and teaching loads. Wherever measures can be taken to increase the student-teacher ratio, the potential for lowering unit costs is great because staff salaries account for such a large share (about two-thirds across all E&T levels in 1994) of current expenditure in the sector.

Section C looks more closely at general (primary and secondary) education and considers a different concept of "unit cost." The shift is from *cost per student-year* to *cost per graduate,* taking into account two expensive educational phenomena -- repetition and dropout. Section D introduces the notion of *quality* into the discussion of internal efficiency in general education in Vietnam and raises questions about (1) the number of instructional hours that students at this time are exposed to during the course of a school year, and (2) the mix of pedagogical inputs purchased with the public and private resources that flow into education -- in other words, how much is spent on wages, how much on textbooks and so on.

Section E turns to higher education, looking at evidence on economies of scale and the prospects for achieving efficiency gains through institutional consolidation. This analysis draws on data from 100 public sector universities and colleges surveyed in 1995 as part of the Higher Education Institutional Finance Survey (HEIFS), the first such survey in Vietnam, undertaken under the auspices of VEFSS.

COST PER STUDENT-YEAR BY LEVEL/TYPE OF EDUCATION

Fiscal Costs

Figure 4.1 presents VEFSS estimates for 1994 of average unit costs per student in public E&T institutions. Fiscal subsidies per student, presented as the bottom portion of each bar, rise sharply with level of education, from VND 121 thousand (about $11) per student per year in pre-school education to VND 1.8 million ($161) in tertiary education. Estimates of unit fiscal costs in VOTECH are problematic, because of the large and not very reliably reported number of trainees in *short-term* VOTECH programs. Based, however, on this study's estimates of the total number of these plus *regular* VOTECH students, fiscal unit costs in vocational E&T appear to be nearly the same as those in upper secondary education (about VND 480,000), and those in technical education, nearly the same as in tertiary.

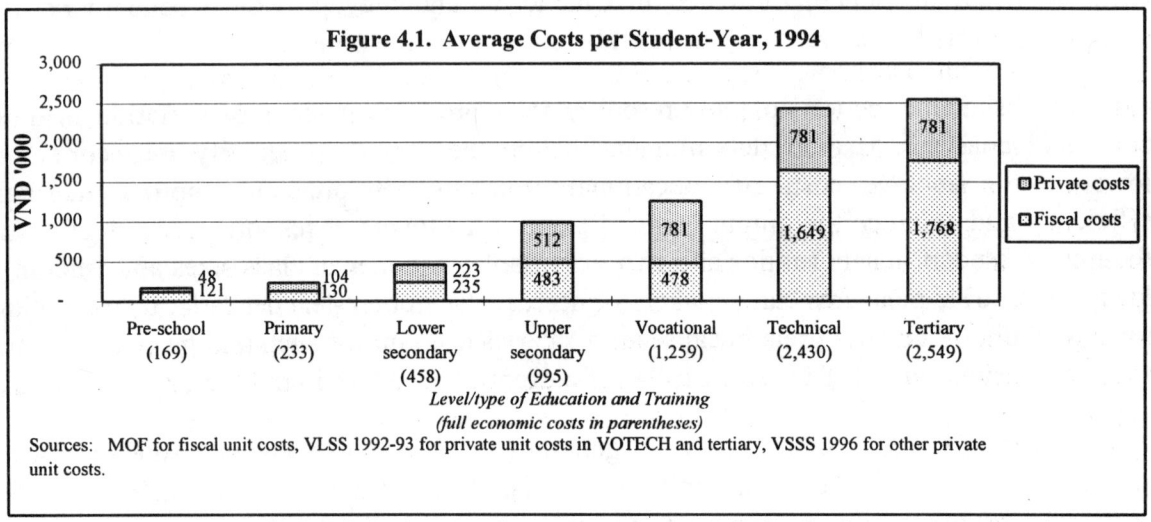

Figure 4.1. Average Costs per Student-Year, 1994

Sources: MOF for fiscal unit costs, VLSS 1992-93 for private unit costs in VOTECH and tertiary, VSSS 1996 for other private unit costs.

Private Costs

Data from household surveys show that private expenditures are significant at every level of E&T in Vietnam. This indicates the high degree of cost recovery already achieved in Vietnamese E&T.[23] As with fiscal costs, private outlays increase as one moves up the education ladder. Estimates for general education in 1994 rise from VND 104,000 per primary school student, to VND 223,000 at lower secondary and VND 512,000 at the upper secondary level. These estimates are obtained by deflating the

---

[23] The estimates of private costs are based on household surveys. Earlier information was used In the case of tertiary education and VOTECH (VLSS 1992-93), and later information in the case of school education (VSSS 1996) -- the first inflated and the second deflated so as to apply to 1994. The cost of meals consumed while attending school, although reported by households as a cost of sending household members to school, are excluded here given that individuals must eat whether or not they are students.

values reported in the Vietnam Social Sector Survey (VSSS 1996). At present, the only available data on private expenditure in VOTECH and tertiary education are from the first Vietnam Living Standards Survey (VLSS 1992-93), which did not differentiate between VOTECH and tertiary education. Inflated to 1994 prices, VLSS suggests an average private outlay of VND 781,000 per student per year. This indicates a relatively low level of cost recovery compared to general education.

Economic Costs

Putting the fiscal and private costs together yields an estimate of the full cost (or economic cost) per student-year at each level of E&T. In 1994, the economic cost per student-year roughly doubled at each of the steps moving from primary (VND 233,000), to lower secondary (VND 458,000), to upper secondary (VND 995,000) and finally to tertiary education (VND 2.5 million, or about $225).

STUDENT-TEACHER RATIOS

Since education is such a labor-intensive industry, if one is looking for ways to reduce unit costs in an effort to enhance internal efficiency, the first thing to examine is how teachers and other staff are utilized. In most education systems, wages and salaries account for at least half of current government spending, and in some systems, especially those in poor countries, the proportion spent on wages and salaries reaches 80 or even 90 percent of the total. The share in Vietnam in 1994, according to MOF information, was 63 percent. This is quite low by international standards. In tertiary education and VOTECH, the share was even lower (about 38 percent), but in basic education, it was 80 percent, much closer to the norm seen in most developing countries. Thus, in Vietnam as in most countries, utilizing teachers effectively is an important policy concern for reasons of budget.

To influence the student-teacher ratio, which is a highly aggregated indicator, policymakers must understand that the average ratio observed over a large geographic unit (e.g., all of Vietnam) hides considerable variation at lower levels (the country's seven regions, 53 provinces, 500-some districts or 10,000-some communes). Also, to influence the ratio in any given situation, there are at least two components that must be considered, class-size and teaching load. We will look first at these components of the student-teacher ratio.

The student-teacher ratio (S/T) can be seen to be the product of average class-size (S/C) multiplied by the average teaching load of teachers in the system (C/T),

$$(4.1) \qquad S/T \quad = \quad (S/C) \quad x \quad (C/T)$$

Put differently, it is the quotient of average class-size divided by the average number of teachers per class (T/C),

$$(4.2) \qquad S/T \quad = \quad (S/C) \quad / \quad (T/C)$$

Table 4.1 presents the relevant ratios for general education in each year between SY91 and SY95. For VOTECH, the component variables are not available, and only the "bottom-line" student-teacher ratio is reported.

Table 4.1. Utilization Ratios by Level/Type of Education and Training, SY91-SY95

Level/Type of E&T	School-Year				
Ratio	SY91	SY92	SY93	SY94	SY95
Primary					
Student-class (*S/C*)	33.8	33.9	33.9	33.7	33.5
Teacher-class (*T/C*)	0.96	0.98	0.96	0.95	0.96
Student-teacher (*S/T*)	35.2	34.6	35.3	35.5	34.9
Lower Secondary					
Student-class (*S/C*)	35.9	36.2	37.5	38.9	40.4
Teacher-class (*T/C*)	1.9	1.8	1.7	1.6	1.6
Student-teacher (*S/T*)	18.9	20.1	22.1	24.3	25.3
Upper Secondary					
Student-class (*S/C*)	36.4	39.1	40.7	43.0	45.1
Teacher-class (*T/C*)	2.6	2.6	2.3	2.1	1.9
Student-teacher (*S/T*)	14.0	15.0	17.7	20.5	23.7
Vocational					
Student-teacher (*S/T*)	15.9	9.7	11.7	10.0	13.6
Technical					
Student-teacher (*S/T*)	12.4	12.1	11.9	11.8	14.7

Source: MOET.

Most students (or their parents) and teachers alike are in favor of smaller classes, but research evidence suggests that, over a surprisingly wide range of class sizes, this variable is not actually a very powerful contributor to differences in student learning.[24] In rural areas especially, classes may be so small as to be quite inefficient. If ways can be found to increase the average class size -- perhaps by merging smaller schools within the same community into one large school or, in very isolated communities, by merging age groups within the same school (multi-grade teaching or, an even more radical measure, admitting students into the first grade only in alternate years) -- it may be possible to achieve significant cost savings. These savings can then be used to purchase non-salary inputs needed to raise education's quality.

---

[24] The actual findings do differ across research studies, reflecting differences in the age-level of the students being researched and also the subjects they are studying, but the weak relationship between class size and average cognitive achievement of students is commonly observed. The true relationship between class size and student learning is likely to be curvilinear. Below some threshold (say, 40 students), class size is not significantly related to student achievement. Above this threshold, larger classes may affect student achievement negatively, holding constant other pedagogical inputs, but even in a situation where the average class size is above the threshold, the most cost-effective intervention may not be to reduce class size, but rather to spend marginal resources on another pedagogical input (such as textbooks or the improvement of facilities). The correct choice is likely to be quite context-specific.

Another way to use teachers more effectively in some situations is to raise the average number of classes that teachers in the system teach. In primary education in most countries including Vietnam (see Table 4.1), the ratio of teachers to classes is close to one. In other words, each primary class is taught by a single teacher. At higher levels, however, where teachers specialize in the teaching of different subjects, the ratio of teachers to classes is usually well above one. In Vietnam in SY95, it was 1.6 in lower secondary and 1.9 in upper secondary education.

The student-teacher ratios reported in Table 4.1 are graphed in Figure 4.2. In most cases, the trend was flat, or it rose slightly, reflecting the growth of enrollments over this period (cf. Chapter 2). In VOTECH, the trend between SY91 and SY94, what little trend there was, was downward, reflecting the falling enrollments over this three-year period. In SY95, VOTECH enrollments recovered somewhat, and the student-teacher ratio rose as a result. The student-teacher gains in lower and upper secondary education reflected improvements in both components underlying the student-teacher ratio, average class size and average teaching load (cf. Table 4.1). Average class size went up (from about 36 students to over 40 students in lower secondary, and from 36 to above 45 in upper secondary). At both levels, the teacher-class ratio fell, which is to say that teaching loads (class-teacher ratios) went up. In lower secondary education, the teacher-class ratio fell from 1.9 to 1.6, and in upper secondary, from 2.6 to 1.9. These are quite dramatic improvements over a relatively short period.

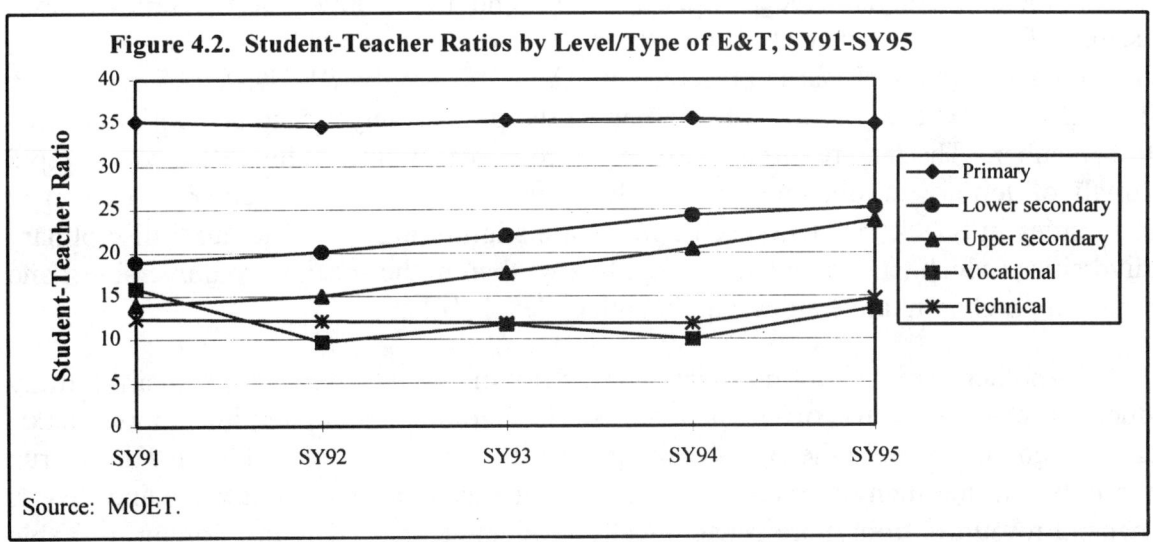

Figure 4.2. Student-Teacher Ratios by Level/Type of E&T, SY91-SY95

Source: MOET.

Naturally, the ease of achieving high student-teacher ratios is greater in areas of the country where population density and/or enrollment rates are high. Figure 4.3 shows enrollment rates at the three levels of general education in each of Vietnam's seven regions in SY95. As might be expected, the Northern Uplands Region (first column of each school-level group), which is relatively sparsely populated and somewhere in the middle of the seven regions in terms of education participation rates, shows relatively low student-teacher ratios, whereas the Red River Delta Region (second column), which is the most densely populated area of Vietnam and has high enrollment rates, shows higher student-teacher ratios. The correlation across regions, however, is far from perfect. The most sparsely populated region of all is the Central Highlands (fifth column), with only 53 people per square kilometer (as compared with 1,124 in the Red River Delta), and yet student-teacher ratios are quite close to the national averages at each level of education in the Central Highlands.

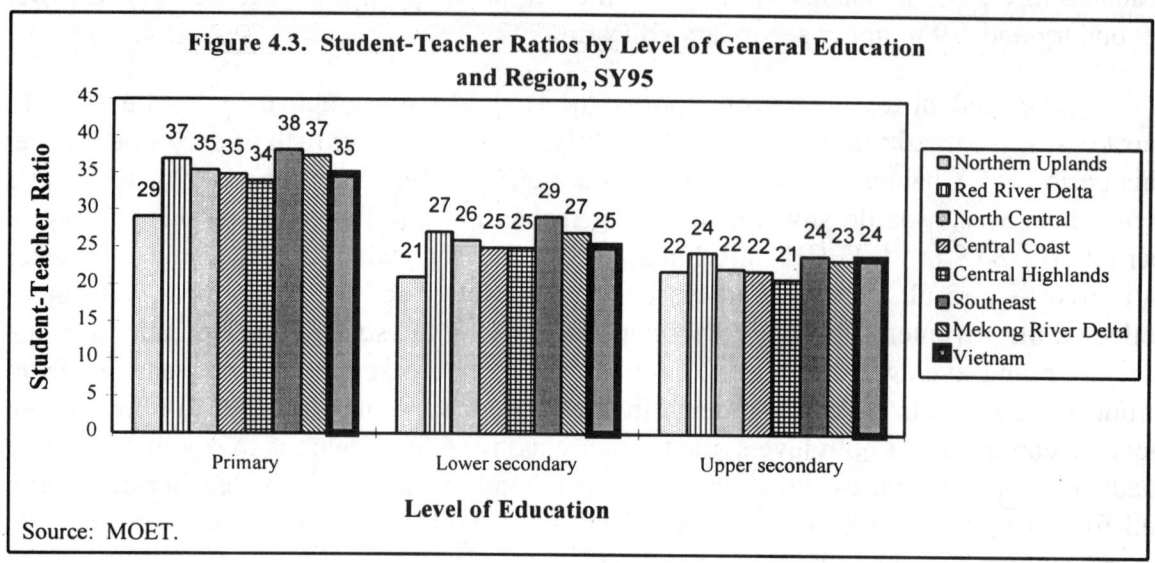

Figure 4.3. Student-Teacher Ratios by Level of General Education and Region, SY95

Source: MOET.

Not surprisingly, student-teacher ratios tend to be lower at the tertiary level because of the need for increased specialization in teaching at this level. The situation in Vietnam's 110 public HEIs is presented in Table 4.2 for the SY91-SY95 time period. The ratio was extravagant at the beginning of the period, only 5.5 students per teaching staff member. The picture improved over the four-year period. This reflected the rapid growth of tertiary enrollments, especially after the opening of Vietnam's two open universities in SY94. Student-teacher ratios are slightly higher in the multi-disciplinary universities (which tend to be larger -- see below) than in the specialized universities, and in general, higher in universities than in college-level HEIs.

Another variable to take into consideration when trying to contain tertiary education costs is the use of *non-teaching* staff. Certainly, some administrators, clerks, janitors, gardeners and other non-teaching staff are necessary to enable an HEI to run smoothly, but too many in these categories is a luxury that raises unit costs and diverts financial resources from more pedagogically productive uses. The last column in Table 4.2 reports the ratio of non-teaching staff to teaching staff in Vietnam's higher education sector. One sees that, on average across all HEIs, there were *six* non-teaching staff for every *ten* teaching staff in tertiary education in SY95.[25] Whether this is an inefficiently high ratio is something for HEI administrators and policymakers in Vietnam to consider and decide upon. Almost certainly, the one-to-one ratio (approximate) in the college-

---

[25] This compares with a ratio of eight non-teachers to ten teachers in SY91 and SY92 (not shown in Table 4.2).

level HEIs managed by central government ministries seems high, and by contrast, the one-to-ten ratio in the open universities is a relatively parsimonious use of non-teaching staff.

Table 4.2. Student-Staff Ratios in Higher Education Institutions, SY91-SY95

University or College Level Type of Institution Name of Institution	Student-Teacher Ratio					Ratio of non-teaching staff to teaching staff, SY95
	SY91	SY92	SY93	SY94	SY95	
Universities	**5.6**	**6.6**	**7.6**	**10.1**	**14.3**	**0.5**
Multi-disciplinary universities	*6.0*	*7.3*	*8.0*	*10.1*	*13.7*	*0.5*
National University of Hanoi	3.4	4.0	3.3	6.2	8.3	0.5
National University of HCM City	7.9	12.1	14.9	17.1	23.5	0.4
Da Nang Regional University	7.8	6.2	1.4	6.4	10.5	0.5
Hue Regional University	5.7	5.6	4.9	8.1	9.0	0.5
Thai Nguyen Regional University	7.3	5.0	6.0	5.5	6.8	0.6
Other multi-disciplinary	5.4	6.6	8.9	9.0	12.8	0.5
Specialized universities	*5.3*	*6.0*	*7.2*	*9.9*	*12.2*	*0.7*
Agro-forestry	4.9	6.0	7.2	7.8	8.3	0.8
Culture and art	3.0	3.2	2.6	5.2	7.3	0.7
Economics and law	8.7	12.7	17.0	26.6	32.3	0.7
Health and sports	5.3	4.7	5.1	5.5	6.3	0.7
Industry	4.2	4.5	4.9	7.5	9.7	0.7
Pedagogy	4.9	4.2	5.5	6.9	8.8	0.7
Open universities	*...*	*...*	*...*	*n.a.*	*37.8*	*0.1*
Colleges	**5.3**	**5.0**	**5.3**	**6.1**	**8.0**	**0.6**
Central teacher training colleges	5.1	5.0	4.1	5.4	7.6	0.8
Other central level colleges	4.9	9.2	8.2	10.8	6.7	1.1
Provincial teacher training colleges	5.4	4.8	5.1	6.2	8.2	0.5
Other provincial colleges	4.7	4.8	7.1	3.8	6.9	0.5
All Institutions	**5.5**	**6.3**	**7.2**	**9.3**	**13.0**	**0.6**

... = not applicable (open universities not yet established);.

    n.a. = information not available

Source: MOET.

COST PER GRADUATE IN GENERAL EDUCATION

To complete any cycle of Vietnam's education system requires several years of successful study. The cost of producing a graduate of primary, lower secondary or upper secondary education depends on the cost per student-year times the average number of years required to produce a successful graduate. As we have seen, the primary education cycle in Vietnam consists of five years, G1 to G5, but Vietnam's education system is like most in the world -- not all children who enter G1 continue in school and finish G5, and some who do eventually finish spend more than five years doing so, repeating one or more grades along the way. Dropout and repetition are costly in terms of the resources required to produce a successful graduate of the system. As we will see in this section, the cost of producing a primary school graduate in Vietnam is significantly higher than five times the cost of one student-year. The same is true for both lower and upper secondary education. The cost of education in Vietnam could be reduced to the extent that "flow-through efficiency" is improved by reductions in dropout and repetition rates,.

Table 4.3 presents repetition and dropout rates by level of general education (primary, lower secondary and upper secondary) for all of Vietnam and by region. The information presented is not based on following a single cohort of students through the education system. Rather it is a cross-sectional "snap-shot" of the situation recently, but to measure repetition and drop-out it is necessary to observe at least two years of student enrollments. In this case, the table shows repetition and dropout between SY94 and SY95.

Table 4.3.   Repetition and Dropout Rates in General Education between SY94 and SY95, for Vietnam and by Region

| Rate | Primary | | | | | Lower Secondary | | | | Upper Secondary | | |
Region	G1	G2	G3	G4	G5	G6	G7	G8	G9	G10	G11	G12
Repetition Rate												
Northern Uplands	12.6%	7.5%	4.5%	4.9%	2.1%	3.2%	1.8%	1.5%	1.3%	3.8%	3.1%	2.0%
Red River Delta	3.2%	2.0%	1.8%	1.9%	0.5%	1.8%	1.4%	1.0%	0.4%	1.0%	0.6%	0.2%
North Central	5.1%	3.6%	3.1%	3.0%	1.9%	2.0%	1.6%	1.5%	1.1%	0.9%	0.8%	0.2%
Central Coast	14.3%	9.1%	6.1%	6.4%	2.2%	5.1%	2.7%	1.8%	1.7%	1.6%	0.9%	0.2%
Central Highlands	10.3%	7.4%	5.5%	5.5%	2.9%	3.3%	3.4%	2.5%	1.9%	2.8%	1.6%	0.3%
Southeast	8.1%	5.0%	4.3%	5.8%	2.6%	5.3%	5.0%	3.9%	1.7%	1.8%	1.0%	0.2%
Mekong River Delta	15.1%	11.0%	7.6%	7.9%	4.7%	6.5%	3.9%	3.0%	3.8%	3.6%	1.9%	1.1%
Vietnam	**10.2%**	**6.6%**	**4.8%**	**4.8%**	**2.3%**	**3.5%**	**2.4%**	**1.8%**	**1.4%**	**2.0%**	**1.3%**	**0.6%**
Dropout Rate												
Northern Uplands	3.3%	1.2%	0.1%	13.1%	5.1%	9.4%	10.4%	8.8%	2.4%	6.3%	2.7%	10.1%
Red River Delta	7.3%	8.7%	6.6%	8.1%	2.4%	6.2%	7.6%	4.9%	2.4%	3.6%	3.9%	4.7%
North Central	5.9%	4.7%	2.9%	15.1%	6.8%	8.4%	9.1%	7.9%	10.0%	3.1%	1.4%	6.1%
Central Coast	5.4%	4.2%	2.9%	9.4%	7.8%	13.2%	13.3%	13.2%	11.5%	10.0%	4.1%	5.3%
Central Highlands	12.6%	8.0%	3.0%	17.4%	8.7%	28.8%	27.6%	29.5%	18.0%	17.4%	15.1%	9.3%
Southeast	5.8%	0.3%	0.1%	7.4%	6.8%	10.5%	8.6%	7.7%	1.9%	8.1%	7.0%	2.3%
Mekong River Delta	15.5%	5.6%	4.8%	14.3%	15.2%	16.7%	16.1%	15.3%	7.5%	12.5%	8.0%	16.1%
Vietnam	**8.5%**	**4.3%**	**2.8%**	**11.6%**	**7.3%**	**10.4%**	**10.7%**	**9.3%**	**5.6%**	**6.8%**	**4.5%**	**7.0%**

Source: MOET.

In Vietnam, both repetition and dropout tend to be highest in the first year of each cycle. The highest repetition rate (10 percent) is in G1. This suggests that first-year Vietnamese students, some of whom will have difficulty adjusting to a classroom situation for the first time in their lives and who may have long distances to walk from their homes to their schools, will repeat the first year rather than enter the second year inadequately prepared. This may be the right decision pedagogically, given a choice between "wasting" resources by letting children repeat the first year and "wasting" resources by promoting them to the next year, for which they are not prepared. First-year repetition is relatively low in the Red River Delta and Central North Regions, which are the regions that have the highest participation in kindergarten, which provides children with a "head-start" when they enter G1. Repetition rates tend to fall off continuously in the higher grades. It is practically non-existent (about one-half of one percent) in G12. By this grade, slow learners have been weeded out of the system, so that Vietnam has no bulge in repetition rates in the last year. This is in contrast to the situation in some countries where students and their families try to gain a competitive edge in the examinations for university entrance.

Drop out rates, on the other hand, tend to fall in Vietnam after the first year in each of the three cycles, but they rise again close to the end of the cycle. As shown in Table 4.3 this applies to primary and upper secondary education, but not to lower secondary. In general, dropout rates in Vietnam are high, especially so in the Central Highlands and Mekong River Delta, where they rise above 10 percent in many grades. The cumulative effects of dropout are seen in Table 4.4, which shows what would happen to a hypothetical cohort of 10,000 students who enter G1. Nationally, if 10,000 students entered, 6,810 would finish primary, the rest having dropped out at some point during the five-year cycle. Of this number, 5,482 would enter lower secondary education, and 3,722 would complete this cycle. Finally, given current dropout rates, only 1,904 of the original 10,000 would complete upper secondary education. The highest retention is in the North Central Region (3,018 completing upper secondary out of 10,000 entering the first grade of primary) and the lowest, in the Central Highlands Region (with only 436 of the original 10,000 completing upper secondary, an alarmingly low ratio).

Table 4.4.   Cohort Survival Rates in General Education by Region

	Primary		Lower Secondary		Upper Secondary	
	Entering	Ending	Entering	Ending	Entering	Ending
Northern Uplands	10,000	7,820	6,889	4,940	3,038	2,473
Red River Delta	10,000	7,040	6,463	5,183	2,835	2,501
North Central	10,000	6,800	6,208	4,259	3,369	3,018
Central Coast	10,000	7,160	5,714	3,245	1,681	1,370
Central Highlands	10,000	5,650	3,079	878	692	436
Southeast	10,000	8,050	5,007	3,655	2,091	1,742
Mekong River Delta	10,000	5,160	3,380	1,795	1,339	896
Vietnam	**10,000**	**6,810**	**5,482**	**3,722**	**2,308**	**1,904**

Source: MOET.

Four other indicators of flow-through efficiency, all derived from the dropout and repetition rates presented in Table 4.3, or from the promotion rate, which is related to these two,[26] are defined in Box 4.1. S, the proportion of entering children who complete a given education cycle of n years, in other words, the proportion who "graduate," is a measure of the effectiveness of education. G, the average number of years completed, is a broader measure of effectiveness because it takes into account not only those who complete the cycle but also those who drop out and the point at which they drop out along the way. T is a closely related measure indicating the average time that an entering student will spend in school before either completing or dropping out. Finally, Y is an important summary measure of flow-through efficiency. It measures the number of student-years required to produce one completing (or "graduating") student.

---

[26] Since there are only three possibilities (the child is promoted, repeats or drops out), the sum of the three rates equals 1. The promotion rate (p) is therefore related to the repetition rate (r) and dropout rate (d) as follows: $p = 1 - (r + d)$.

Box 4.1. Four Internal Efficiency Indicators

- proportion of students who complete *n* grades (*S*):

$$(4.1.1) \qquad S = \frac{p_1}{(1+r_1)} * \frac{p_2}{(1+r_2)} * \dots * \frac{p_n}{(1+r_n)}$$

- expected (average) grade attained per student (*G*):

$$(4.1.2) \qquad G = \frac{p_1}{(1+r_1)} + \frac{p_1 p_2}{(1+r_1)(1+r_2)} + \dots + \frac{p_1 p_2 \cdots p_n}{(1+r_1)(1+r_2)\dots(1+r_n)}$$

- expected duration of schooling per student (*T*):

$$(4.1.3) \qquad T = \frac{1}{(1+r_1)} + \frac{p_1}{(1+r_1)(1+r_2)} + \dots + \frac{p_1 p_2 \cdots p_{n-1}}{(1+r_1)(1+r_2)\dots(1+r_n)}$$

- expected number of student-years per graduate (*Y*):

$$(4.1.4) \qquad Y = \frac{T}{S}$$

where

$p_1 , p_2 , \dots, p_n$ are the promotion rates of grade 1, 2, ... and n,

$r_1 , r_2 , \dots, r_n$ are the repetition rates of grades 1, 2, ... and n.

Sources: Johnstone 1982 (first three indicators); Chau 1996 (fourth indicator).

Table 4.5 presents the results of calculations of all four efficiency indicators for primary, lower secondary and upper secondary education by region of the country and for all of Vietnam. The effects of high dropout and high repetition rates in a region such as the Mekong River Delta are clear. Only 52 percent of those who enter primary in this region ever finish it (as compared with 68 percent nationwide); 53 percent of those who enter lower secondary and 67 percent of those who enter upper secondary in this region finish these levels (as compared with 68 percent and 83 percent nationwide). In the Mekong River Delta, the average number of grades completed by those who enter primary education is 3.4 (as compared with 4.0 nationwide), and the average time spent in primary school by these students is 4.4 years (as compared with 4.6 nationwide). Most telling of all, on average in the Mekong River Delta, 8.4 years of primary education must be provided by the local education authorities (to students, some of whom drop out, some of whom repeat grades and a few of whom actual complete the cycle) in order to produce one "graduate" of the five-year cycle. In Vietnam as a whole, 6.8 student-years are required to produce one primary school graduate (a five-year cycle), 5.1 student-years to produce one graduate of lower secondary (a four-year cycle) and 3.5 student-years to produce one graduate of upper secondary (a three-year cycle).

Table 4.5. Efficiency Indicators in General Education

Education Level Regions	Proportion of cohort graduating (S) (Equation 4.1.1)	Average grade reached (G) (Equation 4.1.2)	Average time spent (T) (Equation 4.1.3)	Student-years per graduate (Y) (Equation 4.1.4)
Primary education				
Northern Uplands	78%	4.5	5.0	6.4
Red River Delta	70%	4.0	4.4	6.2
North Central	68%	4.1	4.6	6.7
Central Coast	72%	4.2	4.9	6.8
Central Highlands	57%	3.6	4.3	7.7
Southeast	81%	4.5	4.9	6.1
Mekong River Delta	52%	3.4	4.4	8.4
Vietnam	**68%**	**4.0**	**4.6**	**6.8**
Lower secondary education				
Northern Uplands	72%	3.2	3.5	4.9
Red River Delta	80%	3.4	3.7	4.6
North Central	69%	3.2	3.6	5.2
Central Coast	57%	2.8	3.4	5.9
Central Highlands	29%	1.8	2.6	9.2
Southeast	73%	3.2	3.6	4.9
Mekong River Delta	53%	2.6	3.2	6.1
Vietnam	**68%**	**3.1**	**3.5**	**5.1**
Upper secondary education				
Northern Uplands	81%	2.7	2.9	3.6
Red River Delta	88%	2.8	2.9	3.3
North Central	90%	2.8	2.9	3.3
Central Coast	82%	2.6	2.8	3.4
Central Highlands	63%	2.1	2.6	4.1
Southeast	83%	2.6	2.8	3.4
Mekong River Delta	67%	2.3	2.7	4.1
Vietnam	**83%**	**2.6**	**2.9**	**3.5**

Source: MOET.

The extra years required to produce graduates, over and above the number of years that would be required were there no dropout or repetition, may or may not be "efficient" in the sense of maximizing the *learning* that occurs per unit of money spent. This study is silent on this question because it has no measure of learning as such.

However, the additional years are certainly "inefficient" in the sense of raising the *economic cost of producing graduates*. Table 4.6 presents calculations of the costs per graduate by education level and by region. The regional breakdown of private unit costs is based on VLSS data (Glewwe and Jacoby 1996), inflated to reflect price changes between 1992-93 and 1994. The breakdown of fiscal costs is based on MOF information on total fiscal costs (VEFSS 1996d) divided by MOET information on student enrollments (VEFSS 1996a).

Table 4.6. Costs per Graduate, 1994

| Education Level | Costs per Student-year ('000 VND) | | | Student-years per Graduate | Costs per Graduate ('000 VND) | | |
Region	Fiscal	Private	Economic		Fiscal	Private	Economic
Primary education							
Northern Uplands	160	42	202	6.4	1,030	270	1,301
Red River Delta	111	64	175	6.2	688	397	1,085
North Central	110	50	160	6.7	741	337	1,078
Central Coast	135	99	234	6.8	918	673	1,591
Central Highlands	157	65	222	7.7	1,201	497	1,698
Southeast	163	176	339	6.1	1,001	1,081	2,081
Mekong River Delta	108	126	234	8.4	912	1,063	1,975
Vietnam	**130**	**104**	**233**	**6.8**	**883**	**706**	**1,589**
Lower secondary education							
Northern Uplands	276	92	368	4.9	1,352	451	1,803
Red River Delta	231	150	381	4.6	1,063	690	1,753
North Central	265	126	391	5.2	1,378	655	2,033
Central Coast	163	270	433	5.9	962	1,593	2,555
Central Highlands	213	181	394	9.2	1,960	1,665	3,625
Southeast	206	345	551	4.9	1,009	1,691	2,700
Mekong River Delta	196	362	558	6.1	1,196	2,208	3,404
Vietnam	**235**	**223**	**458**	**5.1**	**1,199**	**1,137**	**2,336**
Upper secondary education							
Northern Uplands	365	173	538	3.6	1,314	623	1,937
Red River Delta	343	369	712	3.3	1,128	1,214	2,342
North Central	368	212	580	3.3	1,207	695	1,902
Central Coast	196	545	741	3.4	670	1,864	2,534
Central Highlands	524	123	647	4.1	2,127	499	2,627
Southeast	348	659	1,007	3.4	1,169	2,214	3,384
Mekong River Delta	730	678	1,408	4.1	2,978	2,766	5,745
Vietnam	**483**	**512**	**995**	**3.5**	**1,671**	**1,772**	**3,443**

Sources: For private costs, VLSS 1992-93 as reported in Glewwe and Jacoby (1996); for fiscal costs, VEFSS (1996a and 1996d).

The results are very interesting. The average cost of producing a primary school graduate across all of Vietnam in 1994 was approximately VND 1.6 million (about $143). In the Southeast Region, however, the cost was 31 percent higher than this (VND 2.1 million), not because primary schools in this region are less efficient (they require 6.1 student-years to produce a graduate as compared with 6.8 student-years nationwide) but because more is spent per student-year (VND 163 thousand in fiscal costs and VND 176 thousand in private costs as compared with VND 130 thousand and VND 104 thousand nationwide). On the other hand, the second highest cost per primary school graduate is found in the Mekong River Delta. Here the fiscal cost per student-year is well below the national average, but as we have already seen, flow-through efficiency is low in the Mekong River Delta, and it is this factor that leads to an above-average cost per graduate. The lowest costs per primary graduate are in the Red River Delta and North Central

Regions, where flow-through efficiency is about average but where fiscal and private costs are lower than average.

Similar stories can be extracted from Table 4.6 for lower and upper secondary education. Variation around the mean becomes more pronounced, however, as one moves up the education ladder. The highest cost per upper secondary school graduate is in the Mekong River Delta, and this is 67 percent higher than the national average. The lowest is in North Central Region, where it is 33 percent of the highest.

QUALITY DETERMINANTS IN GENERAL EDUCATION

Internal efficiency is not just a matter of achieving the lowest cost per student-year, nor even a matter of achieving the lowest cost per graduate. The lowest-cost education system would be one that hired no teachers and purchased no instructional materials. But this could not be called *education*, let alone *efficient education*, since it fails to address the fundamental objective of any education system, which is to transmit useful knowledge and skills to the students who pass through the system. For students to learn at school, there must usually be an input of teacher time, and also inputs of many non-salary factors. For the school to be efficient, these factors must be combined *in the right proportions, given relative factor prices*.

This section considers two issues in relation to the quality of Vietnam's system of general education. The first is *instructional hours* and whether or not Vietnamese students spend enough time over the course of the school year to cover the official curriculum and to reach cognitive achievement levels that are acceptable by international standards. The second issue is the *mix of pedagogical inputs*, both teaching and non-teaching inputs, and whether or not this mix is efficient. It is *inefficient* if student achievement could be raised, not by spending more on education, but by allocating differently what is already being spent. Moreover, it is *inequitable* if a high proportion of the total spending on pedagogical inputs is expected to be covered by families, and not by the state, and if poor families do not have the necessary income to meet their share of the costs.

Instructional Hours

How many hours do students in Vietnam actually spend in school? The evidence suggests that the number is very low by international standards and that it will need to be increased if student achievement is to be raised significantly. Instructional time is limited at present owing to both a short school day and a short school year. Several factors contribute to the short school day, which rarely exceeds four hours in schools across Vietnam.

In order to expand enrollments in crowded areas, given that school buildings are (in the short run) fixed in size and their capacity to accommodate students, Vietnam's local education authorities have resorted to double- (and sometimes even triple-) "shifting." In other words, classes are held in the mornings for one group of students and in the afternoons for a second group. Wherever there is double-shifting, inevitably each shift lasts only a few hours. The school day is short in many remote areas of Vietnam too, presumably because of the long distances to be walked by children between home and school. Moreover, because many school teachers in Vietnam "moon-light," that is, work at a secondary job before or after their primary teaching job, few are willing or able to spend more than just a few hours in the primary job. This fact is relevant to the question of whether or not teachers in Vietnam are properly remunerated (cf. paras. 2.47-2.49 in Chapter 2).

The short school day is a problem in and of itself, but the negative effect of this on student achievement is compounded by the fact that the school year is also very short -- 165 days as compared with an international norm of 180 or more. Taking four hours to be the average school day in Vietnam, and assuming that students actually receive instruction during all 165 days included in the official calendar (an optimistic assumption given miscellaneous school closings and both teacher and student absences), this leads to the conclusion that the average instructional year in Vietnam totals 660 hours, which is only about three-quarters of the worldwide average of 880 for primary education:[27]

The issue of too little instructional time should be tackled by addressing each factor in turn. First, there is little reason for having an official school calendar that keeps schools open less than half the year. Twenty or more days should be added to the school calendar to bring Vietnam closer to the international norm. Second, in those places where the school day is only about four hours, it should be increased by at least one hour. These two changes alone would increase the number of instructional hours in the year by about 40 percent, to 925 hours. This could have an enormous impact of student achievement and may even pay for itself in part, by reducing repetition and dropout.

Even so, the cost implication of these changes is significant. To implement a longer school day may require the elimination of double shifting in many places. This cannot happen without new school construction, including the rehabilitation of some facilities now underutilized because they are run down and not conducive to learning. Moreover, to increase instructional hours without paying teachers more than they now get amounts to a reduction in their hourly remuneration. Teachers who now moonlight in order to achieve a reasonable living wage will not agree to finance the cost of these measures to enhance education quality, nor should they be asked to do so. Realistically, teachers' annual salaries would need to be adjusted upward, probably by the same percentage amount as hours have been increased (or more, if simultaneous measures are taken to upgrade teachers' skills), in return for which teachers would be expected to work a "full day" and a longer school year. To the extent that some teachers now teach two

---

[27] This average is based on 110 countries in the 1980s. The average increases by income level: for low income countries, it was 870 hours, for middle income 880 and for high income countries 914 (Benavot and Kamens 1989, as reported in Lockheed and Verspoor 1991).

shifts, this would no longer be possible. This implies more incremental costs, to recruit and/or train the additional teachers needed.

Input Mix

Does Vietnam's education system combine teachers and other inputs in the correct proportions? This question is impossible to answer definitively in the absence of test information on student achievement. The discussion here will simply present information on the allocation of costs across different categories of inputs in primary and secondary education and then conjecture as to whether the allocation seems reasonable in the light of international experience.

Table 4.7 takes the unit cost estimates for general education in Figure 4.1 above and breaks these down both by the source of funds and by the object of spending (use of funds). The table shows that for every VND 100 of *government* spending on general education in Vietnam, between VND 70 and 80 is spent on teachers salaries, depending on the level -- primary, lower secondary or upper secondary. This is a lower percentage than in many countries, and it leaves VND 20 to 30 for the purchase of other pedagogical inputs, including learning materials, school maintenance and part of the administrative overhead needed to run both the individual school and the national education system.

Table 4.7.   Disaggregated Unit Costs for General Education, 1994 ('000 VND)

Source of Funds	Primary			Lower Secondary			Upper Secondary		
Object of Spending	Amount	Shares		Amount	Shares		Amount	Shares	
State Budget	*130*	*100%*	*56%*	*235*	*100%*	*51%*	*483*	*100%*	*49%*
Wages/salaries	104	80%	45%	188	80%	41%	348	72%	35%
Non-salary items	26	20%	11%	47	20%	10%	135	28%	14%
Households	*103*	*100%*	*44%*	*223*	*100%*	*49%*	*512*	*100%*	*51%*
Fees/voluntary contributions[a]	24	23%	10%	50	22%	11%	115	22%	12%
Textbooks and school supplies	36	35%	15%	63	28%	14%	113	22%	11%
Uniforms	24	23%	10%	41	18%	9%	61	12%	6%
Out-of-school tutoring	12	12%	5%	53	24%	12%	188	37%	19%
Transportation and other	7	7%	3%	16	7%	3%	35	7%	4%
Total Unit Costs	**233**	**--**	**100%**	**458**	**--**	**100%**	**995**	**--**	**100%**

[a]Fees/voluntary contributions from households are used at the school level and are channeled to school or to various current expenditure categories, including sometimes teachers salaries. Household spending on meals for students during school hours is not included here as a cost of education.
Sources: MOF; VLSS 1992-93; and VSSS 1996.

In primary education, government expenditure on non-salary items amounts to VND 26,000 (a little more than $2). Much more than this is spent, however, by *households* with family members in school. On average, VND 24,000 is spent on "voluntary" contributions to the school by a family with a child enrolled in primary education, VND 36,000 on textbooks and school supplies, VND 24,000 on a school uniforms, VND 12,000 on out-of-school tutoring and VND 7,000 on transportation and other education-related costs. The total is VND 103,000 (about $9), but of course some families spend more than this and other families less. By upper secondary, the average family spends a total of VND 512,000 (more than $46) per year for a child in school, the largest component of which (37 percent) goes for out-of-school tutoring. Poor families, however, do not have the income needed to meet such high private costs, with the result that a relatively small percentage of children from poor homes continue in school past primary, and those who do continue spend far less on pedagogical inputs than children from middle-income homes spend (VLSS 1992-93).

ECONOMIES OF SCALE AND SCOPE IN TERTIARY EDUCATION

Internal efficiency, as evidenced by high unit costs, is an issue at the tertiary level. Given the small average size of higher education institutions, the inevitable result is that student-teacher ratios and facility utilization rates are lower than necessary. The expansion of higher education in Vietnam has taken the form of a proliferation of small, "mono-disciplinary" universities and colleges.

HEIFS, this study's source of *institution-level* data on the costs and sources of financing for higher education, was implemented in 1995 and provided estimates of institutional costs in SY93-SY95. Since estimates for the last of these three years were based on budgeted rather than actual expenditure figures, however, this section of the report will present information for SY94 only. Already by SY94, tertiary education had undergone a period of rapid expansion enrollment, especially in the period after SY91 (see section on tertiary enrollments in Chapter 2). The issue of too-small average institutional size would have been even more serious had this study been conducted just a few years earlier, since the number of institutions, which has risen during this decade, has risen less slowly than the number of students. In fact, the recent consolidation of a number of smaller institutions to create two National Universities and three Regional Universities has begun to address the issue of small HEI sizes in five of Vietnam's large urban centers.

Of the 100 higher education institutions surveyed in HEIFS, only seven are classified as multi-disciplinary. Each of the remaining 93 offers programs in just one field of study and is thus classified as a "mono-disciplinary" HEI. The large number of mono-disciplinary HEIs in Vietnam is a legacy of the historical development of tertiary education, heavily influenced by the Soviet model of small, highly specialized, vocationally oriented institutions under the detailed control of a single line ministry and with the primary purpose of training manpower for that ministry to meet its planned manpower requirements and production targets.

This model does not seem appropriate given Vietnam's changed policy environment. The transition from central planning to a market approach is accompanied by accelerated economic growth and rapid change. It is more difficult for specialized institutions to shift their focus in response to changing labor market demands than it is for multi-disciplinary institutions, which can be more flexible. Moreover, as mono-disciplinary HEIs are generally smaller, they tend to have lower student-teacher ratios and to make less efficient use of specialized facilities such as libraries, laboratories and equipment. As a result, the mono-disciplinary HEIs tend to have higher unit costs than larger, more diversified HEIs in Vietnam.

Economies of Scale and Scope

The HEIFS revealed that the average student size of the 100 HEIs in SY94 was 4,254 students (see Table 4.8).[28] The cumulative distribution shows that about a fifth of the 100 HEIs (18) enrolled fewer than 500 students, nearly half (44) fewer than 1,000, and two-thirds (66) fewer than 2,000. Only seven (not counting the two new open universities, which were not included in the HEIFS sample) enrolled 5,000 or more students, and two enrolled 10,000 or more. As started above, the size of an institution is related to the scope and range of its instructional programs. All but one of the seven multidisciplinary universities enrolled at least 2,000 students, whereas 70 percent of the mono-disciplinary institutions were smaller than these.

Table 4.8. Distribution of Public Higher Education Institutions by Size and Scope, 1994

Institutional scope	Size (number of FTE students enrolled)									Mean size of HEIs in category
	0-249	250-499	500-999	1000-1,999	2,000-2,999	3,000-4,999	5,000-9,999	10,000+	Total	
Mono-disciplinary	3	15	26	21	12	11	4	1	93	4,054
Cumulative percent	3%	19%	47%	70%	83%	95%	99%	100%		
Multi-disciplinary	0	0	0	1	2	2	1	1	7	6,911
Cumulative percent	0%	0%	0%	14%	43%	71%	86%	100%		
Both	3	15	26	22	14	13	5	2	100	4,254
Cumulative percent	3%	18%	44%	66%	80%	93%	98%	100%		

Source: HEIFS 1995.

There are also important differences *between regions* in the average size of HEIs. The North Central Region, for example, has several very small institutions, with 500 or fewer students, and the majority of HEIs in the Mekong River Delta, Central Highlands and North Central Regions enroll fewer than 2,000 students, but over half of the HEIs in the Southeast Region enroll more than 2,000, and over a fifth, more than 5,000.

The inefficiency of having very many small specialized institutions is confirmed by an analysis of the unit costs across institutions in the HEIFS dataset. The analysis leads to the conclusion that *both* small size *and* limited scope have negative effects on average institutional cost, each of these effects independent of the other. Average recurrent cost per student-year was found to be about 25 percent higher in mono-disciplinary HEIs than in multi-disciplinary HEIs, and this effect of program scope remained statistically significant even when institutional size was included in the analysis and thus controlled for. However, the negative effect of small size was the stronger of the two effects. Unit costs (average current fiscal expenditures per student-year) were found to be *six times higher* in the three smallest HEIs (fewer than 250 students) than in the two largest (more than 10,000).

A key factor contributing to the large cost differences is the difference in student-teacher ratios. According to the HEIFS dataset, the average student-teacher ratio (defined

---

[28] HEIFS did not include Vietnam's two Open Universities, which opened in SY94 with relatively small enrollments, but which already by SY95 had a combined enrollment of over 52,000 students.

as the number of FTE students per teaching staff member in the institution) was below 9 in public HEIs. This is low in comparison with other countries in the Asia region. A World Bank study reported an average student-teacher ratio (*not* adjusted for FTEs) of 14 in public HEIs in Asia, with country averages ranging from 5 in China to more than 40 in Korea (Tan and Mingat 1989). In the HEIFS dataset, HEIs with fewer than five FTEs per teacher had average unit costs four-to-five times higher than HEIs with 25 or more.

Ordinary least squares regression analysis was conducted to estimate the parameters of the cost function underlying the observed variation in unit costs. The analysis controlled for the average qualifications or average experience of teaching staff, as a proxy measure of higher education's *quality* at the level of the individual HEI. The regressions controlled also for fixed effects of "institution type" (multi- versus mono-disciplinary, and if mono-disciplinary, the area of specialization) and for fixed regional effects. The analysis confirmed the existence of significant economies of scale in Vietnamese higher education. The negative relationship between an institution's size and average per-student cost remained strong even when the student-teacher ratio was controlled for.[29]

The cost function was estimated according to alternative specifications (linear, quadratic and hyperbolic), and the regression results are presented in Table 4.9. All specifications give clear support to the economies-of-scale hypothesis, but the best-performing function was the hyperbolic model, in which unit cost is determined by the *inverse* of institutional size, implying that, as size increases, cost decreases continuously but by smaller and smaller increments. The adjusted R^2 and F statistics are higher for the regression equations based on the hyperbolic model than for those based on the linear (cost decreases by constant increments) or quadratic (cost decreases to a minimum point, and then increases as size increases further) models.

---

[29] Teaching staff numbers (as measured by the student-teacher ratio) and teacher quality (percentage of teachers with Ph.D. degrees and percentage with 20-plus years of teaching experience) are proxies for the quality of instruction provided by a given HEI, but they also influence the salary bill and contribute directly, therefore, to differences in unit costs. It might be argued that to control for student-teacher ratios "over-controls" and underestimates the negative effect of institution size on unit costs.

Table 4.9.   Multiple Regression Estimates of Higher Education Cost Function

			Explanatory Variables Regression Coefficients[a]						
Model			$Size^2$ divided by 10,000	(1/size) times 10,000	Student-teacher ratio	Percentage of teachers with:			
						Ph.D. degrees	20+ yrs of experience		
Number	Type	Size						Adj. R^2	F statistic
Model 1	Linear	-0.131 *						0.230	3.256 #
Model 2	Quadratic	-0.287 *	0.139					0.237	3.172 #
Model 3	Quadratic	-0.129	0.117		-68.5 #			0.377	4.957 #
Model 4	Quadratic	-0.271 #	0.115			6.998		0.175	2.148 #
Model 5	Quadratic	-0.284 *	0.142				8.507	0.240	3.045 #
Model 6	Hyperbolic			449.6 #				0.325	4.626 #
Model 7	Hyperbolic			31.7 #	-56.6 #			0.436	6.404 #
Model 8	Hyperbolic			58.7 #		7.666		0.285	3.311 #
Model 9	Hyperbolic			48.0 #			13.558 #	0.350	4.722 #

Note: All regression equations controll for fixed regional effects and fixed effects of institution type.

[a]Significance levels: * = 0.05, # = 0.10.

Source: HEIFS 1995.

Figure 4.4 plots observed unit costs of the 100 institutions against institution size. It also shows the regression equation based on Model 7, other factors held constant at the sample means. The regression line shows very clearly the average relation between costs and enrollments in Vietnamese higher education -- the larger the size of a HEI, the lower is its unit cost. Average recurrent cost per student-year falls sharply until enrollment reaches the range of 1,000-1,500 FTE students. After this, unit costs continue to decline as size increases, but much less steeply.

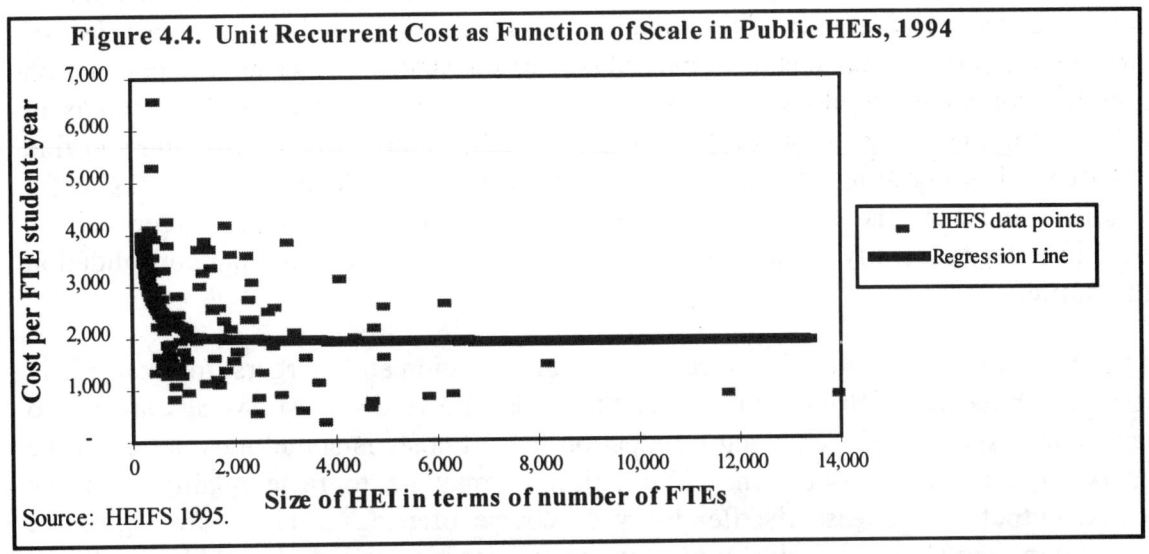

Figure 4.4. Unit Recurrent Cost as Function of Scale in Public HEIs, 1994

Cost per FTE student-year

- HEIFS data points
- Regression Line

Size of HEI in terms of number of FTEs

Source: HEIFS 1995.

There are good reasons, not captured in the regression analysis, for keeping most HEIs in Vietnam in the 1,000-3,000 student range at this time and not trying to eke out any remaining scale economies in the 3,000-10,000 range. One reason is to achieve a regional balance of higher education opportunity throughout Vietnam. Private costs of room and board and transportation, which are not measured in this analysis of institutional costs, increase as the distance from home to the place of study increases. Students from remote provinces of Vietnam should not have to face higher costs of study than students (who are often more affluent) living in populous areas. Moreover, there is probably an argument for some degree of regional diversity in range and content of courses offered.

However, the HEIFS dataset indicates convincingly that a large number of HEIs in Vietnam at this time are too small and miss out on an opportunity to operate at much lower per-student costs. Carefully managed institutional mergers, already an object of Vietnamese policy for higher education, could result in significant cost savings. Care must be taken to ensure that the mergers are not just *token mergers* and do, in fact, lead to more favorable student-staff ratios, fuller utilization of facilities and the elimination of duplicative administrative overhead. If teaching staff possess narrowly specialized skills, and they possess lifetime job tenure, then institutional mergers will not necessarily reduce staffing costs. Simply declaring that two former institutions are now "one" institution, but changing nothing in the way the two operate, will *not* result in economies of scale.

As stated, institutional consolidation is already the Government's announced policy for higher education. There are HEIs resulting from recent mergers that can serve as different models for future consolidation. For example, the National University in Ho Chi Minh City was created by merging previously specialized and separate HEIs in the natural sciences, social sciences and teacher training. Hanoi National University, on the other hand, combined two specialized institutions (for foreign languages and teacher training) with an already established multi-disciplinary university. In both cities, there remain other separate institutions that have not been included (to date) in the newly merged National Universities (for example, there are self-standing universities of technology in both cities). Whether or not these separate HEIs should be brought in with the rest is a policy decision still to be taken. The proposed new Regional University in Hue will combine specialized colleges of agriculture, medicine, teacher training and fine arts with a university of technology and an existing multi-disciplinary university. Careful monitoring and analysis of the cost savings actually achieved in each merger will be needed in order to identify the most efficient way to undertake institutional consolidation in the future.

International experience of institutional consolidation and mergers, for example in Australia, China, Great Britain and the Netherlands, shows that cost savings are by no means automatic. Indeed, achieving a reduction in unit costs is sometimes not even the primary motive for consolidation. The objective may be to raise quality, enhance research outputs or increase the flexibility of course offerings. These are legitimate objectives in their own right. However, their satisfaction may in fact depend indirectly on the achievement of economies of scale, and on a reduction of unit costs, *not adjusting for the quality of a student-year*. The cost savings brought about by the more efficient utilization of educational inputs may be immediately re-directed toward the achievement of other objectives. Whereas the cost per student-year has *not* fallen, the cost per quality-adjusted student year *has* fallen. In other words, it is possible that student *learning* has risen (and what the HEI accomplishes in terms of its many other institutional objectives has risen), even though the *number* of students and total institutional costs have stayed the same. In this sense, consolidation has indeed resulted in enhanced efficiency.

Even if the principal objective of consolidation is to reduce costs, the magnitude of the cost savings will depend on many factors. As already stated, it will depend on the degree of duplication (of facilities, staff and administrative overhead) that existed before the merger and on the extent to which resources can be successfully reallocated or cut from the budget. It will also depend on the type of program offered by the institution, particularly which fields of study are emphasized. In 1995, average current costs in HEIs specializing in fine arts, culture and sports were about three times higher, and in HEIs specializing in agro-forestry and fisheries, six times higher, than costs in HEIs specializing in economics and finance. This was partly related to differences in size. Many of the first group of HEIs had enrollments below 500, and all of the second group had enrollments below 3,000, whereas six of the seven HEIs specializing in economics and finance had enrollments larger than 3,000. But the cost differences also reflect differences in the HEIs' use of expensive, specialized equipment.

In summary, the VEFSS study of economies of scale and scope in higher education suggests that further consolidation of small specialized institutions could lead to more efficient utilization of staff, facilities and administrative resources, and therefore to significant cost savings. However, to fully realize these savings will require careful specification of objectives and analysis of alternatives.

Cost Structure

Another important aspect of internal efficiency is the composition of unit costs. Despite low average student-teacher ratios, the proportion of current expenditure devoted to staff salaries and financial benefits is low by international standards. In 1993, it was only 44 percent, even though this estimate does not include scholarships (which represent about 8 percent of all current expenditure in support of tertiary education but which are excluded from the calculations of unit costs on the grounds that they are transfer payments rather than tertiary education production costs). Non-salary expenditure, including books, teaching materials, and the non-salary component of administrative services, accounted for over half (56 percent) of total current expenditure.[30]

The relatively low share of current expenditure devoted to teachers' salaries, despite high teacher-student ratios in Vietnam, reflects the low salaries of professional workers in the civil service. Low salaries mean that it is difficult for HEIs to attract and retain qualified staff, particularly younger staff, and indeed MOET statistics show that of the total teaching staff in universities and colleges, only 18 percent in SY95 held post-graduate degrees. The rest possessed only bachelor's degrees or college diplomas. Moreover, many teachers, perhaps most, hold one or more jobs in addition to their primary job in the HEI, so that the high teacher-student ratios are almost certainly not an accurate measure of effective teacher inputs.

---

[30] The purchase and repair of small works and equipment is excluded from this definition of current expenditure. These are counted as capital expenditure in order to be consistent with GFS accounting conventions, although they are still classified as current expenditure in Vietnam's own budget laws.

A recent study for the Asian Development Bank (Mingat 1995) shows that, in the early stages of industrialization, Japan and Korea adopted a very different policy for tertiary education, combining low teacher-student ratios with relatively high teacher salaries. This resulted apparently in efficient utilization of teachers and a high quality of tertiary education.

In sum, it would seem that universities and colleges in Vietnam suffer from a dual problem of high costs and uneven quality -- as a result of their small size, narrow specialization, and inefficient utilization of teachers, equipment and facilities. The policy of consolidating institutions and programs within institutions to exploit economies of scale and scope could yield substantial savings. But these benefits will be achieved only if the restructuring and mergers are well designed and carefully implemented. Other necessary steps to improve higher education efficiency and raise quality include the upgrading and better utilization of teaching staff.

5. EXTERNAL EFFICIENCY AND EQUITY

Priorities for education expansion and financing should be guided by considerations of external efficiency and equity. Since the proclamation of *Đoi Moi* a decade ago, the Vietnamese Government has ushered in an ambitious program of economic reform. Such reform creates disequilibria in other sectors, and perhaps nowhere more so than in the education and training sector. This reflects the inertia of educational institutions, as well as the long gestation period of educational investments, with students spending 2-3 years in school to become functionally literate, and another 13-14 years, at least, to complete all steps leading to a university degree.

Not surprisingly, the current system of E&T in Vietnam exhibits many symptoms of low external efficiency and inequitable access and financing. The skills demanded by employers in Vietnam's transition economy are not necessarily those commonly taught in Vietnam's educational institutions (World Bank 1993b). Many VOTECH and university graduates experience difficulty finding jobs today, even though other skills are in short supply. Government may want to consider changes in the curriculum, as well as changes in the system of education financing, so as to encourage study that leads to marketable skills.

Child labor has become more prevalent during the recent period. This fact may help explain the temporary decline in secondary education enrollments between SY88 and SY92. Fortunately, this trend seems now to have been reversed, but large numbers of school-age children remain out of school. The reasons, no doubt, include both "push" (direct costs of schooling) and "pull" (opportunity costs of schooling) factors. To address both sets of factors, Government might consider a policy of targeted subsidies to assist poor children to remain in school and also to compensate their families for the loss of income earned on their labor.

Since SY92, enrollments have increased at most levels of education. However, educational attendance is related to family income, and this relationship becomes more pronounced as one moves up the education ladder. In addition, Government subsidizes a larger share of the costs of education at higher levels of the system. Taking into account the larger unit costs at the upper grades of school and in tertiary education, this means that public spending on education benefits children from wealthier families disproportionately. Again, targeted public subsidies could be used to improve access to education for the poor.

The statistical data needed to address labor market issues in Vietnam are often unreliable and sometimes missing totally. This chapter analyzes recent employment and earnings trends from whatever labor market information could be found, and where nothing was available, the study has assisted Government to generate new data in these areas. The main data source for this chapter is the Vietnam Living Standards Survey

(VLSS), a multi-purpose, nationally representative household survey supported by UNDP and carried out by GSO in 1992-93. VLSS surveyed 4,800 households throughout Vietnam and provided data on the employment and earnings of individuals at the time with different levels and types of education.[31] The Higher Education Graduate Tracer Study (HEGTS) and Skill Development and Labor Market Study (SDLMS) are recent initiatives undertaken under the auspices of VEFSS. They are generating new information on the creation and utilization of labor market skills in Vietnam.

EXTERNAL EFFICIENCY OF EDUCATION AND TRAINING

Education is known to be an important determinant of earnings in market economies. The higher an individual's educational attainment, the higher that individual's expected starting salary, and the steeper his or her rise in earnings capacity over time, especially during the early working years. Although research on the education-earnings link is limited in the centrally planned economies, including economies in transition, what evidence there is suggests that the returns to schooling are low by comparison with what has been observed in market economies (see discussion of China, below). The returns to education tend to increase, however, as market reforms take hold (see discussion of Slovenia, below).

The VLSS dataset provides estimates of the returns to schooling of those Vietnamese workers employed in the wage labor force. Strictly speaking, VLSS does not provide comparable information for the large number of self-employed workers, for whom labor earnings are difficult to assess. Given the importance, however, of self-employment in Vietnam, total household income of self-employed workers will be analyzed below. Estimates of the returns to education in the self-employment sector of the economy will be estimated, but at best these will be indicative, since it is not possible with the VLSS data to provide satisfactory controls for the contributions of physical capital to household income.

Employment and Earnings Characteristics of Workers

At the time of VLSS data collection, the largest number of Vietnamese workers (66 percent) were in agriculture (Table 5.1). Manufacturing (12 percent) was the next largest sector, followed by wholesale and retail trade, including restaurants and hotels (11 percent). The vast majority of workers in Vietnam (79 percent) were self-employed (Table 5.2). Private firms accounted for 11 percent of the labor force, and the public sector broadly defined, for 9 percent.

---

[31] It should be emphasized that VLSS 1992-93, while the best source of household-level information currently available for the country of Vietnam as a whole, is limited in its value because the information is already several years old, and the Vietnamese economy is undergoing rapid change. A new VLSS will be undertaken beginning at the end of 1996.

Table 5.1. Employment by Industry

Industry	No. of Obs.	Percent
Agriculture	6,506	65.5%
Mining	56	0.6%
Manufacturing	1,156	11.6%
Electricity	20	0.2%
Construction	244	2.5%
Wholesale/Retail Trade	1,078	10.8%
Transport	214	2.2%
Finance	23	0.2%
Services	642	6.5%
Total	**9,939**	**100.0%**

Source: VLSS 1992-93.

Table 5.2. Employment by Sector

Sector Sub-sector	No. of Obs.	Percent
Public	**921**	**9.3%**
Government	413	4.2%
State Enterprise	329	3.3%
Social Organization	47	0.5%
Cooperative	132	1.3%
Private	**9,016**	**90.7%**
Self-employed	7,857	79.1%
Domestic Firms	1,136	11.4%
Foreign/Mixed/JointVenture	23	0.2%
Total	**9,937**	**100.0%**

Note: 2 missing cases.

Source: VLSS 1992-93.

In comparison with many low income countries, Vietnam's wage labor force is well educated (Table 5.3). The mean educational attainment of wage workers was 7.8 years in 1992-93. Only 22 percent of the sample had not completed primary education; 12 percent had done some VOTECH; and 8 percent and 7 percent had finished secondary and tertiary education. The typical wage worker was 31 years old, had 17 years of work experience, and worked 46 hours in a week. More than 40 percent of the wage labor force worked in the public sector. The mean monthly earnings of wage workers was VND151,690 (about $15).

Table 5.3. Characteristics of Employed Wage Workers, Age 15-65 Years

Variable	Mean or proportion	Standard Deviation
Age (years)	30.81	10.97
Male	0.60	
Public Sector	0.42	
Earnings (1993 VND/month)	151,690	151,890
Work Intensity (hours/week)	46.24	13.70
Work Experience (years)	16.96	11.26
Education (years)	7.85	4.16
No education	0.22	
Completed Primary	0.50	
Completed Secondary	0.08	
Attended VOTECH	0.12	
Completed Tertiary	0.07	
Number of Observations	2,259	

Source: VLSS 1992-93.

Among Vietnam's wage workers, educational attainment did not differ very much between men and women (Figure 5.1). The education difference was much greater between rural and urban workers. Only 20 percent of rural wage workers had completed more than primary education, as compared with 40 percent of urban wage workers. Similarly, those working in the public sector had more education than those working in the private sector. Even small state enterprises rarely employ workers with less than ten years of schooling (Ronnås and Sjöberg 1995). This reflects the policy, only recently abandoned, of a guaranteed job in the public sector for anyone who had finished secondary, technical or tertiary education.

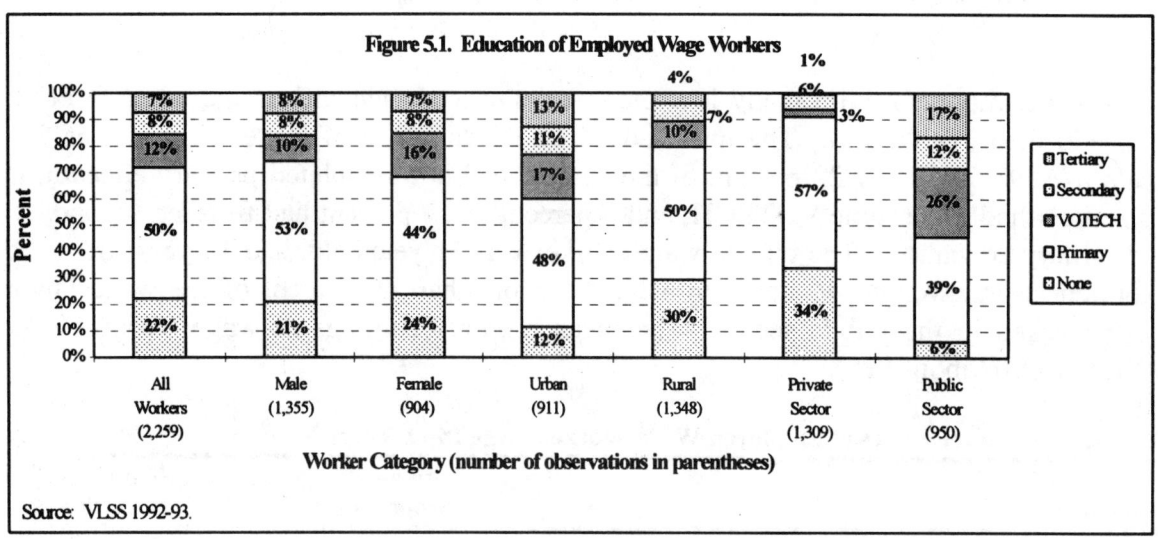

Wage differences across education groups are small in Vietnam by comparison with most market economies (Figures 5.2-5.4). A wage worker in 1992-93 who had completed tertiary education earned two or three times more than one who had completed primary education, but this is a small difference in a country where primary graduates outnumber tertiary graduates seven to one. VOTECH graduates who were male or rural, or who worked in the private sector, earned less than secondary graduates in the same categories, but more otherwise. The pattern of earnings across the various groups was a bit erratic as shown in Figures 5.2-5.4, because the VLSS sample included relatively small numbers of observations, but generally earnings did increase with education.

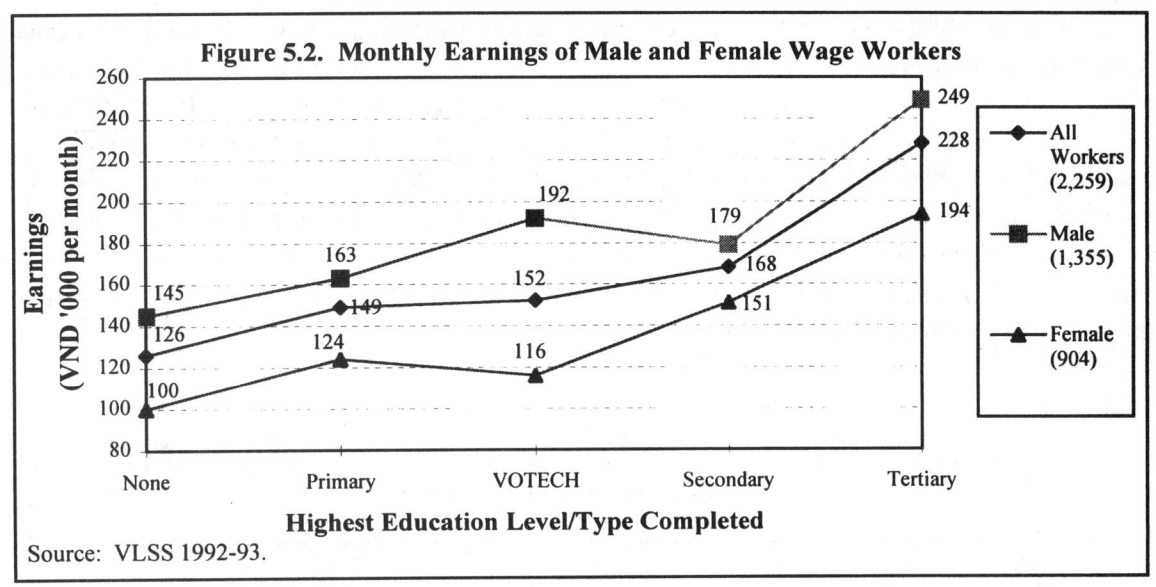

Figure 5.2. Monthly Earnings of Male and Female Wage Workers

Source: VLSS 1992-93.

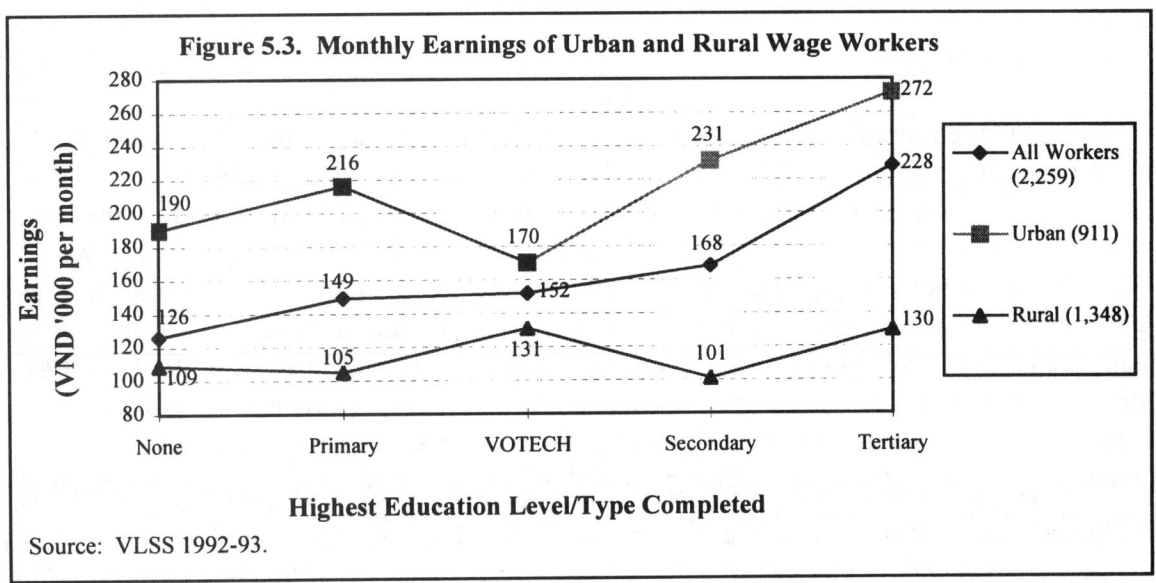

Figure 5.3. Monthly Earnings of Urban and Rural Wage Workers

Source: VLSS 1992-93.

Labor Market Policies

Đoi Moi policies accord a lead role to the private sector in Vietnam's future economic development and in the transition to a market economy. Employment growth is now highest in the private sector, which must absorb most new labor market entrants and also workers released by government and state enterprises. Between 1989 and 1993, about 4.7 million jobs were created in the private sector. A reduction of 0.9 million jobs in the state sector implies a net increase of 3.8 million jobs, or approximately 0.95 million jobs per year (World Bank 1995b). Current public sector remuneration policy compresses earnings differentials across education groups. Public workers in 1992-93 with no education were paid 188,000 VND per month on average. This was as much as public sector workers who had completed primary or secondary education or attended

VOTECH were paid, and it was more than workers in the private sector earned with any of these educational qualifications.

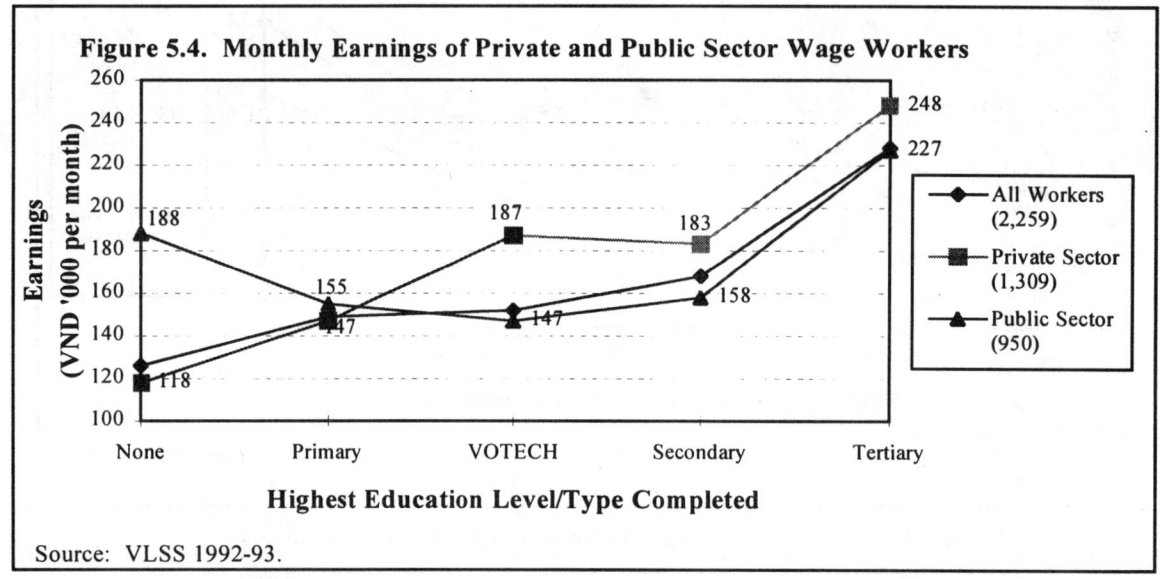

Figure 5.4. Monthly Earnings of Private and Public Sector Wage Workers

Source: VLSS 1992-93.

The Government's development strategy places priority on investment in human capital (Socialist Republic of Vietnam 1995e). There are, however, problems in relation to labor. As part of the economic reform program, some 1.5 million workers who were working in government offices and state owned enterprises have been retrenched (World Bank 1995b). In conjunction with high population growth, which reflects high birth rates and the return of many migrants and refugees, the loss of jobs has resulted in increased unemployment. Real wages have declined since the start of *Đoi Moi* (ILO 1994). Moreover, modern labor practices are new to Vietnam. A labor law and labor code were adopted in 1995. These cover a wide range of labor issues including labor contracts, unions, collective bargaining, training, social insurance, and working conditions and safety regulations (see World Bank 1995b for a full description).

Public Sector Reform. In 1990, Government began the difficult process of dismantling the old public sector wage system. No longer will remuneration of public sector workers be based on length of service alone, nor will jobs be guaranteed for life. In order to achieve these market principles, the Government announced plans to place all government workers on contract, but the process of change has been slow (Hiebert 1993; Norlund 1993).

In 1993 Government announced plans to monetize the wages of all public servants. In the past, only a fraction of a government employee's compensation was received in cash. Up to 90 percent was in the form of bonuses and in-kind payments (ILO 1994). New state workers will, however, no longer be able to purchase rationed goods at artificially low prices, nor will they be given subsidized housing, health care, education and social insurance. Salaries will be set according to market rates. The salary structure will compensate government workers according to education level, job responsibility and performance. Government has also announced plans to de-compress public sector wages. The full impact of these reforms may not be seen for years, however, since those hired prior to 1994 are largely exempted.

In the past, graduates of secondary and tertiary education, including higher-level VOTECH graduates, were assigned jobs in the public sector. Only primary school graduates and those without any education operated in a labor market of sorts. A reliance on market signals to allocate educated labor was announced, however, as government policy at the 1991 Party Congress (Ronnås and Sjöberg 1995).

Regulations Governing the Private Sector. Private firms are now free to set wages without government interference. In the parastatal sector, subsidies were reduced in 1989 and further privatization measures introduced in 1990, but state owned enterprises still negotiate salary levels for employees with their parent ministries rather than with workers directly (Lindauer and Haughton 1996).

Although an official minimum wage is set by Government, it is only minimally effective given the apparent reluctance to enforce this and many other labor regulations. However, for foreign and joint ventures, the minimum wage almost certainly does have an effect. Not only is it easier to monitor the relatively small number of foreign firms, but the minimum wage is set much higher for foreign firms than the market wage or the minimum wage for local firms. Between 1993 and 1996, the minimum wage for all enterprises was VND 120,000 (about $12) per month. The minimum wage for firms with any foreign ownership was $35 per month in Hanoi and Ho Chi Minh City and $30 elsewhere. A new minimum wage law was enacted in April and took effect in July 1996. It raises the minimum wage for foreign firms to $45 in Ho Chi Minh City and Hanoi; $40 in Hai Phong, Vinh City, Hue, Da Nang, Bien Hoa, Can Tho, Hatay, Nha Trang and Vung Tau; and $35 in other places (VEFSS 1996b).

Labor Mobility. Although labor mobility is not *officially* restricted, work permits are legally required in most places, and those wishing to move their place of residence are supposed to get residence permits. These regulations do not, in practice, prevent many rural inhabitants from "trying their luck" in urban labor markets. In the main cities, job seekers queue each morning in markets and along central boulevards, such as Dong Xuan Market and Nga Tu So in Hanoi, joining what has come to be known as the "labor bazaar" (VEFSS 1996b). These informal labor markets have emerged spontaneously in response to uncontrolled rural-urban migration, and they have given rise to illegal employment services, middlemen and charges of exploitation. MOLISA estimates the number of rural job seekers in Hanoi at about 170,000, and 800,000 in Ho Chi Minh City.

Benefits of Education and Training

Rates of returns to investment in education are estimated here, perhaps for the first time since the reforms of *Đoi Moi* returned the Vietnamese economy onto a market-oriented track. The rate of return estimates here are based primarily on wage data from the 1992-93 VLSS. Since many of the labor market reforms did not come on stream until later, and their impact may not begin to be felt until even later, VLSS information is supplemented, wherever possible, with more recent data, including new survey data generated under the auspices of VEFSS. Moreover, in an effort to reach robust conclusions, several different methods have been used to assess the benefits of education and training relative to the costs of investing in these programs.

The general picture, drawing upon different methods and the most recent information available, is that rates of return to education and training in Vietnam are low by international standards. Worldwide, another year of schooling increases earnings by about 10 percent (Psacharopoulos 1994). The findings for Vietnam, detailed below, suggest a lower rate of return, only about 5 percent -- higher for some levels of education and for some categories of workers, but lower for others.

This is not to say that rates of return to education and training in Vietnam may not go up (or may not *already* have gone up since VLSS) in response to the country's recent economic reforms. The impact of the reforms will be to allocate jobs based on market demand rather than government decree. The wages paid should begin to reflect much better the relative supply of, and demand for, particular skills. Rates of return were probably higher in some parts of Vietnam in the distant past. A study of rural wages in South Vietnam in 1964 showed that an additional year of schooling there was associated with an earnings difference of 16.8 percent (Stroup and Hargrove 1969).

The more recent picture in Vietnam is consistent with evidence from other centrally planned economies and economies in transition. Estimates of rates of return to education in China during the 1980s range from just 1 to 5 percent (Jamison and van der Gaag 1987; Byron and Manolato 1990; Meng 1995). In an analysis of rural industrial workers in China, Gregory and Meng (1995) sub-divided their sample into two groups -- those who were allocated jobs by the State and those who found their own jobs. Returns to schooling for the first group were small and not significant statistically, but the second group, who found work on their own, realized significantly larger returns.

Low rates of return have been found in other command economies, for example, those in pre-transition Eastern Europe and Central Asia. Psacharopoulos (1994) reports rates of return to education of 2.9 percent in Poland in 1986 and 4.3 percent in Hungary in 1987. More recent evidence from the same region, while limited, suggests that successful reform raises the returns to human capital. In Slovenia between 1987 and 1991, workers with four years of university education had the largest increase in earnings, followed by those with two years of university education. The group, however, that gained the least, relative to those with no education, were those with vocational degrees and certificates (Orazem and Vodopivec 1995).

Complete Method -- Constructing Age-Earnings Profiles. The complete method for estimating education rates of return is to construct average net earnings profiles for working individuals at different levels of educational attainment:

$$(5.1) \qquad \sum_{t=0}^{n} [(B_t - C_t) / (1 + r)^t] = 0$$

$$(5.2) \qquad \sum_{t=0}^{n} [(B_t) / (1 + r)^t] = \sum_{t=0}^{n} [(C_t) / (1 + r)^t]$$

where B_t and C_t are the benefits and costs of the particular educational investment (for example, completing secondary education following completion of primary education) in year t, n is the expected life of the investment (40-50 years for most educational investments), and r is the rate of return -- which is that discount rate which reduces the present value of the net benefit stream to zero, or alternatively, that rate which equates the present value of the benefits with the present value of the costs of the investment.

The benefit of an educational investment is measured as the average additional earnings received by (for example) the graduates of secondary school, over and above the graduates of primary school, controls being provided for other determinants of earnings. The cost of the investment comprises: (1) the direct costs -- for the individual, these include all expenditures related to school attendance, and for society, the full resource costs of providing the educational service, including any subsidized costs not borne by the individual or the individual's family, plus (2) the average earnings foregone as a result of the investment.

Figure 5.5 illustrates the information needed to estimate a rate of return to secondary education using the complete discounted net earnings method. The earnings (SS) of a secondary education graduate after completing secondary school are shown, as well as the hypothetical earnings (PP) of the same individual had he or she stopped studying and begun working right after completing primary school. The direct costs of the investment appear below the horizontal axis. The indirect costs, or foregone earnings, are shown as the *negative* earnings differential while the individual is studying. The benefits of the investment are shown as the *positive* earnings differential after the individual finishes secondary school and begins working.

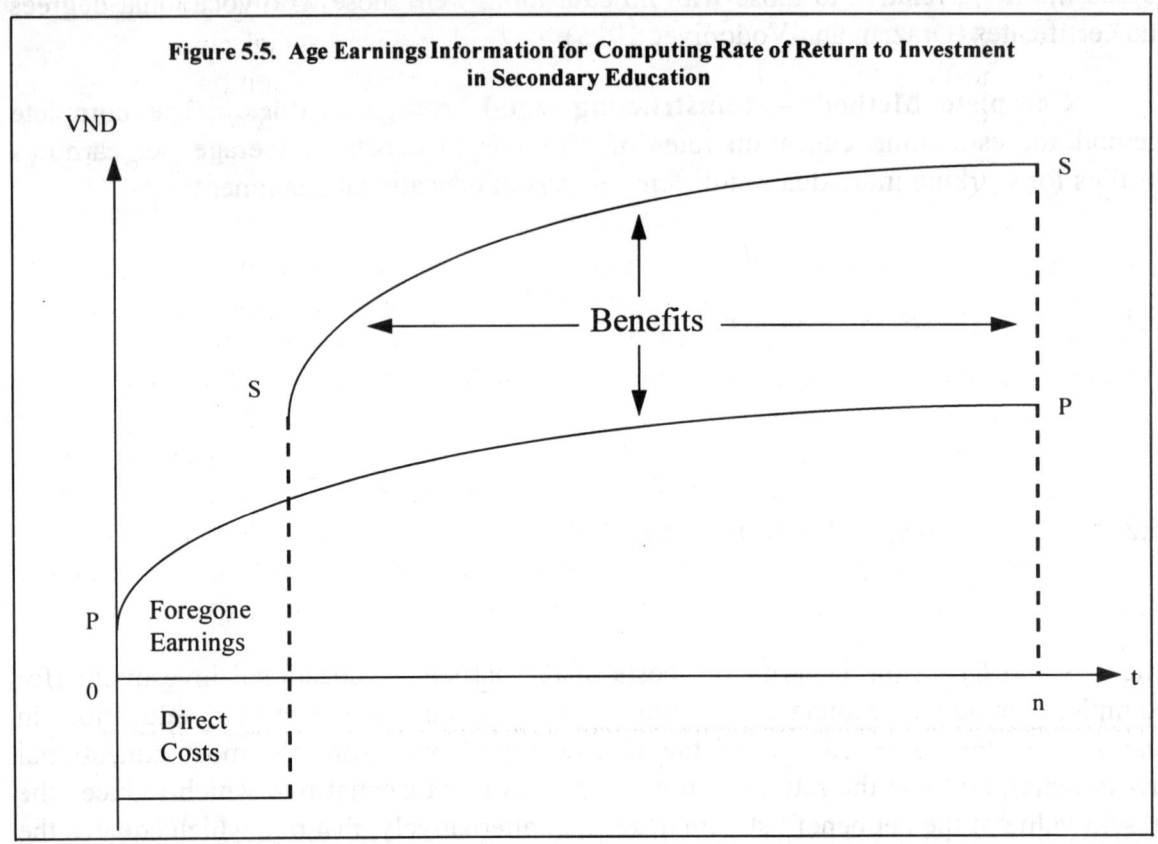

Figure 5.5. Age Earnings Information for Computing Rate of Return to Investment in Secondary Education

Source: VEFSS Team

Theoretically the social rate of return should also include any external benefits -- benefits not captured by the individual student or, if education is treated as a family investment, by the individual and his or her family. Unfortunately, not only is the size of education's external benefits nearly impossible to determine, but some policymakers and researchers question even their existence, rendering the rate of return literature the subject of some debate even 40 years after the re-birth of this methodology around 1960 (Schultz 1961). Of course, the same uncertainty as to precise social rates of return applies equally to investments in most other sectors. Some education economists have argued that adding external benefits to estimates of social rates of return would result in estimates about twice as large as those measured according to standard methods (Haveman and Wolfe 1984; Wolfe 1995).

The complete method, while straight-forward and requiring fewer "as if" assumptions than other, more elegant methods used by economists to estimate education rates of return, is quite data demanding. One needs to have sufficient observations in every age-education cell (55 year-olds who have completed university degrees, for example) to construct "well-behaved" age-earnings profiles -- profiles that do not cross and that are concave to the horizontal axis. Strictly speaking, the 1992-93 VLSS dataset does not satisfy the stringent data criteria demanded by the complete method. Nevertheless, the VEFSS research team was able to construct credible age-earnings profiles by removing extreme outlying observations and "smoothing" the data with moving averages. This made it possible to estimate private and social rates of return to primary, secondary and tertiary education. No VOTECH rates were computed because of the wide range of VOTECH programs in Vietnam, with relatively few observations in any one program, and because the 1992-93 VLSS did not adequately distinguish among the various VOTECH programs.

The results of this analysis are presented in Table 5.4. The estimates in the table should be treated with caution. The number of observations in some age-education groups is small. Moreover, the VLSS 1992-93 data set is now several years old, and the Vietnamese economy has undergone rapid and often dramatic change. There is, however, no alternative data set of comparable scope for conducting this kind of analysis, and information from a four-year old VLSS is better than no data at all.[32] The findings in Table 5.4 may be valid still in relative terms (i.e., the rank order of rates of return to different levels and types of education), but the point estimates should be seen as indicative only. Readers must bear these caveats in mind as they look at Table 5.4 and subsequent findings in Chapter 5, since the VLSS data set is used throughout.

Table 5.4. Rates of Return to Education Based on Age-Earnings Profiles (in annual percent)

Education Level	Private Rates of Return		Social Rates of Return[c]
	Low Cost Estimates[a]	High Cost Estimates[b]	
Primary (vs no education)	18.5	13.5	10.8
Secondary (vs primary)	5.5	4.5	3.8
Tertiary (vs secondary)	7.8	6.2	3.0

[a]Costs = foregone earnings only.

[b]Costs = foregone earnings plus household expenditures.

[c]Costs = full resource costs.

Source: VLSS 1992-93.

The first two columns are estimates of private rates of return, the first measuring costs as foregone earnings only, and the second, adding the expenditures on fees and other, school-related items (for example, transportation, books and required school uniforms) reported on average by households in the VLSS dataset. The third column is based on estimates of the full resource costs (equivalent to private costs plus all subsidized costs) and reports "social rates of return." What does the table suggest? First, that rates of return were high for primary education (above 10 percent), and lower for both secondary and tertiary education. Ignoring external benefits, not easily measured, this implies that primary schooling was the best educational investment in Vietnam earlier in the 1990s both for individuals and for society. The returns to secondary and tertiary education, while positive, appear to have been below the "good investment"

---

[32] A new VLSS will be carried out later in 1996.

threshold, given the value of alternative investments as indicated by the market rate of interest.

Second, the differences between private rates of return based on foregone earnings alone and those based on foregone earnings plus household monetary outlays were greater for primary education than for secondary and tertiary education, and the differences between private and social rates were low for secondary education but relatively high for primary and tertiary education. Tertiary education in particular seems to have been less profitable as a social investment, which takes full economic costs into account, than as a private investment. To the extent that positive externalities do exist, this would have brought the private rate of return and the "true" social rate of return closer together. However, these findings suggest that the subsidies going to primary education in Vietnam are too low, especially in light of the fact that primary is the only education attained by a majority of the poorest Vietnamese households, and that the subsidies going to secondary and tertiary education are too high, in relative terms at least (as compared with the subsidies going to primary). Government might consider a different pricing policy that benefits the poor at the expense of the rich and that encourages the consumers of post-primary education to be more discriminating in choosing among alternative programs of study.

Reverse Method -- Estimating Switching Values. As noted, the VLSS data set did not really include enough individuals in all of the age-education groups to support a proper rate-of-return analysis using the complete method. In the absence of a sufficiently large sample of working individuals, or in a centrally planned or transition economy where it is difficult to argue that wage differences reflect productivity differences, much can still be said with cost data alone. Information on costs can be used to estimate "switching values." In the language of project appraisal, a switching value is the value that an element of an investment with an acceptable rate of return must reach, moving in a unfavorable direction, in order to push the project below the minimum level of acceptability and switch the appraisal decision from a "go" to a "no go." A simple but useful application of switching values in education is the "reverse cost-benefit analysis." This consists of finding the minimum productivity differential required to bestow an education investment with an acceptable social rate of return. The question is framed in the following manner: Given the cost of producing a graduate, what productivity differential is required to make the investment profitable to society? If the discount rate is 10 percent, the required differential using the reverse cost-benefit method can be estimated according to Equation (5.3):

(5.3) $D_{S/S-1} = 0.10[t_S(C_S + W_{S-1})]$,

where $D_{S/S-1}$ is the required productivity differential between a person who has graduated from schooling level S and one who has graduated from level $S-1$; t_s is the number of years required to complete level S (seven years, say, for secondary education, assuming no grade repetition); C_S is the per student direct resource cost of each year of the investment, and W_{S-1} is the earnings foregone during each year of the investment.

Reverse cost-benefit results are presented in Table 5.5. *Column 1* indicates which educational investment is being evaluated, and with reference to which completed level of education. For example, the analysis assumes that the decision to invest in VOTECH is made upon completion of primary schooling. Unit costs, which combine fiscal costs and household expenditures, are presented in *column 2*.[33] *Column 3* presents the average annual earnings of individuals at each education level, derived from the VLSS dataset. *Column 4* indicates the assumptions made as to how many years are required to complete an education investment. For example, VOTECH is assumed to require five years beyond primary education, although in fact some VOTECH programs take more time than this, and some take less. Primary education is a special case. Although five grades of instruction are involved in primary education, it is assumed here that very young children do not forego earnings. For analytical purposes, the indirect cost of primary education is taken to be *just one year* of income earned by an individual with no education. *Column 5* presents the productivity differentials required to realize a 10 percent social rate of return on the education investments -- i.e., the "switching value" whose formula was given in equation (5.2). *Column 6* gives the observed earnings differentials, derived by subtracting one value from another in *column 2*. *Column 7* presents the observed differentials in *column 6* as percentages of the "required" values in *column 5*.

Table 5.5. Earnings Differentials Required to Realize 10 Percent Rate of Return

Education level (and investment reference level)	Variables in Equation (5.2)					Observed as percent of required (VND'000)
	(C_S) Cost per student year (VND'000)	(W_S) Average earnings (VND'000)	(t_S) Assumed cost periods (years)	(D_S) Required differential (VND'000)	$(W_S - W_{S-1})$ Observed differential (VND'000)	
None	...	1,512	...	...	...	...
Primary (vs none)	192	1,788	C_S: 5 W_S: 1	247	276	112%
Secondary (vs primary)	436	2,016	7	1,557	228	15%
VOTECH (vs primary)	1,331	1,824	5	1,560	36	2%
Tertiary (vs secondary)	2,745	2,736	4	1,904	912	48%

Source: VLSS 1992-93.

The results suggest that in Vietnam earlier in the 1990s most E&T investments were marginal investments. Primary education satisfied the 10 percent rate of return test, given the assumption of just one year's foregone earnings, but secondary and tertiary education did not. VOTECH appears to have been an extremely bad social investment, given the high cost of producing it (VND 1.3 million per student year, about $118) and given the very small observed earnings differential between those who completed primary school and those who graduated from a VOTECH institution (VND 36,000 per year, $3-4). Given the high cost of VOTECH, the productivity differential would have needed be VND 1.6 million per year in order for the investment to realize a 10 percent rate of return.

---

[33] Unit costs were discussed more fully in Chapter 4.

In the case of VOTECH, the difference between the required and the observed differentials was not even close. In the case of secondary and tertiary education, the difference was closer. One might argue that Vietnam's economic reforms will result in a less compressed wage structure, so that graduates of secondary and tertiary education will earn more than they did at the time that the VLSS survey was conducted. The earnings of a tertiary graduate vis-à-vis the earnings of a secondary graduate would need only to double in order to make the investment in tertiary education profitable, according to Table 5.5.

Moreover, the assumptions used here in conducting the reverse method are quite conservative. The indirect costs (foregone earnings) of investing in an education program are measured by the average earnings of individuals who have completed the program just below it. But earnings increase with age. If, instead of using the average earnings of all workers regardless of age, the analysis had used only the earnings of school-age workers, who are young and just entering the labor force, the measured costs of the education investments would be lower, and the switching value or "required differential" would also be lower.

Earnings Function Method. The human capital earnings function (HCEF), formally derived and written up by Jacob Mincer (1974), provides another estimate of education's rate of return. This method is less data demanding that the complete method described above. The basic Mincerian function is given in Equation (5.4):

$$(5.4) \qquad \ln Y_i = \alpha + \beta S_i + \gamma EXP_i + \phi EXP^2_i + \varepsilon_i$$

where S_i is the years of schooling completed by the i-th individual, EXP_i the years of work experience of that individual, EXP^2_i the square of the experience variable, and ε_i a stochastic error term. Hours worked per week is added as a control variable, on the assumption that this is institutionally determined or reflects exogenous differences in taste.

In Mincer's semi-log specification, the coefficient on S (β) is interpreted to be the average private rate of return that accrues to an additional year of schooling -- constrained in the basic version of the model to be a constant.[34] In other words, the percentage increase associated with an additional year of schooling is assumed to be the same at

---

[34] The HCEF provides estimates of private rates of return but not social rates of return. The model does not require the detailed enumeration of education's direct costs, which is a reason for its popularity with labor economists -- it can be estimated based on earnings information alone. For the β coefficients in the HCEF to be interpreted as private rates of return, it is necessary to assume that the direct outlays made by the student's family in the form of fees and other education-related expenses are exactly offset by the student's part-time earnings while in school. In other words, the model measures the cost of educating one student who is in school by the average earnings of other individuals, with the same characteristics, who are not in school.

every step on the education ladder. This assumption can be relaxed in extended versions of the human capital earnings function.

Estimates of rates of return accruing to private investments in E&T, derived from the HCEF regression estimates and using the VLSS sample of wage workers in Vietnam in 1992-93, are presented in Annex 5.1 at the end of the report. Based as they are on the same dataset, the HCEF results are naturally consistent with the results presented above. They suggest that sending a child to school was only a middling investment for individual households in Vietnam, given the earnings of wage workers in the early 1990s. On average, across all levels and types of schooling, for both boys and girls, and for those working in both the public and private sectors, schooling yielded about a five percent return on the earnings foregone by the household. Schooling was an excellent private investment, however, for certain student categories.

The private rate of return was quite high for investments in primary education, and higher for tertiary than for either secondary or VOTECH. The *rate* of return was higher for the investments made in girls' schooling than in boys', and higher for the education of those individuals who ended up working in the public sector, provided that their education did not stop after primary school. To realize the high rates of return to primary education, the primary school graduate must have chosen to work in the private sector. *Rates* of return to education were slightly higher in the North of Vietnam than in the South, although the returns to experience were higher in the South. Finally, the return to an additional year of schooling was greater for younger Vietnamese workers than for those who had started working more than five years before 1992-93, before the start of the recent economic reforms.

Self-Employed Workers

The estimates of the returns to schooling presented above are based on individuals working in the formal sector and receiving a regular wage. But wage workers account for only about 20 percent of the entire Vietnamese labor force. The rest is made up of self-employed workers who run their own businesses or work in family-run businesses. Most of these individuals (about 80 percent, or 65 percent of the entire labor force) work as subsistence farmers.

Studies worldwide have shown that farmers with more education produce larger farm yields than farmers with less education, other factors held constant (Moock 1994; Lockheed et al. 1980). A recent production function study of paddy rice farming confirmed this finding for Vietnam. Paddy yields were shown to be 7 percent higher on farms headed by men or women who had completed 3-4 years of education than on other farms headed by individuals with less education. Yields were 11 percent larger on farms where the heads had finished all of primary school. Additional education was not found to have a significant impact on paddy yields, but it did increase significantly an individual's chances of finding off-farm employment (World Bank 1996c).

Figure 5.6 shows the type of employment and the educational attainment of all household heads in the VLSS dataset. On average, the 3,195 self-employed household heads in 1992-93 had completed fewer years of education than had the 737 wage-employed heads. Only 22 percent of the self-employed had continued in school beyond primary education, whereas 30 percent of the wage-employed had done so; 9 percent of the second group had completed tertiary education, as compared with just 1 percent of the first group.

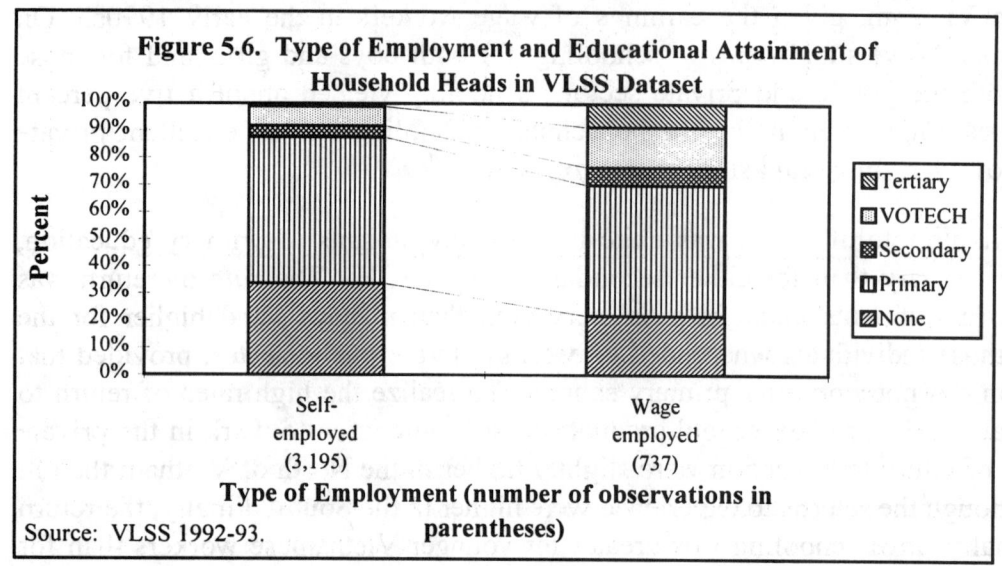

Figure 5.6. Type of Employment and Educational Attainment of Household Heads in VLSS Dataset

Source: VLSS 1992-93.

Figure 5.7 shows household consumption (as a measure of household income) by employment type and educational attainment of household head. Where the household head had no education, family income was nearly the same whether the individual worked in wage employment or was self-employed. Household income went up with the head's educational attainment, but the increments were smaller when the head was self-employed.

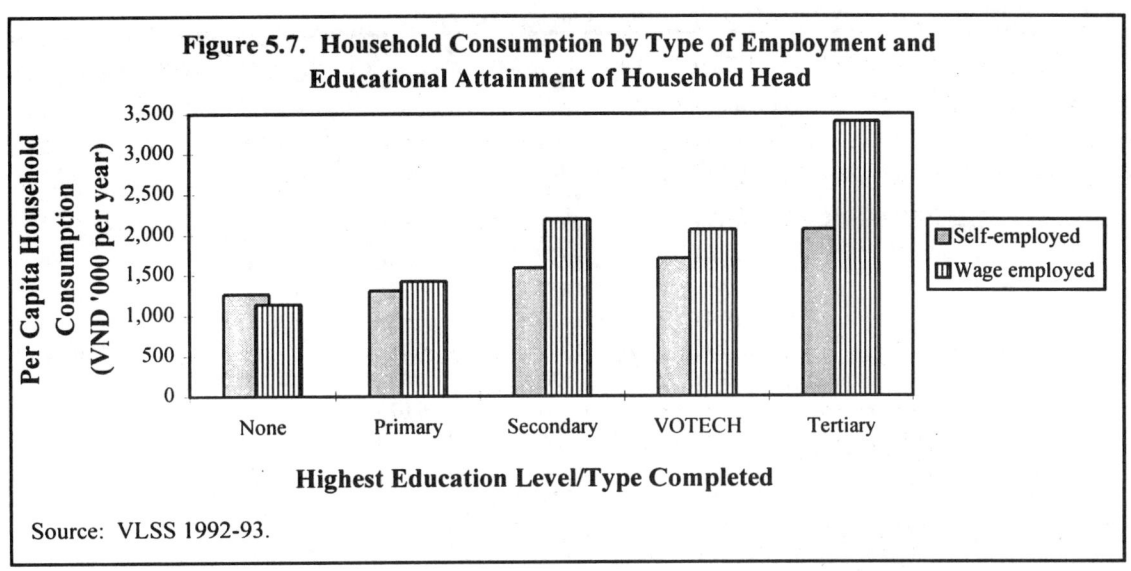

Figure 5.7. Household Consumption by Type of Employment and Educational Attainment of Household Head

Source: VLSS 1992-93.

To control for other factors that influence household consumption levels, including gender of the household head, differences in the physical capital endowment of the household and important ethnic and regional differences, multiple regression equations were estimated. The results are presented in Table 5.6. The first regression, for all 3,932 households, included two dummy variables indicating different types of self-employment -- family-run farms, and other self-employed households not dependent on agriculture as the primary source of income. Per capita consumption on family-run farms was about 14 percent lower than in households headed by wage-employed individuals, but in other self-employed households, it was about 16 percent higher. Next the same regression was run for each of the two self-employment groups. Because these regressions did not, however, control for physical capital inputs contributing to self-employment income, they were run again with value of the household capital stock in the case of the 649 non-agricultural households and with area of land ownership in the case of the 2,363 agricultural households for which this information was available.

Table 5.6. Determinants of Household Consumption by Employment Type

Variable[a]	(1) All Households	(2) Agriculture Self-employed	(3) Other Self-employed	(4) Agriculture Self-Employed	(5) Other Self-employed
Constant	6.354	6.312	6.232	6.361	6.459
Completed primary	0.193	0.180	0.199	0.167	0.171
	(9.5)	(8.1)	(3.3)	(7.5)	(2.9)
Completed secondary	0.248	0.122	0.279	0.103	0.268
	(6.4)	(2.6)	(3.0)	(2.1)	(2.9)
Attended VOTECH	0.251	0.157	0.289	0.128	0.293
	(8.4)	(4.1)	(3.7)	(3.3)	(3.9)
Completed University	0.394	0.204	0.138 *	0.154 *	0.140 *
	(6.3)	(1.9)	(0.8)	(1.3)	(0.9)
Age	0.005	0.003 *	0.013 *	0.003 *	0.007 *
	(1.2)	(0.7)	(1.0)	(0.6)	(0.6)
Age-squared/100	0.005	0.007 *	-0.007 *	0.007 *	-0.002 *
	(1.1)	(1.5)	(0.5)	(1.4)	(0.1)
Self-employed agriculture	-0.137				
	(6.2)				
Self-employed other	0.162				
	(5.9)				
Land owned (sq. meters/10,000)				0.109	
				(4.2)	
Capital assets (VND/10,000)					0.053
					(6.5)
Male	-0.137	-0.119	-0.108	-0.120	-0.136
	(7.1)	(5.3)	(2.2)	(5.3)	(2.9)
Chinese (Hoa)	0.472	0.404	0.482	0.025 *	0.315
	(7.1)	(2.7)	(4.5)	(0.1)	(2.9)
Other Ethnic	-0.258	-0.271	-0.089 *	-0.264	-0.082 *
	(9.8)	(10.1)	(0.6)	(9.9)	(0.5)
Hours worked (natural logarithm)	0.095	0.046	0.173	0.028 *	0.153
	(5.2)	(2.1)	(4.1)	(1.3)	(3.7)
R-squared	0.265	0.213	0.159	0.220	0.213
Number of observations	3,932	2,546	649	2,363	649

Note: The dependent variable is the natural logarithm of household consumption. *t*-statistics are given in parentheses. All coefficients are significant at the 10 percent level except where indicated by asterisks (*).

[a]The regressions control also for the region in which the household is located.

Source: VLSS 1992-93.

Because education was entered into the regressions in Table 5.6 as a series of sequential dummy variables,[35] the coefficient on any of the dummy variables indicates the expected percentage difference in per capita household consumption where the head of household had completed this level of education, relative to another where the head of household had not done so but had completed the level just below it. In other words, the coefficient on secondary education in the first regression (0.248) tells us that the expected per capita consumption of family members in a household headed by a man or a woman who had completed secondary school was about 25 percent higher than in another household headed by an individual who had only completed primary school. However, given the foregone earnings costs associated with investment in secondary education, the implied rate of return was only between 3 and 4 percent.

[35] For a fuller discussion of dummy variables as used here, see Footnote 2 of Annex A.5.1.

The results in Table 5.6 suggest that completing more education is associated with higher household consumption in all types of households. In self-employed households, however, the higher level of consumption associated with tertiary education (although the difference is as large as many of the others) was not statistically significant -- see especially equations (4) and (5), since these regressions controlled for the household's ownership of physical capital, which is correlated with educational attainment. The low statistical significance does not mean necessarily that tertiary education was not also a determinant of consumption levels in self-employed households. It may simply reflect the fact that, in the VLSS dataset, only 38 self-employed households were headed by tertiary graduates.

Public versus Non-Public Education

The private costs to a Vietnamese household of sending a child to a semi-public or private school tends to be higher, but not necessarily much higher, than sending the child to a public school (see Figure 5.8 for comparisons based on the VLSS dataset). The question remains as to whether the difference in costs yields future benefits. One way to answer this question is to examine whether individuals who attended semi-public or private schools in the past earn more than otherwise similar workers who attended public schools. The results of a simple wage regression suggest that this may be the case. Those who in the past attended private schools earn 30 percent more today than those who attended public schools, while those who attended semi-public schools earn 33 percent more. Although these estimates are consistent with the hypothesis that private schools offer instruction of higher quality, this conclusion should be treated with considerable caution. Those working in the early 1990s were educated earlier, in some cases, many years earlier. Even if the analysis here had been able to control properly for other factors that may have affected earnings, all this really would tell us is that Vietnam's private and semi-public schools were better in the past. Whether the private and semi-public schools recently established in Vietnam offer higher (or lower) quality instruction today than Vietnam's public schools is an important question that cannot be answered satisfactorily with the cross-sectional earnings information contained in the VLSS dataset, but it is an area that deserves further study.

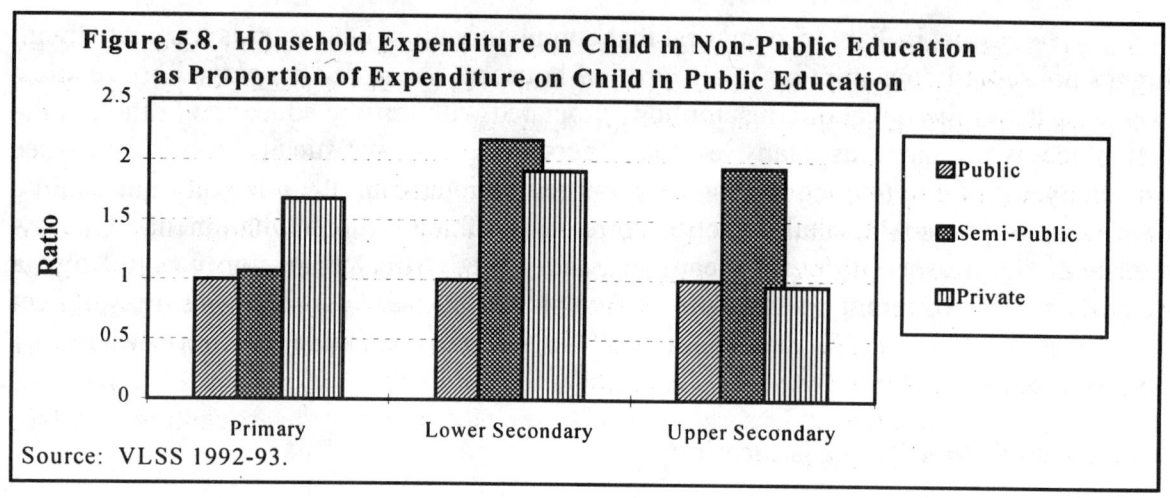

Figure 5.8. Household Expenditure on Child in Non-Public Education as Proportion of Expenditure on Child in Public Education

Source: VLSS 1992-93.

Higher Education Graduates

The Higher Education Graduate Tracer Study (HEGTS) was designed as part of VEFSS, in order to examine the labor market outcomes of recent graduates of Vietnam's universities and colleges. Traced in the nationwide survey were 1,829 individuals who graduated in 1990 and 1993 from all of Vietnam's public higher education institutions -- a 4.3 percent sample of the graduates in these two years. The graduates' earnings were assessed at the time of the survey, the field work for which took place in December 1995 and January 1996. The sampling frame was designed to ensure institutional representativeness as well as representative numbers in different subject areas. Only a preliminary analysis of the dataset was available in time for this report, and these results are described here.

Male graduates earn 8.5 percent more than female graduates, holding constant other determinants of earnings. Age, marital status and whether or not one has children are not related to differences in earnings for this group of workers. Self-reported university performance (academic status at graduation) is a significant predictor of earnings. Those who achieved "excellent" performances as undergraduates earn 30 percent more (those who achieved "good" performances 4 percent more) than those whose performances are judged to have been just "average." Graduates whose jobs require English language proficiency earn more than others, as do those whose jobs require computer skills, particularly spreadsheet knowledge. Those who worked while studying earn 10 percent more today than those who did not work as students. Holding a second job currently, over and above the main job, is associated with 27 percent lower earnings in the main job. This is taken to mean that graduates seek other jobs, especially when earnings from the main job are too low to support themselves and their families.

The inclusion of family characteristics in the analysis sheds light on an important question in the research on human capital, and this is the importance of father's and mother's education on the future earnings of a child. In the HEGTS dataset, father's education has little or no influence on a graduate's earnings today, but mother's education is a significant determinant of earnings. Graduates whose mothers completed secondary school (university) earn 16 percent (20 percent) more than other graduates whose mothers only completed primary school or did not go to school.

Sector of employment is also an important determinant of earnings for this sample of graduates. Those who are self-employed earn 26 percent more than those who work for government. Those working for domestic private firms earn 33 percent more than those working for government, and those working for foreign companies or joint ventures, 73 percent more. It should be noted that in 1993 there were very few university graduates who did not work for government, according to the VLSS dataset, but 20 percent of recent university graduates were working in the private sector at the beginning of 1996, according to the HEGTS dataset.

Many foreign languages have been imposed on Vietnam over the centuries -- Chinese, French, Russian. Today, English has emerged as the dominant language for business in the East Asia region (McGurn 1996), and there is considerable incentive for Vietnamese to learn English, especially as Vietnam joins ASEAN and the economy opens up. In 1994, the Government issued a decree urging public servants to learn English. Periodically, official fears do surface that the English language and other foreign influences are undermining Vietnam's cultural heritage. These concerns, however, tend to be short-lived.

According to preliminary HEGTS results, those graduates with more than elementary proficiency in the English language earn 8 percent more than do others. Proficiency in French and in Russian, the most common languages other than English spoken by recent Vietnamese graduates, is only weakly related to higher earnings. It is no surprise, therefore, to find that graduates spend time and considerable money of their own learning English and other productivity enhancing skills such as the use of computers. Table 5.7 presents a cost-benefit analysis of private investments in post-graduate training. The results suggest that English language training will increase the lifetime earnings of recent graduates enough to yield a rate of return of between 5 and 8 percent on the individuals' investments. Computer training, with the exception of computer programming, is even more profitable, yielding rates of return well above 8 percent. The ability to work with spreadsheets seems to be a particularly good investment at this time.

Table 5.7: Private Costs and Benefits of Foreign Language and Computer Skill Courses

	Average cost of training	Discounted lifetime earnings increase[a]		Net present value of investment	
		@5%	@8%	@5%	@8%
Language skill courses					
English	736	892	618	156	-118
French	442	..[c]	..[c]	Negative	Negative
Computer skill courses					
Word Processing[b]	190	336	238	146	48
Spreadsheets	199	1,225	844	1,026	645
Programming language	442	..[c]	..[c]	Negative	Negative
Database management	224	401	273	177	49

Note: All figures in VND '000.

[a] Over 40 years

[b] Based on only 22 observations.

[c] Regression coefficient small and not statistically significant.

Source: HEGTS 1995-96.

Students who did not work part-time while studying spent, on average, an additional two weeks searching for work after graduation before they found full-time jobs. Students who graduated in 1993 spent five weeks less time searching for work than those who graduated in 1990. The more recent graduates are also 20 percent more likely to be employed today.

EQUITY

Promoting equity is a fundamental principle of Vietnamese society, and poverty reduction has been a central goal of government policy. Vietnam's high levels of literacy and school participation attest to the strenuous efforts made in the past to enhance opportunities for all individuals and to achieve a more equitable distribution of consumption across households. Inevitably, however, certain groups lag behind. These are the poor, the weak and the disadvantaged. Nowhere has the need been eliminated for relative labels such as these. No matter how rich a society may become, some individuals and some households are always poorer than others. Perfect equality is not only impossible to achieve but would be inefficient, many would argue, even if possible.

The extremes of rich and poor can, however, be pulled much closer together through a variety of policy instruments. There are good examples, within the East Asia region, of nations that have eradicated poverty and achieved a high degree of equality within one generation, without sacrificing economic growth. The purpose of this section of the VEFSS report is to analyze the available data on relative poverty and disadvantage in Vietnamese society and to highlight those areas where there is clear scope for poverty reduction and equity enhancement by means of policy changes in relation to E&T.

Incidence of Poverty by Schooling Level

Schooling and literacy are important indicators of quality of life in their own right, and they are key determinants of the poor's ability to access better income-earning opportunities. The section above on external efficiency presented evidence of education's relation to higher employment rates and higher earnings. Just as education apparently increases earnings, it follows that it should also reduce the probability of being poor and, for those born poor, increase the probability of escaping this condition.

Households with uneducated heads are more likely than other households, in Vietnam and elsewhere, to have incomes and consumption levels that fall below the poverty line, however poverty may be defined in a given context. Using the World Bank's definition of poverty as constructed for Vietnam (World Bank 1995c), and using VLSS data to measure per capita household consumption, one sees that 65 percent of Vietnamese households headed by individuals who had never gone to school were "poor." At the other end of the spectrum, the incidence of poverty in households where the heads had completed tertiary education was only 11 percent. The poverty rate for all Vietnamese households according to the Bank's definition was 51 percent.

This relationship between education of household head and poverty is shown in Figure 5.9. Of course, it should be stressed that correlation does not necessarily imply causality. Although education probably does raise incomes, there are prior causative factors that help explain both educational background *and* household income.

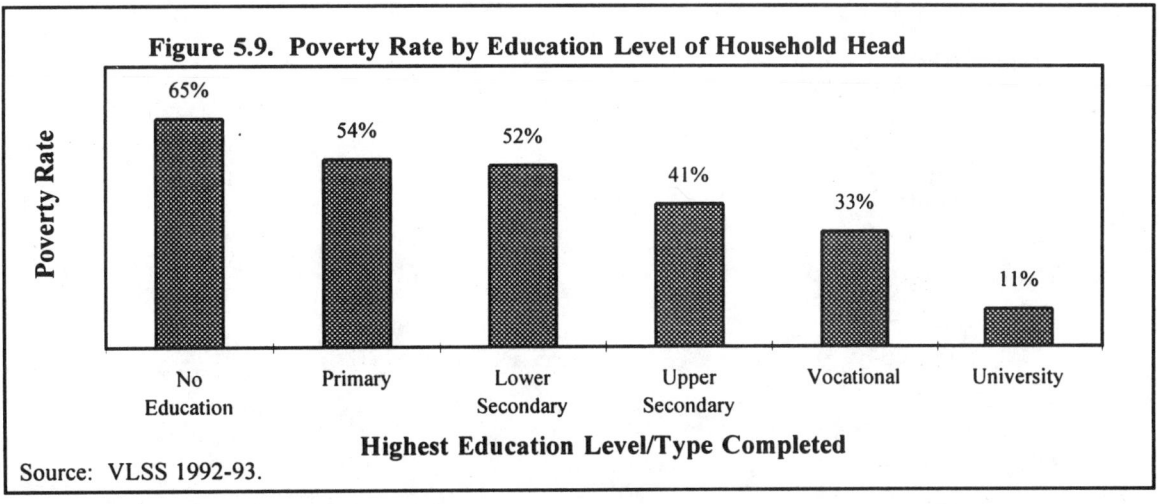

Figure 5.9. Poverty Rate by Education Level of Household Head

Source: VLSS 1992-93.

Poverty and Access to Schooling

Whereas most people do agree that schooling helps to raise household income and lower the probability of becoming or remaining poor, the reverse is also true. Very poor parents often lack the disposable income necessary to cover the direct costs of sending their children to school. Moreover, and ironically, although the indirect costs of school attendance tend to be lower for poor children, because they do not have equal access to income-earning opportunities relative to rich families, they often have no choice but to spend all of their time "earning," which leaves no time for "learning" and, in particular, attending school. This is the development economist's "vicious circle of poverty," seen at the level of the individual poor household.

Vietnam's high aggregate enrollment rates divert attention from quite large differences in school participation across income groups. It is only in primary education that most (but even at this level, not all) poor children are enrolled as students. In 1993, the primary school enrollment rate of children in the bottom quintile (poorest 20 percent) of Vietnamese households was 68 percent. For the middle quintile it was 81 percent, and for the richest 20 percent of the population, it was 86 percent.

The same comparisons are illustrated in Figure 5.10 for all four levels of education.[36] What is apparent from the four graphs is that the relative gap between richest and poorest households becomes progressively more pronounced as one moves up the education ladder. Already by lower secondary education, only 19 percent of children in the bottom quintile were enrolled as students in 1992-93, whereas 56 percent of those in the richest 20 percent of households were still in school. By upper secondary education, the enrollment of children in the poorest group had dropped to 2 percent. The VLSS dataset showed no children from the poorest group enrolled in universities and colleges. The richest 20 percent accounted for more than half of all those enrolled in upper secondary and tertiary education.

---

[36] Because they are computed from household survey data (VLSS), and not from the school census data collected by MOET, for which it is impossible to know the actual ages of those enrolled, the rates in Figure 5.10 are net rates and not gross. A *gross enrollment rate* divides the total number of children enrolled in the particular level of education, many of whom may be over-age and some under-age, by the total number of children in the population who are of the officially correct age for this level of education. The *net enrollment rate* "nets out" those children who are both over-age and under-age and is, in fact, a truer measure of an education system's coverage of the target population group.

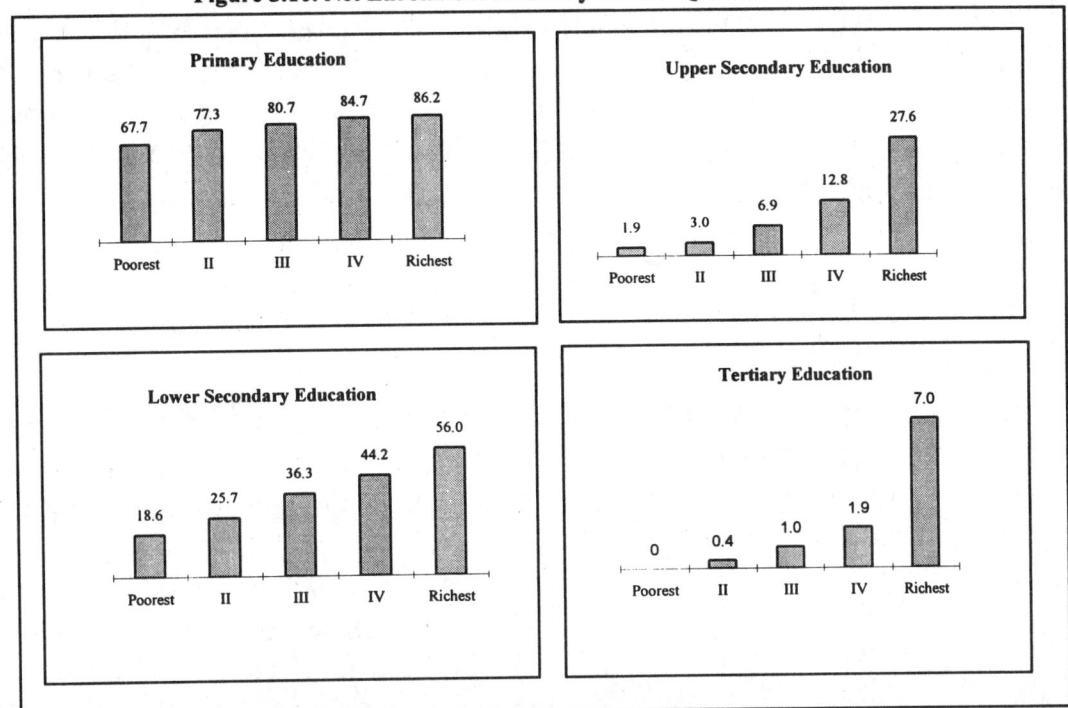

Figure 5.10. Net Enrollment Ratios by Income Quintiles

Note: Percent of target age group enrolled on vertical axis; income quintile on horizontal axis.
Source: VLSS 1992-93.

Determinants of Schooling

In Vietnam, about 90 percent of all children eventually do attend school, if only for a few years at the primary level. As shown above, household income is strongly associated with school attendance. A probit analysis of the VLSS dataset reveals that an increase in per capita household consumption of one standard deviation around the mean raised the probability of a child's being enrolled in school by 2.7 percentage points. Parental education, particularly mother's education, is significantly related to school attendance, even when household consumption is held constant in the probit equations. The probability of a child's being enrolled in school was 8.9 percentage points (2.4 percentage points) higher in the case of a child whose mother (whose father) had completed three more years of schooling herself (himself). Finally, girls in Vietnam were less likely to attend school than boys, other things being equal. The probability of finding a boy enrolled was 8 percentage points higher in the VLSS data set than the probability of finding a girl enrolled, holding other determinants of school enrollment constant at their means. This gender difference is surprising, given the high enrollment rate of Vietnamese children in general.

Child Labor. An important reason for a poor family not to send its children to school is that they are needed at home for the income they can generate in the family business or on the family farm. Despite official restrictions against child labor, children under the age of 12, according to the VLSS dataset, accounted for 6 percent of the labor force of Vietnam; those under the age of 15 accounted for 15 percent. Child labor is especially widespread in rural areas, where almost a third of children between the ages of 6 and 14 are employed, and enrollments for this age group are just 78 percent, much lower than the nationwide average (Toan et al., 1994). A recent study on the economic value of children points to the importance of raising mother's schooling level and general education level of the community, both of which result in lower fertility and reduced child labor (Gallup 1995).

Ethnicity. The ethnic Vietnamese, or Kinh, make up 87 percent of Vietnam's population. There are, however, 54 recognized ethnic groups in the country. Two (the Tay and Thai) have populations exceeding one million, and 12 more have populations greater than 100,000. Each group has its own language and cultural traditions. The provinces with the highest concentrations of ethnic minorities tend to be those with the lowest per capita incomes and lowest educational attainment levels (Fong 1994).

Some ethnic groups live in remote mountainous areas, making it difficult for the government to provide them with social services. Many children come to school for the first time to hear a teacher speaking in a language they have never before heard. In the past, Government tried to promote the assimilation of ethnic minorities by providing education in the public schools only in the Vietnamese language. Now there is an attempt to teach at least the first few grades in seven major ethnic languages, to ease the transition into school and to increase retention rates (Van et al. 1993). It is difficult, however, to find qualified teachers who can teach in the minority languages (United Nations 1995). In some areas, moreover, children from different minority groups are found in the same classrooms.

A few minority groups are concentrated in cities, and not all are economically disadvantaged. The ethnic Chinese (or Hoa) play a dominant role in private industry, especially in Ho Chi Minh City. In the VLSS data set, per capita household consumption was twice as high in households of Chinese origin than in all Vietnamese households, and three and a half times larger than in other ethnic minority households. The Chinese community, which makes up just over 1 percent of Vietnam's population, is responsible for about $4 billion of business output annually, which is about 20 percent of Vietnam's total business output (*The Economist* 1996). Enrollment rates in Chinese households were about at the national average in the VLSS data set.

Benefit Incidence of Public Subsidies

Assessing how well public spending on education is targeted to the poor requires a profile of who attends publicly financed schools at each level of the system, together with measures of the per-student subsidies received by students at each level. Household data (in this case VLSS data) were used to estimate the distribution of public school enrollments by household income groups, and public finance data (from MOF) and school enrollment data (from MOET) were used to estimate subsidies per student. The general picture emerging was as follows: (a) in general, enrollments of rich children were higher than enrollments of poor children; (b) the higher the level of education, the greater was the rich-poor difference in enrollments; and (c) the total costs of education went up with education level. The net conclusion from these four facts, all of which have been discussed elsewhere in the report, is that (with the exception of primary education, where public subsidies are slightly pro-poor) the distribution of public subsidies in Vietnam is biased in favor of the rich. The pro-rich bias is particularly pronounced in the case of tertiary education, subsidies for which are distributed even less equally than the per capita household consumption (the VLSS measure of household income). The subsidy per student is 30 times higher in tertiary education than in primary education. Yet there are very few poor students who attend tertiary education.

These patterns are illustrated in Figure 5.11. For each level of education, the graph known as a Lorenz curve has been constructed. This shows the percentage of total subsidies at this level of education received by the poorest 20 percent of the population, by the poorest 40 percent of the population, and so on. (Figure 5.11 shows as well the distribution of per capita consumption). Obviously, the "poorest 0" and the "poorest 100" percent of the population must necessarily receive 0 and 100 percent of total subsidies (consume 0 and 100 percent of total consumption), meaning that the Lorenz curve always coincides with the diagonal line at both its ends. A Lorenz curve that coincided with the diagonal line at every point along the way would represent a situation of perfect equality. The more concave any Lorenz curve is *below* the diagonal line, the more unequal is the distribution of subsidies (or consumption) in favor of the rich.

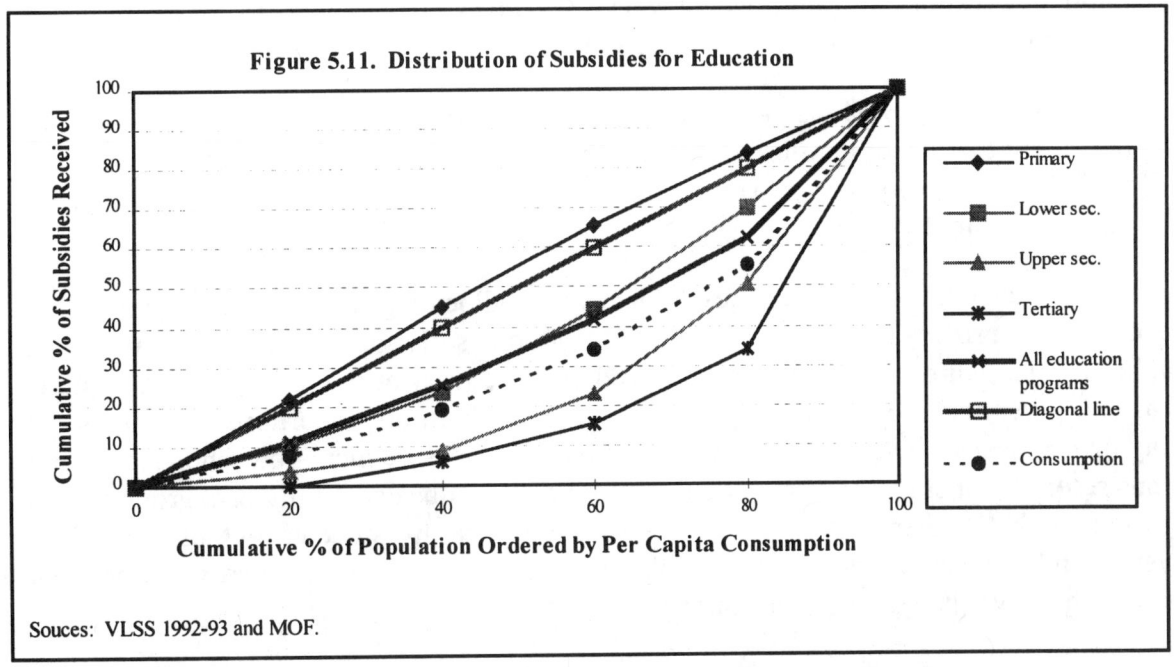

Figure 5.11. Distribution of Subsidies for Education

Souces: VLSS 1992-93 and MOF.

A Lorenz curve that is *above* the diagonal line represents a pro-poor distribution, as is (marginally) true for primary education subsidies in Vietnam. Most of the education subsidies that benefit the poor are delivered through the primary education program. Subsidies for tertiary education, on the other hand, are grossly pro-rich. The poorest 80 percent of the population received only about one-third of the subsidies from Government that went to public colleges and universities. This means that the richest 20 percent of the population, those least in need of government support, received two-thirds. This pattern suggests the need for directing a higher percentage of government subsidies on those education programs that tend to benefit the poor (as does primary education), especially if it can be shown that these programs yield a high social rate of return (again, as does primary education -- see above).

This goal can be served by a number of different policies, including all of the following:

- redouble the Government's efforts to *expand primary education facilities*, so as to reach those children not now served;

- where primary school places that are accessible to poor households already exist, but where large numbers of children, nevertheless, remain out of school (generally the poorest of the poor, from families where the parents did not go to school either) -- *encourage the remaining children to enroll by targeting special subsidies to them* so as to lower the costs (both direct and indirect) for them of school attendance;

- *re-allocate existing subsidies from higher levels to lower levels* of the education system -- so as to increase access as already discussed, but also to raise the quality of public education at the lower levels -- an investment likely to pay efficiency dividends as well as enhancing equity; and

- continue to *encourage the development of private alternatives to public education*; to the extent that richer families, in particular, begin to choose these private alternatives, the subsidies already going to education will re-distribute themselves automatically in favor of poorer families.

To achieve the third policy objective (reallocating from tertiary and upper secondary to primary and lower secondary), without suffering a loss of quality at the higher levels, will probably require increased cost recovery at the higher levels. This is feasible, given that wealthy children attend these levels in disproportionate numbers. It may be necessary, however, to introduce as a parallel measure increased scholarships and loans reserved for students who come from poor and uneducated family backgrounds. To the extent that higher cost recovery pushes some wealthy students out of the public system and into the private or semi-public system, this is consistent also with the final policy objective (increased privatization).

Public and Non-public Education -- Financing versus Provision

Because private and semi-public education has only recently been re-introduced in Vietnam, private and semi-public enrollments today account for only a small part of total enrollments (although they are growing rapidly). Most students still attend schools that are owned and managed by public authorities. In terms of *education financing*, however, as distinct from *education provision*, privatization is well advanced in Vietnam. In fact, the situation in Vietnam stands in sharp contrast to that which prevails in Korea, a country that has achieved rapid economic growth in recent years while at the same time reducing income inequality. Figure 5.12 provides comparative information for the two countries.

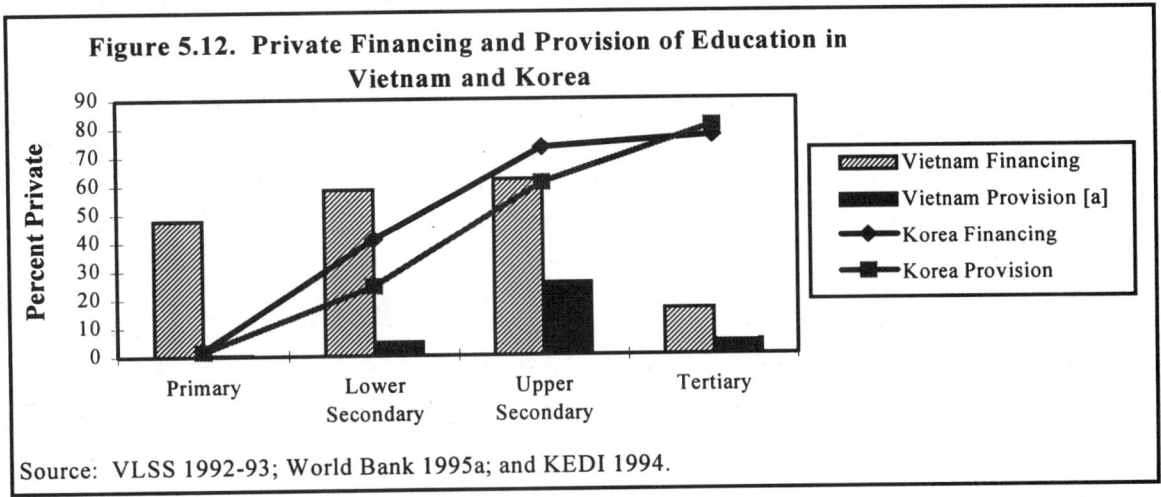

Figure 5.12. Private Financing and Provision of Education in Vietnam and Korea

Source: VLSS 1992-93; World Bank 1995a; and KEDI 1994.

In Korea, the proportion of private provision across education levels reflects closely the proportion of private financing. In terms of both financing and provision, the private role in Korea rises from practically none at all at the primary level, to a very substantial one at the tertiary level. In Vietnam, although school enrollments outside the public system are still small at every level, non-government financing is large. As a share of the total, private financing is lowest at the tertiary level, where only 24 percent of total costs are covered by households. As discussed above, because tertiary education is attended by few poor individuals in Vietnam, this is an inequitable situation that Government should address in its development of new policies for the E&T system.

6.   FUTURE DIRECTIONS FOR EDUCATION FINANCE

The first five chapters of the VEFSS report have provided a description of the education and training sector in Vietnam, and of societal and economic trends as these relate to developments in the E&T sector. Many of the findings in the report are based on data not previously available to researchers and policymakers in Vietnam, or on new analyses of data that existed but had not been used to address issues of who provides E&T services, how much these services cost, who finances these costs, and what returns can reasonably be expected on the public and private investments made.

In the remainder of this chapter, the report looks first, in Section A, at Vietnam's accomplishments in E&T vis-à-vis the experience of other countries in the East Asia Region, in particular, the experience of the High Performing Asian Economies (HPAEs) whose exceptional performance was analyzed in a World Bank study (1993a) and against which Vietnam may wish to measure its own performance. In Section B the chapter looks to the future and assesses the likely affordability of two alternative enrollment trajectories for the E&T sector over the decade ahead. Finally, the chapter concludes with Section C, in which the VEFSS team proposes a menu of policy options related to the three public policy instruments articulated above. Vietnamese policymakers may wish to consider and choose from this menu in deciding on the national policy framework that will guide sector developments into the 21st century.

VIETNAM IN RELATION TO THE HIGH PERFORMING ASIAN ECONOMIES

The experience during the past thirty years of several of Vietnam's regional neighbors demonstrates that sound, deliberate and predictable (consistent) social and economic policies over an extended period of time can lead to high economic growth and an equitable distribution of income. The remarkable experience of these countries has been called the "East Asian miracle," documented in a recent study carried out by the World Bank (1993a).

The East Asian Miracle study focused especially on eight "high performing Asian economies" (HPAEs). The development timetables of the eight countries were, of course, different. Japan's economic miracle began in the 1960s, followed more than a decade later by the arrival of Asia's "Four Tigers" (Hong Kong, the Republic of Korea, Singapore and Taipei-China), and quite recently by the emergence of three "newly industrializing economies" or NIEs (Indonesia, Malaysia and Thailand). Despite timing that spanned more than three decades, the HPAEs have, however, followed many of the same development recipes. The East Asian Miracle study concluded that the creation and maintenance of a strong human resource base were critical factors in explaining the HPAEs' remarkable economic performance. Before each of the eight countries "took off" economically, its education enrollment rates had reached levels well above the average of other countries at comparable income levels in the rest of the world (Mingat

1996). Table 6.1 presents the gross enrollment rates (GERs) of the HPAEs at ten-year intervals since 1950 and the GDP per capita of each of the eight in 1960, expressed in 1992 US dollars, as well as the average annual rate of economic growth between 1960 and the 1990s.

Table 6.1. Gross Enrollment Ratios and GDP per Capita in High Performing Asian Economies, 1950-1992

| | Gross Enrollment Ratio (percent) | | | | | | | | | | | | | | | GDP/capita | |
| | Primary | | | | | Secondary | | | | | Tertiary | | | | | 1960 (in 1992 US$) | 1960-92 (annual growth) |
	'50	'60	'70	'80	'92	'50	'60	'70	'80	'92	'50	'60	'70	'80	'92		
Hong Kong	50%	++	++	++	++	13%	30%	46%	64%	n.a.	1%	4%	7%	11%	20%	2,167	6.3%
Indonesia	41%	60%	74%	++	++	2%	6%	16%	29%	43%	--	1%	2%	3%	10%	191	4.0%
Japan	++	++	++	++	++	66%	79%	90%	93%	98%	6%	9%	17%	31%	46%	4,677	5.8%
Korea	88%	96%	++	++	++	16%	27%	41%	78%	90%	1%	4%	8%	16%	42%	647	7.6%
Malaysia	57%	74%	87%	93%	93%	5%	17%	30%	48%	60%	--	1%	2%	4%	8%	824	3.9%
Singapore	77%	++	++	++	++	7%	32%	46%	58%	70%	2%	6%	7%	8%	22%	1,992	6.7%
Taipei-China	88%	97%	++	++	++	11%	29%	52%	77%	88%	1%	4%	7%	10%	21%	1,063	7.2%
Thailand	73%	83%	83%	99%	97%	6%	12%	17%	29%	36%	2%	2%	2%	13%	19%	365	5.2%

++ = 100 percent or above; -- = below 1 percent; n.a. = not available.
Source: Mingat 1996.

Certainly, unique historical and cultural factors contribute to a country's public policy choices. The HPAEs did not implement all of the same policies in the same order or in the same way. Moreover, policies that worked well for the HPAEs should not be adopted blindly elsewhere. The impact of particular public policies may differ depending on country circumstances. While useful as general models, the successful policies of the HPAEs need to be adapted to country-specific goals and circumstances. However, bearing all of these caveats in mind, the following are generalizations about the education policies of the HPAEs.

- All of the HPAEs *emphasized primary education* strongly. Coverage in terms of both access and quality, at this level especially, was high, and the eight HPAEs achieved impressive pupil retention and achievement rates in comparison with other countries. With net primary enrollment rates between 90 and 100 percent, Japan, Korea, Taipei-China and Hong Kong had already achieved UPE by the 1960s, Singapore by the 1970s, and the three NIEs by the 1980s. Of those students who entered Grade 1, the proportion who reached Grade 4 was well above the Asian mean (which was 80 percent in 1980 and 87 percent in 1990) in all of the HPAEs, except for Indonesia, where flow-through efficiency was lower and close to the regional average. International studies of comparative cognitive achievement among 9-10 year-olds suggest that learning in Japan, Korea, Singapore and Taipei-China are consistently higher than the "international mean" and generally above (or on a par with) the mean for OECD countries. Achievement in Indonesia was found in one study to be below the international mean, while comparative information on the other three countries is not available (Robitaille and Garden 1988; Lapointe, Mead and Askew 1992; Elley 1992; Schleisher and Yip 1994; as reported in Mingat 1996).

- The HPAEs provided *basic education essentially free of user charges*, but they relied on *substantial cost recovery at higher levels*, especially tertiary, to help finance the costs of education. Private financing as a proportion of the full direct costs of education rises in the HPAEs as students in these countries move up through the education system. On the one hand, the HPAEs have mobilized considerable public financing, and targeted this to lower levels of the education system and to low-income groups, while on the other hand, they have supplemented these subsidies with high levels of private financing in the form of reasonable fee levels in public education and via the development of a strong private E&T system to parallel the public system. In Japan about 80 percent of the costs of upper secondary and tertiary education is financed from user fees, and in Taipei-China about 90 percent.[37] Private enrollments have accounted for at least 40 percent of upper secondary enrollments and at least 60 percent of tertiary enrollments in Japan, Korean and Taipei-China since before 1970. Private enrollments are lower in Singapore -- about 30 percent in upper secondary and virtually none in tertiary. Comparable information is not available for Hong Kong and for the three NIEs (Cheng 1995; Kaneko 1995; Low 1995; Paik 1995; as reported in Mingat 1996).

- The HPAEs *emphasized school-based VOTECH in secondary education*. At some time in the past, Japan, Korea and Singapore all had between 40 and 50 percent of their secondary school enrollments in VOTECH courses. However, the *students enrolled in vocational and technical courses have fallen as a proportion of total enrollments* as GDP per capita in the HPAEs went up (Mingat 1996).

- The HPAEs achieved an *efficient input mix*, including quite high student-teacher ratios and reasonably *generous teacher remuneration*. The average student-teacher ratio in secondary education in Japan, Korea, Singapore and Taipei-China was 32.5-to-1 when their GDP levels were at $650 (in 1992 US$), many years in the past. As their income levels rose, the HPAEs could afford and choose to have smaller classes. Today in primary education, the average student-teacher ratio in the eight HPAEs ranges from a low of 18:1 in Thailand to a high 33:1 in Korea, in secondary education from 14:1 in Indonesia to 23:1 in Korea, and in tertiary education from 12:1 in Malaysia to 28:1 in Korea. It should be noted that Vietnam has maintained student-teacher ratios at the high end of each of these ranges, except in tertiary education where, despite a recent rise in the student-teacher ratio, it is still below 15:1. In 1990 in the HPAEs, the average salary of a teacher in primary education ranged from a low of 1.9 times the GDP per capita in Singapore to a high of 3.2 times the GDP per capita in Korea. This range is above the average for all OECD countries (1.6 times GDP per capita; Tan and Mingat 1992), and well above the figure for Vietnam (about 1.2 times GDP per capita; cf. Table 2.8 above).

---

[37]The private share of financing has fluctuated in tertiary education in Taipei-China, approaching 100 percent in 1980 and falling back to 70 percent by 1993.

In general, the HPAEs were successful in achieving high E&T outcomes in terms of quantity, quality and equity. It is difficult to compare Vietnam's current performance with that of the HPAEs twenty, thirty or even forty years ago. To do so in a statistical sense, however, VEFSS ran ordinary least squares (OLS) regression equations to estimate the average relationship between gross enrollment ratios and GDP per capita in the eight HPAEs over a period of more than 40 years, using the data presented in Table 6.1 above.

The time-series data were pooled for the eight HPAEs to create a sample of data points to use in the regression analysis.[38] Identical equations were estimated for primary, secondary and tertiary education. For each level, the relationship between the gross enrollment ratio (*GER*) and GDP per capita (*Y*) was estimated in linear ($GER = a + bY$), quadratic ($GER = a + bY + cY^2$) and logistic ($GER = a + b/Y$) forms, and the best fit chosen. The logistic specification was chosen as the best fit for primary education ($R^2 = 0.61$), and the quadratic for secondary and tertiary ($R^2 = 0.69$ and 0.66, respectively). The results are presented in Figures 6.1-6.3. In each figure, for reasons of visual clarity, the GDP per capita axis is truncated at \$5,000 (1992 US \$), although observations for the HPAEs when they had reached higher income levels were also used to estimate the average trend line.

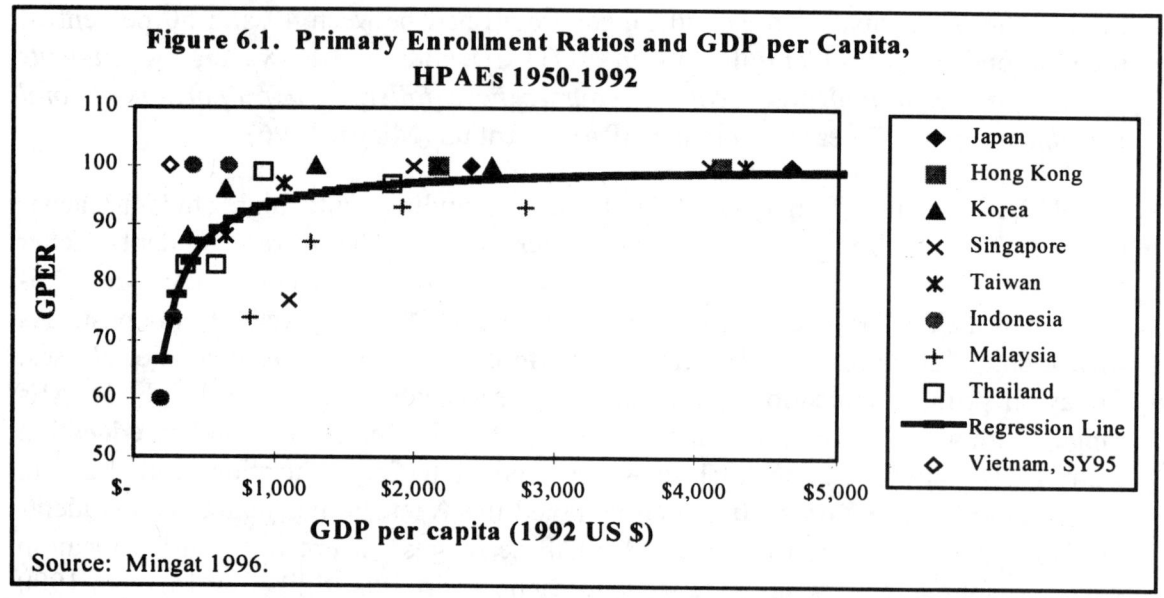

Figure 6.1. Primary Enrollment Ratios and GDP per Capita, HPAEs 1950-1992

Source: Mingat 1996.

---

[38] The data are from Mingat (1996). Income per capita in 1950 was not available for Hong Kong, Indonesia, Malaysia and Thailand, so that the pooled sample consisted of 36 and not 40 data points. The available data did not distinguish between lower and upper secondary gross enrollment ratios.

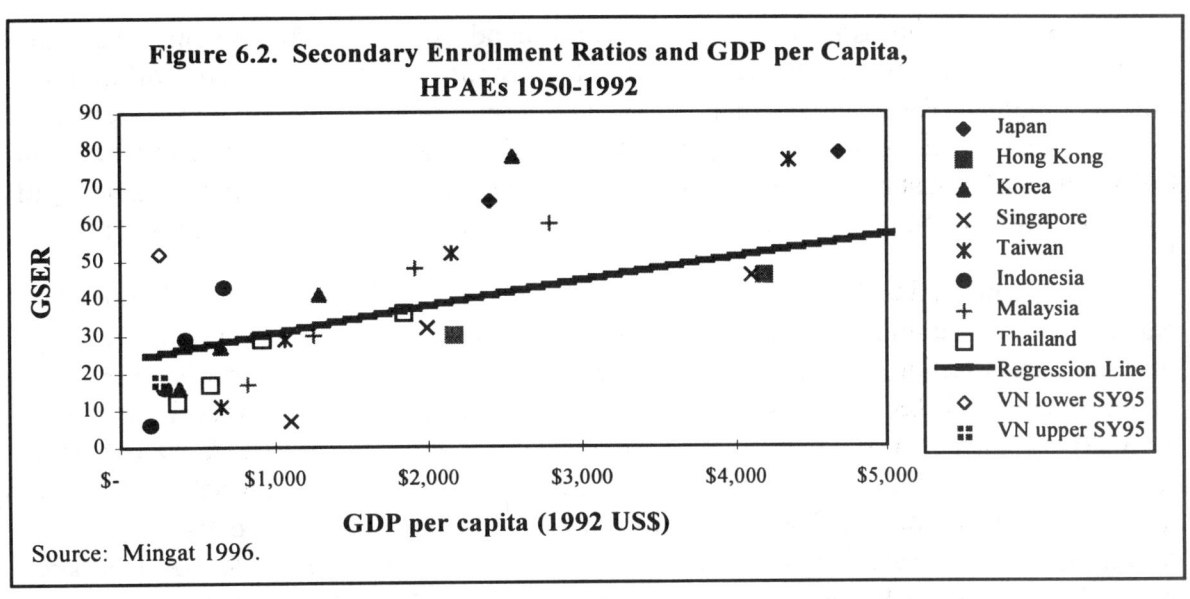

Figure 6.2. Secondary Enrollment Ratios and GDP per Capita, HPAEs 1950-1992

Source: Mingat 1996.

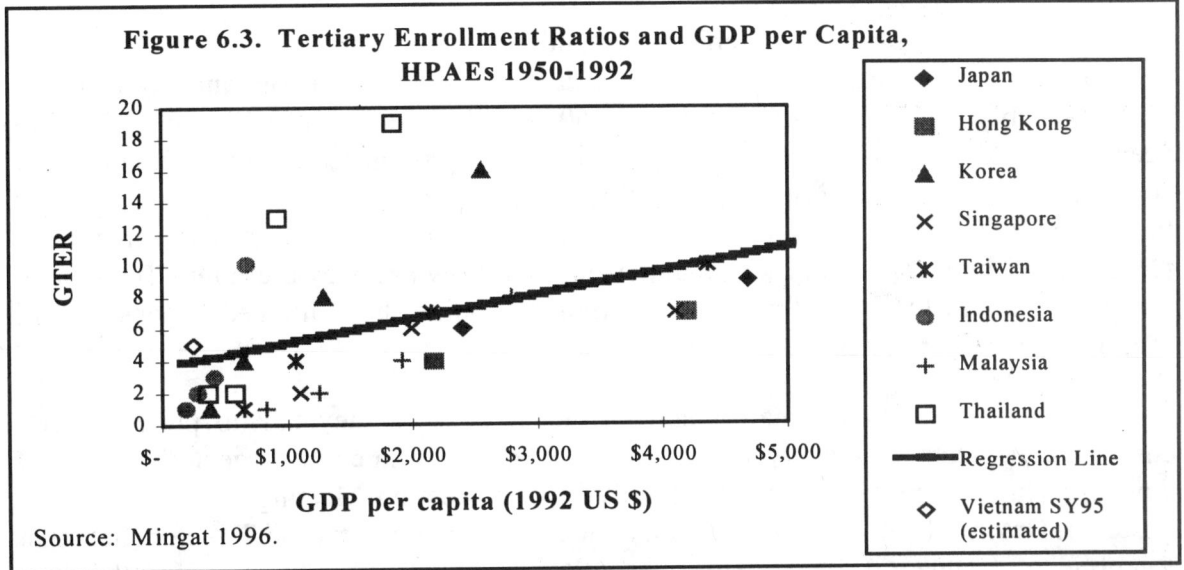

Figure 6.3. Tertiary Enrollment Ratios and GDP per Capita, HPAEs 1950-1992

Source: Mingat 1996.

In each figure, a data point is included that shows Vietnam's income and enrollment status currently (circa 1995), in order to compare its enrollment achievements with the historical experience of the HPAEs. The conclusion is that Vietnam is "right on schedule," or even ahead of schedule, in quantitative terms at least, as compared with the HPAEs when they were, in the past, at the same per capita GDP level that Vietnam has reached today. In primary education (Figure 6.1), Vietnam has achieved virtual UPE, an accomplishment that the "typical HPAE" did not achieve until its income level was many times larger than Vietnam's today. When the "typical HPAE" had reached the GDP per capita of Vietnam today (about $250), it had achieved a gross primary enrollment ratio of not quite 75 percent. The HPAE data for secondary education (Figure 6.2) does not distinguish between lower and upper secondary. At Vietnam's present income level, the "typical HPAE" had achieved a gross secondary enrollment ratio of 25 percent. The present enrollment ratios in Vietnam for lower secondary (GER = 52 percent; NER = 45 percent) and for upper secondary (GER = 18 percent; NER = 15 percent) bracket the HPAE benchmark, suggesting that Vietnam is approximately "on track." Vietnam's enrollment ratio at the tertiary level is currently about 5 percent, whereas the "typical HPAE" had achieved a ratio of 4 percent (Figure 6.3) when its income was at the level of Vietnam's today.

The only HPAE that actually had an income level during the past 40 years that was close to Vietnam's current income level is Indonesia. Indonesia's GDP per capita was about $250 (in 1992 US$) in the late 1960s. At that time, Indonesia's GPER was about 70 percent, its GSER about 15 percent, and its GTER less than 2 percent. Thus, in comparison with Indonesia 30-40 years ago, Vietnam is well ahead today. However, Indonesia's enrollment growth trajectory *since* the late 1960s has been much steeper than that of most of the other HPAEs. This may be inevitable for any country (such as Indonesia, and now Vietnam) that is "running to catch up with the pack," as compared with other countries (such as Japan and the three "Tigers") that are leading the pack.

Although Vietnam has achieved quantitative enrollments that are impressive given its current income, the country may look to its HPAE neighbors and say to itself, understandably: "Had the history of the past 50 years been different, Vietnam could have been -- in fact, *would* have been -- one of the Asian 'Tigers' instead of one of the poorest countries in the East Asia Region today. We lost those years, but we plan to make up for this period, and we will do so quickly and not wait the 50 or more years that it may have taken the 'Tigers' to get from where they were then to where they are now. To achieve our plan, we will move boldly on many fronts, including the continued expansion and improvement of our system of education and training."

This is the message that outsiders often hear when they talk to policymakers, educators, students and everyday citizens. The Government's targets for sectoral development were presented at a Sectoral Aid Coordination Meeting that Government hosted in October 1995 in Hanoi for donor agencies working in the E&T sector (Socialist Republic of Vietnam 1995e). These *quantitative targets* are considered in the next section, from the point of view of fiscal affordability. Given World Bank projections of (a) economic growth and (b) growth of the State Budget, even the Government's ambitious targets for sectoral expansion seem affordable. This conclusion, however, is based on an assumption *that nothing else will change with respect to the way that E&T is financed and produced.* In other words, the analysis of fiscal affordability begins with an assumption that unit costs and cost-recovery ratios (the percentage of full costs financed privately) will both remain as they were in 1994, the baseline year. This assumption is then relaxed in the last section of the report, which reviews a variety of policies, alluded to in earlier chapters, that Government may wish to consider as it addresses quality issues in the sector and pursues its broader goals of economic growth, poverty reduction and equity.

AFFORDABILITY OF QUANTITATIVE ENROLLMENT PROJECTIONS

The question of whether a particular enrollment growth scenario is "affordable" or not must be approached from the two sides of supply and demand. On the "demand" side, the question is how much money will be *needed* to achieve and maintain the enrollment targets specified in the scenario. On the "supply" side, the question is how much will be *available* to finance the operation of an expanded E&T sector. The complete model that was used to address these questions is presented in a set of tables at the end of this report (Annex 6.1). The discussion below extracts key elements of the model in order to demonstrate the affordability or non-affordability of two different enrollment growth scenarios for the period from the middle of the 1990s through the middle of the next decade.

The analysis will focus, in the first instance, on *fiscal* affordability.[39] Hence, the growth scenarios will involve only those students enrolled in Vietnam's public-sector institutions. These public-sector enrollments will be costed using the unit cost calculations described earlier in the report. In Section A of Chapter 4, unit fiscal costs were presented for 1994.[40] To project budget requirements into the future, enrollment targets in each year will be multiplied by the 1994 unit cost figures. Since 1994 information will be used for this purpose, all of the other monetary units in the analysis will also be expressed in 1994 prices.

The budget constraint is presented in Table 6.2. According to Revised Minimum Standards Model (RMSM) estimates prepared by World Bank macroeconomists working with Government counterparts in Vietnam, GDP will grow from VND 170.3 trillion (170.3×10^{12}), approximately US \$15.5 billion, in 1994 to VND 421.8 trillion in 2004, implying an annual real economic growth rate of 9.5 percent over the ten-year period. Assuming that government spending will remain at about 26 percent of GDP, this means that the State Budget will also grow at 9-10 percent a year. Debt repayment is projected to rise at first, and then fall, both in absolute terms and as a percentage of the State Budget; interest payments made up 6.6 percent of the budget in 1994 but are projected to

---

[39] The alternative instruments available for the use of Vietnamese policymakers to meet enrollment targets (cost-recovery and private sector development) will then be considered in light of the findings on fiscal affordability. Clearly, if a particular enrollment growth scenario is shown to be too expensive to be financed from the budget, then it is necessary to do one of the following: (1) recover a higher percentage of the costs of expanding public education from students and other private sources of funding; (2) cut back on the expansion of public sector enrollments and rely on private sector institutions to make up the difference; (3) relax the budget constraint by convincing the central ministries that E&T should be allocated a larger share of the budget than it has been given historically; or (4) do none of the above but, rather, expand enrollments to satisfy the growth targets, and do this without claiming a larger share of the budget -- in other words, to *reduce unit fiscal costs*.

[40] This was the most recent year for which reliable information was available on both the *numerator* (State Budget current expenditure on each level and type of E&T) and the *denominator* (FTE enrollments in each level and type of E&T), the division of which provided the measure of unit fiscal cost (public expenditure per student-year).

be only 2.0 percent in 2004. These will be impressive achievements if they are all realized. The macro-projections reflect the excellent performance of the Vietnamese economy in recent years as well as the World Bank's optimistic judgment about the depth of the economic renovation program and the rapid pace of Vietnam's transition to a market economy.

Table 6.2. Projected GDP, State Budget and Allocations for Education and Training, 1994-2004
(in VND '000,000,000,000 at constant 1994 prices; 1994 actual, 1995 budgeted, 1996 projected)

	1994	1995	1996	1997	1998	1999	2000	2001	2002	2003	2004
A. GDP	170.3	186.5	204.3	223.7	245.0	268.3	293.7	321.5	352.0	385.3	421.8
B. State Budget (I+N)	44.2	45.6	47.2	59.8	65.0	70.8	77.0	83.9	92.6	99.8	109.8
C. State Budget as % of GDP	26%	24%	23%	27%	27%	26%	26%	26%	26%	26%	26%
D. Interest payments	2.92	2.48	3.47	3.23	3.05	2.87	2.71	2.58	2.46	2.34	2.23
E. Discretionary State Budget (B-D)	41.3	43.1	43.7	56.6	62.0	67.9	74.3	81.3	90.1	97.5	107.6
F. E&T (ca. 12% of E and 3% of A)	5.01	5.28	5.29	6.81	7.36	8.06	8.83	9.66	10.65	11.50	12.62
G. Education (71-73% of F)	3.63	3.85	3.83	4.91	5.25	5.75	6.29	6.89	7.56	8.15	8.90
H. Training (27-29% of F)	1.38	1.42	1.46	1.90	2.11	2.32	2.53	2.77	3.09	3.35	3.72
I. Current State Budget	32.9	34.9	34.9	43.0	44.2	48.0	52.0	56.6	60.9	65.2	69.7
J. Discretionary current budget (I-D)	30.0	32.5	31.5	39.8	41.2	45.1	49.3	54.0	58.4	62.8	67.5
K. E&T (13.3% of J)	3.98	4.30	4.17	5.28	5.46	5.98	6.54	7.16	7.75	8.33	8.95
L. Education (77.4% of K)	3.08	3.33	3.23	4.09	4.23	4.63	5.06	5.54	6.00	6.45	6.93
M. Training (22.6% of K)	0.90	0.97	0.94	1.19	1.23	1.35	1.48	1.62	1.75	1.88	2.02
N. Capital State Budget	11.3	10.6	12.3	16.8	20.8	22.8	25.0	27.3	31.7	34.7	40.1
O. E&T (9.1% of N)	1.03	0.97	1.12	1.53	1.90	2.09	2.28	2.50	2.90	3.17	3.66
P. Education (53.8 of O)	0.56	0.52	0.60	0.82	1.02	1.12	1.23	1.34	1.56	1.71	1.97
Training (46.2% of O)	0.48	0.45	0.52	0.71	0.88	0.96	1.06	1.16	1.34	1.47	1.69
Memo Item:											
GDP Deflator	100	119	130	139	148	157	166	174	183	192	202

Source: World Bank estimates prepared by the East Asia 1 Country Operations Division using MOF data and the Revised Minimum Standards Model (see Annex 6.1, Tables 1, 5 and 6).

A major change foreseen in the model over the ten-year period is an increase in capital relative to current spending. Capital's share of the discretionary State Budget would rise from 27 percent in 1994 to 37 percent in 2004. The corollary, of course, is that current spending would fall in relative terms, which reduces the budget available to finance E&T's current costs.[41] Despite this, the current budget for E&T is projected here to increase at an average annual rate of 8.4 percent over the period. This reflects an assumption that E&T's share of the discretionary current budget will remain at 13.3 percent, its level in 1994.[42] This is modest by comparison with other countries in the

---

[41] The analysis here of "affordability" focuses on current expenditure alone. The assumption is that the capital costs of expanding the E&T system will not be a serious constraint in Vietnam. Indeed, even if budget projections did not signal a significant increase in capital spending from the Government's own revenues, the country has relatively easy access to ODA and other sources of capital financing for development projects in E&T and other areas.

[42] The share of E&T in the consolidated (capital plus current) budget has been about 12 percent. In relation to GDP, public expenditure on E&T has been about 3 percent (although when private spending is added to public spending, E&T's share of GDP rises to about 5 percent).

Region,[43] and the Government of Vietnam has indicated that E&T's share will go up in the future. The assumption of a constant 13.3 percent share can thus be seen to be a conservative assumption, presented here as a heuristic device. Give this assumption, the fiscal budget constraint for financing E&T's current costs between 1994 and 2004 is shown as Line K of Table 6.2. Now the question is -- are these annual figures a lot or a little? This, of course, depends on what needs to be financed. As already said, the study will present two different enrollment scenarios, and assess each of these in light of the budget constraint in Line K.

If Vietnam is indeed on schedule, or even a little ahead of schedule, relative to the historical pace set by the HPAEs, then perhaps only modest enrollment increases are called for. A very modest approach, referred to here as the "Baseline Scenario," is essentially a maintenance program -- expanding enrollments, but only at the rate of population growth. In other words, the Baseline Scenario calls for maintaining GERs at their present (1994) levels. The enrollments in each level/type of E&T are then determined by multiplying present GERs by projections of age-specific population figures. These trajectories are presented in Section A of Table 6.3. The alternative, presented in Section B as the "Plan Scenario," consists of the Government's enrollment targets for the period ahead.[44] Not surprisingly, the Plan Scenario is considerably more ambitious than the Baseline Scenario. The Plan targets are higher than those in Section A (implied by population growth alone) -- by between 2 percent (in the case of technical education) and 138 percent (in the case of vocational education). Two other E&T programs for which the Plan shows substantial increases in the enrollment ratios are pre-school and lower secondary education.

---

[43] The Asia mean for public spending on E&T as a percentage of GDP was about 3.8 percent in 1992. Among the HPAEs, Indonesia scored the lowest on this indicator of "fiscal effort" (2.2 percent), and Malaysia and Singapore (5.5 percent and 5.4 percent) scored the highest (Mingat 1996).

[44] These were supplied privately to the VEFSS team and discussed with both MOET and MPI during 1996. They are essentially the same targets presented to the Sectoral Aid Coordination Meeting in October 1995 (Socialist Republic of Vietnam 1995e), though with some minor modifications.

Table 6.3.   **Projected Enrollments and Gross Enrollment Ratios under Two Different Scenarios, 1994-2004**

	1994	1995	1996	1997	1998	1999	2000	2001	2002	2003	2004
A. Baseline Scenario											
Enrollments (in '000,000)											
Education											
Pre-school	1.61	1.61	1.62	1.63	1.64	1.65	1.66	1.64	1.61	1.59	1.56
Primary	9.93	9.97	10.08	10.18	10.29	10.40	10.52	10.62	10.67	10.67	10.62
Lower Secondary	3.24	3.33	3.35	3.37	3.40	3.42	3.44	3.47	3.51	3.57	3.62
Upper Secondary	0.65	0.67	0.68	0.70	0.72	0.73	0.75	0.76	0.76	0.76	0.76
Training											
Vocational	0.28	0.29	0.30	0.30	0.31	0.32	0.32	0.33	0.33	0.33	0.33
Technical	0.13	0.14	0.14	0.14	0.14	0.15	0.15	0.15	0.15	0.15	0.15
Tertiary	0.23	0.23	0.24	0.24	0.25	0.26	0.26	0.27	0.28	0.28	0.28
Gross enrollment ratio[a]											
Education											
Pre-school	19%	19%	19%	19%	19%	19%	19%	19%	19%	19%	19%
Primary	109%	109%	109%	109%	109%	109%	109%	109%	109%	109%	109%
Lower Secondary	49%	49%	49%	49%	49%	49%	49%	49%	49%	49%	49%
Upper Secondary	17%	17%	17%	17%	17%	17%	17%	17%	17%	17%	17%
Training											
Vocational	8%	8%	8%	8%	8%	8%	8%	8%	8%	8%	8%
Technical	4%	4%	4%	4%	4%	4%	4%	4%	4%	4%	4%
Tertiary	5%	5%	5%	5%	5%	5%	5%	5%	5%	5%	5%
B. Plan Scenario											
Enrollments (in '000,000)											
Education											
Pre-school	1.61	1.83	2.14	2.31	2.43	2.51	2.64	2.76	2.90	3.04	3.18
Primary	9.93	10.29	10.83	11.15	11.39	11.59	11.77	11.95	12.13	12.32	12.51
Lower Secondary	3.24	3.74	4.15	4.33	4.45	4.75	5.33	5.98	6.70	7.52	8.43
Upper Secondary	0.65	0.77	0.86	0.90	0.93	0.96	0.99	1.03	1.06	1.09	1.13
Training											
Vocational	0.28	0.32	0.36	0.41	0.45	0.49	0.54	0.59	0.65	0.71	0.78
Technical	0.13	0.13	0.14	0.14	0.14	0.14	0.15	0.15	0.15	0.15	0.16
Tertiary	0.23	0.29	0.31	0.33	0.35	0.36	0.37	0.37	0.37	0.38	0.38
Gross enrollment ratio[a]											
Education											
Pre-school	19%	21%	25%	26%	28%	29%	30%	32%	34%	36%	38%
Primary	109%	113%	117%	119%	121%	122%	122%	123%	124%	126%	129%
Lower Secondary	49%	55%	61%	63%	65%	69%	76%	85%	94%	104%	115%
Upper Secondary	17%	19%	21%	22%	22%	22%	22%	23%	24%	24%	25%
Training											
Vocational	8%	9%	10%	11%	12%	12%	13%	15%	16%	18%	19%
Technical	4%	4%	4%	4%	4%	4%	4%	4%	4%	4%	4%
Tertiary	5%	6%	6%	7%	7%	7%	7%	7%	7%	6%	6%

[a] Gross enrollment ratio (GER) = enrollment divided by age-specific population.

Sources: VEFSS projections based on MOET education data and GSO population data (see Annex 6.1, Table 13).

The cost implications of the two scenarios are presented in Table 6.4. Given the assumption that unit costs will remain constant over time (and not decline as a function of the number of students enrolled at each level of the public E&T system, nor increase in response to explicit measures aimed at raising quality), the Plan Scenario would cost 41 percent more than the Baseline Scenario (VND 7.34 trillion as compared with VND 5.20 trillion) by the year 2004. Current expenditure would increase at an average annual rate of 2.7 percent between 1994 and 2004 under the Baseline Scenario, and 6.3 percent under the Plan Scenario.

Table 6.4.   Projected Public Expenditure on Education and Training under Two Different Scenarios, 1994-2004

	Unit fiscal cost (VND '000)	Projected public expenditure on Education and Training (in VND '000,000,000,000 at constant 1994 prices)										
		1994	1995	1996	1997	1998	1999	2000	2001	2002	2003	2004
Baseline Scenario												
Education		3.08	3.16	3.17	3.34	3.39	3.49	3.59	3.69	3.78	3.87	3.95
Pre-school	120.9	0.20	0.20	0.20	0.20	0.20	0.20	0.20	0.20	0.19	0.19	0.19
Primary	129.8	1.29	1.29	1.31	1.32	1.34	1.35	1.37	1.38	1.38	1.39	1.38
Lower Sec.	235.0	0.76	0.78	0.79	0.79	0.80	0.80	0.81	0.82	0.83	0.84	0.85
Upper Sec.	482.5	0.31	0.32	0.33	0.34	0.35	0.35	0.36	0.36	0.37	0.37	0.37
Other		0.52	0.56	0.54	0.69	0.71	0.78	0.85	0.94	1.01	1.09	1.17
Training		0.90	0.93	0.95	1.01	1.03	1.07	1.11	1.15	1.19	1.22	1.25
Vocational	478.1	0.13	0.14	0.14	0.14	0.15	0.15	0.16	0.16	0.16	0.16	0.16
Technical	1,649.0	0.22	0.22	0.23	0.23	0.24	0.24	0.25	0.25	0.25	0.25	0.25
Tertiary	1,767.8	0.40	0.41	0.42	0.43	0.44	0.45	0.47	0.48	0.49	0.50	0.50
Other[a]		0.15	0.16	0.15	0.20	0.20	0.22	0.24	0.27	0.29	0.31	0.33
Education and Training		3.98	4.09	4.11	4.35	4.42	4.56	4.71	4.85	4.97	5.08	5.20
Plan Scenario												
Education		3.08	3.37	3.60	3.87	3.98	4.17	4.43	4.72	5.02	5.35	5.70
Pre-school	120.9	0.20	0.22	0.26	0.28	0.29	0.30	0.32	0.33	0.35	0.37	0.39
Primary	129.8	1.29	1.34	1.41	1.45	1.48	1.50	1.53	1.55	1.58	1.60	1.62
Lower Secondary	235.0	0.76	0.88	0.98	1.02	1.05	1.12	1.25	1.40	1.58	1.77	1.98
Upper Secondary	482.5	0.31	0.37	0.42	0.43	0.45	0.46	0.48	0.50	0.51	0.53	0.54
Other		0.52	0.56	0.54	0.69	0.71	0.78	0.85	0.94	1.01	1.09	1.17
Training		0.90	1.05	1.10	1.21	1.27	1.34	1.39	1.45	1.51	1.57	1.63
Vocational	478.1	0.13	0.15	0.17	0.20	0.21	0.23	0.26	0.28	0.31	0.34	0.37
Technical	1,649.0	0.22	0.22	0.23	0.23	0.23	0.24	0.24	0.25	0.25	0.25	0.26
Tertiary	1,767.8	0.40	0.52	0.55	0.59	0.62	0.64	0.65	0.65	0.66	0.67	0.67
Other[a]		0.15	0.16	0.15	0.20	0.20	0.22	0.24	0.27	0.29	0.31	0.33
Education and Training		3.98	4.42	4.70	5.08	5.25	5.51	5.82	6.17	6.53	6.92	7.34

[a]Includes post-graduate research and training, approximately 19 percent of total of "other" training.

Sources: VEFSS projections based on MOET education data, GSO population data and MOF expenditure data
(see Annex 6.1, Tables 16 and 19).

Are these quantitative targets affordable from the point of view of the State Budget given: (a) the RMSM budget projections, and (b) the assumptions that unit costs and cost-recovery ratios will remain constant at their observed 1994 levels at all levels of E&T, as will E&T's share of the budget. Figure 6.4 graphs the availability of public spending for E&T (from Table 6.2) and the budget needed to finance operations under the two scenarios (from Table 6.4). The projected allocation for E&T from the State Budget provides a *budget cushion*, even under the Plan Scenario (the only exception being in 1996, when a projected dip in the budget would seem to be making the situation tight and will require a one-year delay in starting the implementation of the Government's plan for sectoral expansion).

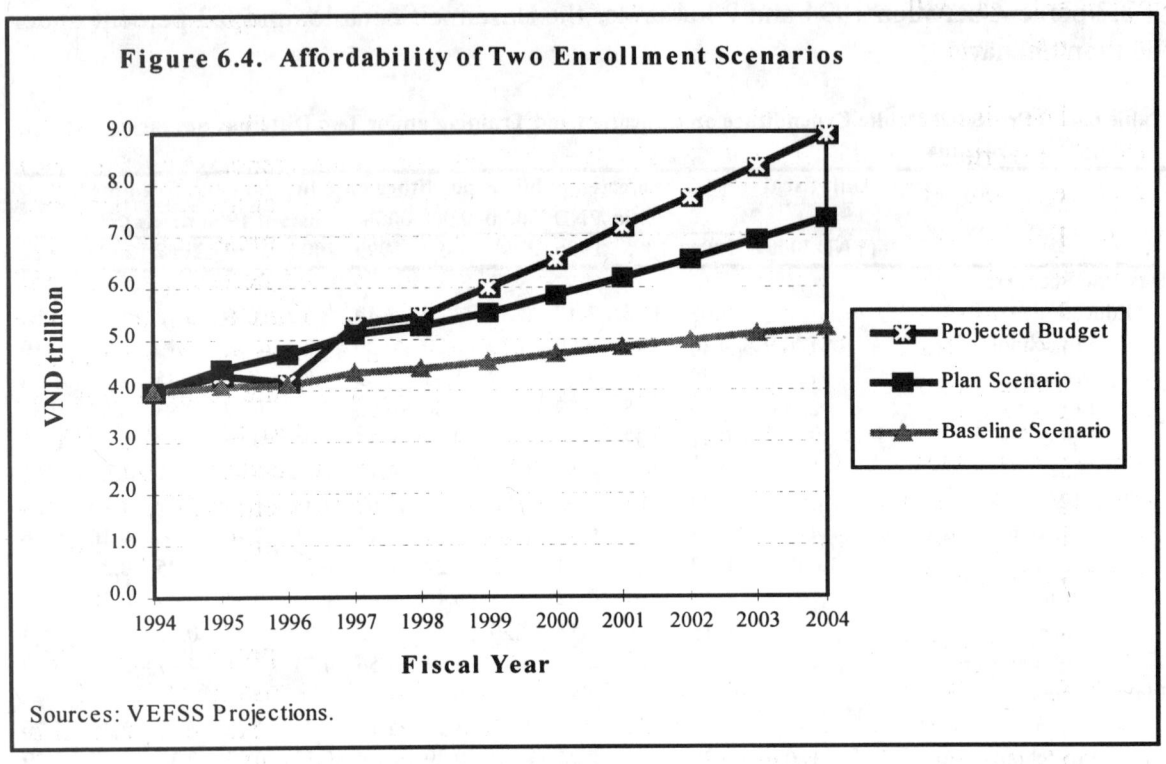

Figure 6.4. Affordability of Two Enrollment Scenarios

Sources: VEFSS Projections.

What should the Government of Vietnam do with this cushion? It could be reallocated to other sectors, but this would be a questionable decision given the fact that E&T's share of the budget is already low by East Asian standards and given the importance of E&T to Vietnam's continued buoyant economic performance and completion of its transition to a market economy. Alternatively, this cushion can be treated as an asset to be used to accomplish other very important *non-quantitative* goals for the sector. These goals include increased equity and quality enhancement. Possible measures for achieving these goals are discussed in the final section of the report.

PROMISING POLICY OPTIONS

If it has been demonstrated to the reader's satisfaction that inadequate budget will *not* be a constraint to achieving the Government's enrollment targets for the E&T sector, perhaps the VEFSS report should end here. In terms of the quantitative targets, the criterion of affordability has been satisfied. However, adequate financing is only one of several factors that must be considered in evaluating a sectoral strategy and investment plan. While a *necessary* condition, it is by no means a *sufficient* condition for moving ahead. In this case, several questions remain unanswered. Are there other ways of using the same resources now earmarked for the E&T sector, options which emerged from the analyses presented in earlier chapters of this report, that promise to pay even larger dividends in terms of Vietnam's social and economic goals in the broadest sense? Does the Government's sectoral strategy adequately address the issues of efficiency and equity discussed earlier? Are there policies, some of which may be relatively cost free to implement, that will provide a more conducive framework for rapid progress and positive results in the sector?

The discussion that follows is, by no means, exhaustive. The purpose of the VEFSS, undertaken collaboratively by the World Bank and other agencies together with the Government of Vietnam, has been to assemble information and stimulate discussion among policymakers, private sector actors and donor agency representatives. The information here and subsequent discussion should help to rule out certain policies and investment options and should identify others as promising avenues to explore. The World Bank invites detailed discussion with its partners in Vietnam on all of the findings and recommendations contained in the chapters above. It expects some of these findings and recommendations to be modified, and many to be elaborated and extended, in response to the views of Government officials and other informed readers. Thus, in the final pages of this final chapter, just a few selected policy options emanating from the above findings and recommendations will be reiterated and highlighted by way of summary and conclusion.

The discussion in this section begins by re-visiting the budget projections in Table 6.4 and reviewing what would happen to expenditure allocations across levels and types of E&T over the decade ahead under the two different scenarios. The budget shares going to different E&T programs under the Baseline Scenario and under the Plan Scenario are summarized in Table 6.5 and presented visually in Figure 6.5.

Table 6.5. Shares of E&T Budget by Level and Type of Education and Training under Two Different Scenarios, 1994, 1999 and 2004

Level/Type of Education	1994 Actual	1999		2004	
		Baseline Scenario	Plan Scenario	Baseline Scenario	Plan Scenario
Pre-school	5%	4%	6%	4%	5%
Primary	32%	30%	27%	27%	22%
Lower Secondary	19%	18%	20%	16%	27%
Upper Secondary	8%	8%	8%	7%	7%
Vocational	3%	3%	4%	3%	5%
Technical	5%	5%	4%	5%	4%
University/College	10%	10%	12%	10%	9%
Post-Graduate	1%	1%	1%	1%	1%
Other[a]	16%	21%	17%	28%	20%
All programs	100%	100%	100%	100%	100%

[a]Includes post-graduate research and training, approximately 4 percent of total of "other" E&T.

Source: VEFSS projections -- see Tables 6.3 and 6.4.

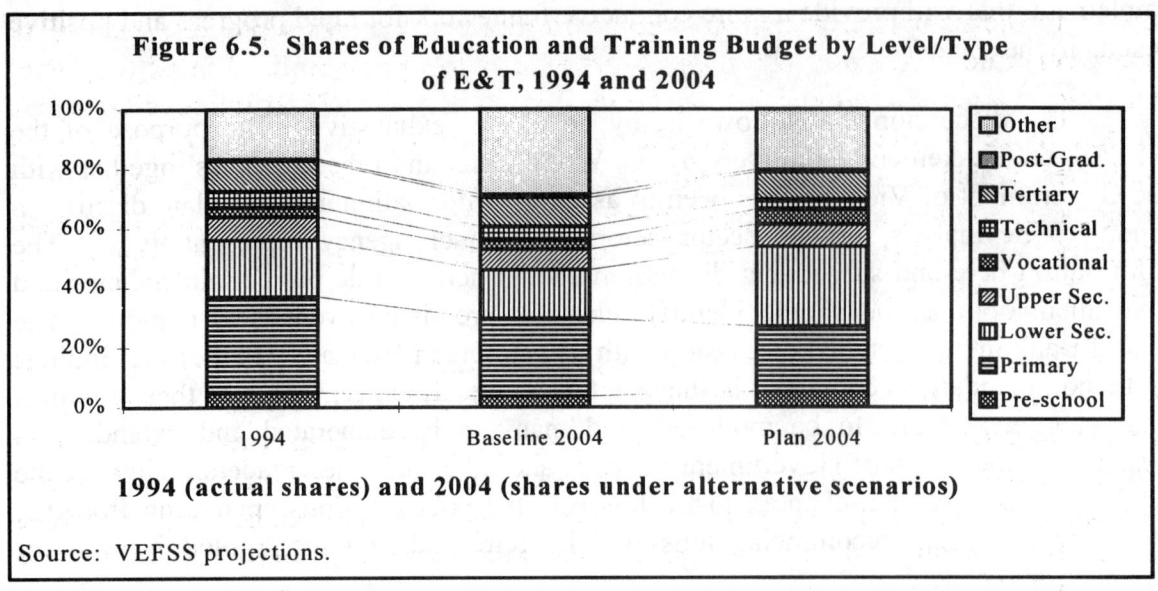

Figure 6.5. Shares of Education and Training Budget by Level/Type of E&T, 1994 and 2004

1994 (actual shares) and 2004 (shares under alternative scenarios)

Source: VEFSS projections.

System of Budget Classifications

One fact that strikes the eye is the relatively large percentage of the VND 3.98 trillion E&T budget in 1994 that falls into the "other" category and the fact that this unallocated share is projected to rise under both scenarios between 1994 and 2004. Given assumptions made in the budget projection model detailed in Annex 6.1, the unallocated category will reach 28 percent of the total budget under the Baseline Scenario by 2004 and 20 percent under the Plan Scenario. Even if some of the modeling assumptions are wrong, the *observed* unallocated share in 1994, which was 16 percent (having risen from about 6 percent in 1991)[45] is high. It stands in the way of sound decision-making by Central Government officials in MOF, MPI and MOET's Department of Planning and Finance. It was explained in Chapter 3 above that the "other" category consists of at least two components: (a) allocations to the centrally financed "targeted programs," which are not assigned in the budget to one level/type of E&T or another (even though some of these programs do indeed focus on particular levels/types), and (b) general overhead (administrative) expenditure, which is difficult to break down by sub-program.

This difficulty, however, highlights a more general problem of the budgeting system and the way that E&T is planned and administered. With assistance from VEFSS, the budget information available in MOF was re-classified to conform with GFS standards. This accelerated a process for standardizing the Government's budget information which was already occurring and which had moved more quickly in some sectors than in others. It is important that GFS classifications should be used in Vietnam, so as to make the Government's financing statistics more transparent, more readily

---

[45] Cf. Table 3.4 in Chapter 3, although that table shows the breakdown of the consolidated budget (current and capital spending combined), whereas the analysis here focuses on current spending alone.

subject to the comparative analysis needed to measure Vietnam's progress relative to other economies and easier for international experts to comprehend. The GFS system, however, is a general system that can be used to classify the budget information across the full range of sectors. This general system is needed for purposes of the central ministries, which must decide on an overall budget and which cannot be expected to understand and monitor sector-specific details. However, these sector-specific details are precisely those that the sectoral ministry needs to manage effectively the programs for which it is responsible.

One recommendation that follows from the experience of VEFSS is that MOET, working with MOF, develop a second level of budgetary classifications that are sector-specific and designed to help MOET discharge its responsibilities as coordinator of sectoral activities. To give one concrete example, management of the E&T sector requires detailed information on teachers -- how many are employed, how many of these are actually teaching and how many re-assigned to administration and other duties, what are the qualifications and experience of those working in different areas and at different levels, and how much they get paid. Obviously, these are details that cannot be included in the annual national budget law, but the details that *underlie* MOF's aggregated budget data should be available in the sectoral ministry. MOET officials, at the central and provincial levels, and eventually at the district and even commune levels, should have ready access to such details, which are of paramount importance for effective administration.

Allocation of Subsidies in General Education

A second stylized fact seen in Table 6.5 and Figure 6.5 is that primary education's share of the E&T current budget is projected to fall from its level in 1994 (32 percent) to a much lower level by 2004, as low as 22 percent under the Plan Scenario. This is no real surprise given that a high proportion of primary school age children in Vietnam are already attending school, meaning that *quantitative* sectoral expansion, if it is to occur, will need to occur primarily in other sub-sectors. The projection model used here simply extrapolates the present fiscal unit costs into the future, multiplying this constant by the rising student numbers.

One key finding of VEFSS has been that public expenditure per student in primary education is low -- in two different senses: (a) *relative to other levels/types of E&T* (public expenditure per student is 13 times higher in technical and tertiary education than it is in primary education), and (b) *relative to private spending on E&T*. On average, across all Vietnamese household, for every VND 100 of government spending on primary education, households spend VND 80. In secondary and in vocational E&T, the ratio is as high or even higher than this. However, in technical education, for every VND 100 of government spending, households spend only VND 47, and in tertiary education VND 44. This pattern suggests an inequitable distribution of public subsidies for education, a conclusion that is reinforced when one looks at the consumption levels of households with family members enrolled at different levels.

Net enrollments rates (NERs) are correlated with income at all levels of E&T, but much less so at the primary level. The NPER of Vietnamese households in the poorest consumption quintile was 68 percent in 1992-93 (when VLSS was carried out, providing the most recent measure of this relationship); it was 86 percent in the richest quintile. In tertiary education, however, the situation is dramatically different. In 1992-93, families in the poorest quintile had virtually no representation in higher education institutions. Participation was marginally higher in the middle three quintiles; the NTER reached 1.9 percent for those in the fourth quintile. The NTER was 7.0 percent, however, for those in the top quintile. These figures suggest that participation in college and university education is a privilege reserved almost exclusively for high income families, a finding that is all too common in many countries.

The high private costs of education certainly contribute to the high dropout rates at the primary level and also explain much of the inter-regional and inter-provincial variation in participation rates. The high participation rates across the board in Grade 1 of primary school reflect government campaigns to encourage enrollment and demonstrate the high value that Vietnamese families place on education, but some poor families soon find that they are unable to afford the "voluntary contributions" and other education-related costs. They are forced as a result to withdraw their children from school. To provide opportunities for poor children to remain in school, Government should consider a program of *targeted subsidies*, directed at poor families who cannot afford the private costs (direct plus indirect) of primary education. Of course, it is difficult to distinguish families who are truly poor from other families who may be less poor but quite happy, nevertheless, to substitute public financing for their own. To minimize the "free-rider" problem, the special subsidies for primary education will need to be targeted, not at individual families, but at communities identified by sample survey methods to have high concentrations of poverty.

Targeted subsidies can also be tied to a specific use, to ensure that critical learning inputs are not compromised when low-income households are unable to meet the expenditures associated with their children's school attendance. Specific-use subsidies are mentioned again below in the context of the discussion on education quality enhancement.

Cost Recovery in Tertiary Education

The shares of public spending allocated to higher and technical education are projected to remain about the same between 1994 and 2004 under both scenarios. Together these programs will continue to claim only about 15 percent of the budget. However, together they account for fewer than 3 percent of all of Vietnam's students. The fact that students at the top end of the E&T system tend to come from wealthier families has already been noted. Not so much for the savings generated, but for reasons of equity, Government is encouraged to consider policies that would increase cost recovery at the upper levels. The VEFSS higher education survey concluded that student fees actually declined between 1993 and 1995 in the 100 HEIs included in the survey, from 44 percent to 24 percent of expenditures. This may have been an accident of the particular three years covered in the survey. The percentage could revert to the 1993 level when the fee structure is next revised. Revising it soon and regularly, however, should be a priority of government policy, as there is virtually no justification for private costs to be higher as a percentage of full economic costs at the basic level than at the highest levels.

Another reason to aim for high levels of cost recovery is that the private rate of return to family investments in tertiary education is also high (especially in relation to the measured social rate of return, which is low when compared with the social rate of return to investment in primary education). Students who attend colleges and universities should be expected to share significantly in the burden of the costs of their education, *both* because they come from wealthy homes to begin with, *and* because they will earn more in later life as a result of having received tertiary training. A final reason for wanting to see more cost recovery in higher education is to guide the HEIs in deciding which programs to expand and which ones to contract or eliminate. Many higher education administrators at this early stage in Vietnam's transition to a market economy are waiting for instructions to be given by the government ministry which has responsibility for the particular HEI. Such signals should now come from the students themselves and from a much broader range of employers in the marketplace, including private sector employers. In a market economy, HEIs should be given substantial autonomy to set their own programs and also to raise and then retain revenues that can be used to enhance the quality of the programs offered and research produced. Greater cost recovery ensures that the outputs of higher education are demand-driven and socially useful.

Whereas achieving a greater degree of cost recovery should be an objective of government policy, complementary measures will need to be adopted to ensure that students from poor homes are not financially constrained from attending higher education courses for which they are academically qualified. Again, a program of targeted subsidies is a possible solution. At this top level of education, unlike in general education, the special subsidies should be granted based on evidence supplied by the individual family of its inability to bear a full load of the private costs of tertiary education. The cost of verifying this information is probably worthwhile at this level, because of the larger subsidies and fewer families involved. An alternative is to expand the student loan program now being piloted in Hanoi, but this program should be modified so that interest paid on student loans is at the full market rate and not subsidized. A mixed program that provides "social scholarships" for needy students and access to loans at market rates for others who do not qualify for scholarship but want assistance would appear to be the most efficient way of achieving a higher level of cost recovery in higher education while, at the same time, expanding opportunities for the poor.

Vocational Education

The two programs that will increase substantially given the Government's targets for the sector are lower secondary education and vocational education and training. Their shares of current public expenditure would go from 19 percent in 1994 to 27 percent in 2004 in the case of lower secondary education, and from 3 percent to 5 percent in the case of vocational education and training.

To give priority to the expansion of lower secondary education is understandable, given that UPE has already, or nearly, been achieved. There is a big gap between the NER in primary education (91 percent) and that in lower secondary (45 percent), and there is now pressure to expand enrollments at the higher of the two levels. To do so is also consistent with the goals declared by world leaders at the inter-agency UN Conference on Basic Education for All, in Jomtien, Thailand, in 1990 (UNDP, UNESCO, UNICEF and World Bank 1990).

Prudence suggests greater caution, however, in implementing the Government's plans for expanding vocational education and training. Implementation should be on a step-by-step basis only, with continuous monitoring and evaluation along the way. The evidence available when this report was prepared suggests that the labor market returns to investment in VOTECH are not adequate to justify VOTECH's high costs, although the data used to address this issue (VLSS 1992-93) are somewhat dated, and they confound two quite different programs -- technical education, on the one hand, and vocational education and training, on the other, lumping the two together as VOTECH; the general finding could be masking large differences between some programs that are cost-effective and others that are not at all so. Also, vocational training is an area where the private sector could play a much larger role. Finally, as with other levels and types of education, the labor market returns to VOTECH may improve as the labor market continues to evolve, but it would be wrong to assume that high returns to VOTECH investments are automatic.

VEFSS supported two survey-based studies of vocational training and labor markets, one in a sample of urban districts (SDLMS) and the other in a small sample of rural districts (RLMVTS). These surveys were completed too late for the data to be fully analyzed and the results adequately reflected in this report. A recommendation here is that Government should now exploit these data to their fullest, to garner information on which to base its program of expansion for vocational education and training. More generally, it is recommended that regular labor market surveys be carried out in the future, along the lines of HEGTS (the VEFSS tracer study of higher education graduates), SDLMS and RLMVTS. Surveys such as these can provide useful information for government policymakers, for administrators at the level of the individual training center and HEI, and for the "consumers" of training -- both students deciding on what to study and employers deciding on whom to employ.

Cost Reductions

Even when budget is not a constraint, Government should always be vigilant in identifying and eliminating wastage in the E&T system. The HEIFS identified scope for lowering unit costs at the tertiary level through a carefully considered and fully implemented program of institutional consolidation. Consolidation is one way to address, inter alia, the high staff-student ratios now found in Vietnam's HEIs. Also, the system of narrowly focused HEIs, each under the control of a different government ministry or specialized agency, should give way to an integrated system of higher education, with broad coordination coming from a single umbrella "commission" or "council," but with considerable autonomy left to individual HEIs in regard to programs and financing.

At the general education level, the principal source of savings will come, not from raising student-teacher ratios, which are already high on average (although much lower in some sparsely populated parts of Vietnam), but from lowering dropout and repetition, which inflate the cost of producing graduates. Dropout rates, as already noted, are likely to fall in response to a program of targeted subsidies that would provide poor students with the financial means to remain in school. Both dropout and repetition are likely to respond to a different set of measures intended to raise the quality of education, i.e., to raise student learning. Improvements in quality will ensure that fewer students are forced out of the system, or back in the system, for reasons of academic failure. Improvements in quality will also result in higher labor market returns to the knowledge, skills and attitudes acquired while studying and, thereby, raise the incentive to continue to the next level of schooling, while also raising the costs of repeating, since to repeat grades in school is to delay labor market entry. Possible policies to raise education quality will now be reviewed.

Quality Enhancement

The projected budget cushion under each of the two scenarios reflects the assumption that unit fiscal costs that were observed in 1994 will remain constant. Certain measures, already discussed, may lower average unit costs, ceteris paribus, and these should be pursued. Many if not most of the measures required to raise quality, however, will require additional government spending per student-year. Costing all of these measures in detail is beyond the scope of this study, although it should be undertaken as a next step. Even without having costed them, it is apparent that these measures could absorb all, or even more, of the budget cushion implied by the projection model -- which then would require a choice to be made between quantitative expansion and quality enhancement. If the macroeconomists' projections are correct, there will be adequate budget to finance E&T's expansion and to meet the Government's enrollment targets until 2004, but only if unit costs remain at their present levels, which in basic education especially, are probably lower than they should be on efficiency grounds.

Several quality enhancing options have been discussed in the chapters above. Before reviewing these, however, it should be noted that all of the evidence in this report on the scope for quality enhancement in Vietnamese E&T has been *indirect evidence* that focuses on the inputs that produce educational outcomes rather than on the outcomes themselves. The VEFSS team was unable to locate direct evidence on the learning outcomes of Vietnamese students and, especially, on measures that would allow comparisons to be made with students in other countries according to internationally agreed definitions of quality. There is a need to put in place mechanisms for setting standards in Vietnamese E&T and for monitoring learning outcomes in relation to these standards and in relation to international norms. Such measures can be used, not only to assess the performance of the E&T system, but also, if linked with proper incentives, to drive the system toward higher levels of performance. The importance of standards and performance monitoring mechanisms was underscored in a recent global review of priorities and strategies for education (World Bank 1995a).

On the input side, one policy option judged here to be very important is to raise the number of hours in the Vietnamese school year to a level that approximates international standards, including the standards set by the HPAEs. This will be expensive, as it involves extending the school year (from 165 days to at least 185 days) and extending the school day (from four hours on average to at least five hours, if not more, especially in the upper grades). The longer school day will make it difficult to maintain the system of double- and triple-shifts that many communities use to achieve fuller utilization of limited physical facilities. This implies civil works, to build new schools and expand/upgrade existing schools. Teachers will also need to be compensated for the additional hours required by reform of the school calendar.

If annual instructional hours go up by 40 percent, then annual teachers' salaries should go up by the same percentage (if not by a greater percentage, because of other measures taken to upgrade teacher qualifications and teacher effectiveness -- see below). So that policymakers in Vietnam do not become complacent in regard to the adequacy of the budget and to emphasize that there will continue to be difficult choices to face in the future, Figure 6.6 is presented to illustrate the impact on the projected E&T budget of implementing an increase in teachers' salaries by 40 percent in primary and secondary education. What had looked like a budget "cushion" in the outer years of the plan period disappears as a result of this one important policy to enhance quality. Instead of enjoying a budget cushion, policymakers in Vietnam would need to look for ways to finance a budgetary gap throughout most of the plan period. This might be made possible by increasing E&T's share of the State Budget, or by implementing the salary increase for teachers in phases. Inevitably, too, some choices will need to be made between this and other policy changes aimed at increasing equity or enhancing quality.

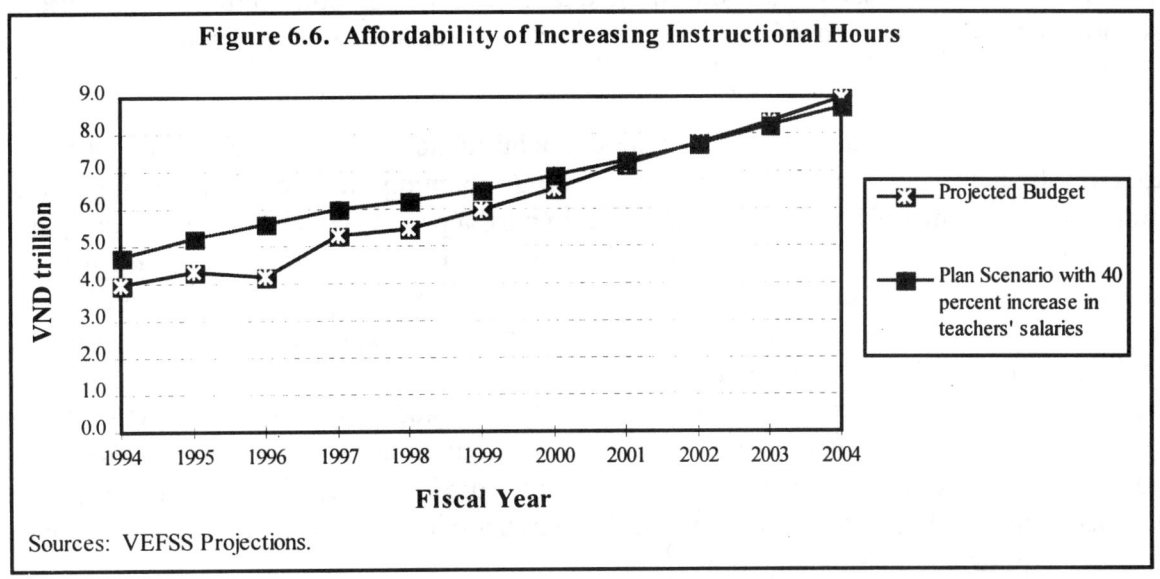

Figure 6.6. Affordability of Increasing Instructional Hours

Sources: VEFSS Projections.

To be fully "qualified," primary school teachers in Vietnam are expected to have graduated from a teacher training college. Only about two-thirds of those now teaching in primary education have actually received this training, and in some regions the proportion is far lower. In the Mekong River Delta, fewer than 40 percent of primary school teachers are fully qualified. Government may wish to consider a massive program of teacher upgrading. This should start with primary education where the problem of low qualifications is now the greatest and where the importance of good teaching is arguably the highest. Primary is the entry level of education that reaches the most children and provides the foundation for secondary and tertiary education. Even teachers who are qualified may be in need of refresher courses, to keep their skills and enthusiasm intact. This implies an expanded program of in-service teacher training. Teacher upgrading and regular in-service teacher training will require additional resources to cover the direct costs of the training and to support salary increments granted to teachers who receive training.

Non-salary inputs are also important factors in determining how much students learn at school. In basic education in Vietnam, despite low teacher salaries, non-salary inputs today account for only 20 percent of current budgetary allocations. In primary education, this only amounts to VND 26,000 (a little more than $2) per student per year. In lower secondary, this figure rises to VND 47,000, which is still too little to buy much in the way of pedagogical inputs. On average, at both levels of basic education, the family of a child enrolled in school currently spends more on textbooks and school supplies alone than Government spends on all non-salary inputs for that child. Given the critical importance of textbooks and other learning materials in the process of education, Government may wish to target some part of public spending specifically on these inputs -- if not for all school children, then at least for children in impoverished parts of the country. The present system loads most of the responsibility for the purchase of learning materials, and much of the responsibility for primary school construction, on families. This leads to inequitable results, as already discussed, since poor families cannot afford these costs, at least not in the quantities required both to maintain a child in school through to the end of basic education and to ensure the child's mastery of the curriculum.

Vietnam is a country that cares about social justice, and it is a country that wants to complete quickly the transition from central planning to a market economy and enhanced economic efficiency. Education is, in part, a private good, but it is, in part, also a social commodity, to the extent that education benefits all of society and not just the individual in whom it happens to be embodied. Education is properly seen, therefore, as a partnership between individual households striving to get ahead, and government looking out for the collective benefit of all of society. A balanced system is sought between one extreme that relies too heavily on households and an opposite extreme that relies too heavily on government. This balance requires constant review, and requires adjustment whenever the scales tip too far in either direction. This is the "art" of public finance, and a purpose of this study has been to assist education policymakers in Vietnam to make equitable and efficient choices.

ANNEXES

ANNEX A. REGIONS AND PROVINCES OF VIETNAM

Zone Region Province	Code[a]	Land Area (km²)	Population, 1994		GDP per Capita, 1994	
			People ('000)	Density (per km²)	('000 VND)	(US $)[b]
NORTH ZONE		**115,471**	**15,784**	**137**	**1,960**	**178**
Northern Uplands		**102,961**	**12,389**	**120**	**1,577**	**143**
Ha Giang	1	7,831	535	68	549	50
Tuyen Quang	2	5,801	645	111	1,010	92
Cao Bang	3	8,445	638	76	981	89
Lang Son	4	8,187	690	84	1,259	114
Bac Thai	5	6,503	1,168	180	1,830	166
Lao Cai[c]	6	8,050	552	69	0	0
Yen Bai	7	6,808	652	96	1,985	180
Lai Chau	8	17,133	521	30	1,414	129
Son La	9	14,210	802	56	796	72
Quang Ninh	10	5,938	900	151	2,919	265
Ha Bac	11	4,616	2,308	500	1,662	151
Vinh Phu	12	4,827	2,249	466	1,617	147
Hoa Binh	13	4,612	729	158	3,008	273
Red River Delta		**12,510**	**14,065**	**1,124**	**2,297**	**209**
Ha Noi	14	921	2,194	2,383	5,005	455
Hai Phong	15	1,503	1,615	1,075	2,995	272
Ha Tay	16	2,148	2,257	1,051	1,422	129
Hai Hung	17	2,550	2,709	1,062	1,891	172
Thai Binh	18	1,509	1,789	1,186	1,678	153
Nam Ha	19	2,492	2,640	1,060	1,534	139
Ninh Binh	20	1,387	861	621	1,276	116
CENTRAL ZONE		**152,449**	**20,283**	**133**	**1,621**	**147**
North Central		**51,174**	**9,726**	**190**	**1,490**	**135**
Thanh Hoa	21	11,168	3,382	303	1,521	138
Nghe An	22	16,371	2,743	168	1,411	128
Ha Tinh	23	6,054	1,309	216	1,278	116
Quang Binh	24	7,984	762	95	1,263	115
T.Thien Hue	25	5,009	995	199	2,097	191
Quang Tri	26	4,588	535	117	1,417	129
Central Coast		**45,192**	**7,558**	**167**	**1,753**	**159**
Quang Nam	27	11,985	1,953	163	1,988	181
Quang Ngai	28	5,177	1,179	228	1,156	105
Binh Đinh	29	6,076	1,407	232	1,386	126
Phu Yen	30	5,278	731	138	1,474	134
Khanh Hoa	31	5,257	947	180	2,707	246
Ninh Thuan	32	3,427	459	134	2,811	256
Binh Thuan	33	7,992	882	110	1,275	116

Zone Region Province	Code[a]	Land Area (km²)	Population, 1994		GDP per Capita, 1994	
			People ('000)	Density (per km²)	('000 VND)	(US $)[b]
Central Highlands		**56,083**	**2,999**	**53**	**1,715**	**156**
Gia Lai	34	16,212	763	47	1,161	106
Kon Tum	35	9,934	256	26	1,630	148
Dac Lac	36	19,800	1,211	61	1,983	180
Lam Dong	37	10,137	769	76	1,872	170
SOUTH ZONE		**63,035**	**24,729**	**392**	**3,459**	**314**
Southeast		**23,467**	**8,878**	**378**	**5,460**	**496**
TP H-C-Minh	38	2,090	4,392	2,101	6,477	589
Song Be	39	9,519	1,114	117	1,869	170
Tay Ninh	40	4,029	888	220	1,908	173
Dong Nai	41	5,864	1,813	309	2,908	264
Ba Ria-Vung Tau	42	1,965	671	341	16,359	1,487
Mekong River Delta		**39,568**	**15,851**	**401**	**2,338**	**217**
Long An	43	4,338	1,252	289	1,874	170
Dong Thap	44	3,276	1,491	455	3,304	300
An Giang	45	3,424	1,971	576	2,316	211
Tien Giang	46	2,339	1,656	708	2,039	185
Ben Tre	47	2,247	1,330	592	1,857	169
Vinh Long	48	1,487	1,062	714	2,117	192
Tra Vinh	49	2,369	958	404	2,040	185
Soc Trang	50	3,191	1,197	375	1,540	140
Can Tho	51	2,965	1,817	613	2,350	214
Kien Giang	52	6,243	1,360	218	3,757	342
Minh Hai	53	7,689	1,757	229	2,249	204
VIETNAM		**330,955**	**71,466**	**219**	**2,382**	**217**

[a] See map at the back of report.

[b] Exchange Rate (August 1994), US$1.00 = 11,000 VND

[c] GDP data for the Lao Cai province is unavailable.

Source: State Planning Committee and General Statistical Office.

ANNEX B. VEFSS -- A COLLABORATIVE AND PARTICIPATORY APPROACH

A substantial part of the effort and other resources that went into VEFSS were used to generate new information, as well as to cross-check publicly available statistics. Much of the data needed for a study of this kind is not routinely collected by any agency of government. Other statistics are ostensibly available, but access to information can be problematic, even for Vietnamese who work in government. By the time that official data are released to the public, the information may be out of date and of only limited value. Some indicators are the responsibility of more than one agency of government, but when data from different sources are compared, the numbers may differ because of different methodologies used. Informational problems of this kind are common in most developing countries, but they are particularly acute in Vietnam, which is still at an early stage of a program of reform that should lead eventually to greater openness, transparency and reliability.

To help address the issues of data availability, consistency and timeliness, the VEFSS team set up four inter-agency working groups, each focusing on one key topic: (1) E&T statistics, (2) public finance, (3) labor market linkages, and (4) private sector development. These counterpart working groups facilitated local information gathering and analysis, and they provided focal points for the Government's interaction and collaboration with VEFSS missions during the study's planning and preparation period. The working groups were managed by a senior-level steering committee chaired by the Ministry of Planning and Investment (MPI) and including members from the General Statistical Office (GSO), Ministry of Education and Training (MOET), Ministry of Finance (MOF) and Ministry of Labor, Invalids and Social Affairs (MOLISA).

In addition to this structure, VEFSS financed four special survey-based studies designed to supplement the information gathering activities of the working groups and fill key informational gaps. These were: (1) the Higher Education Institutional Finance Survey (HEIFS); (2) the Higher Education Graduate Tracer Study (HEGTS); (3) the Skill Development and Labor Market Study (SDLMS); and (4) the Rural Labor Markets and Vocational Training Study (RLMVTS).

HEIFS was a 1995 survey of the institutional costs of Vietnam's public colleges and universities in 1993-95 and of the sources of finance mobilized to meet these costs. The survey covers 100 institutions, practically all of the public higher education institutions in Vietnam in 1995. The survey was carried out by MOET. HEGTS was a retrospective tracer study of 946 individuals who graduated from the same 100 higher education institutions in 1990 and 878 who graduated in 1993. HEGTS was carried out by MOLISA's Institute of Labor Sciences and Social Affairs (ILSSA).

SDLMS was a study of VOTECH institutions and of the demand for VOTECH graduates in eight urban districts, two districts each in Hanoi and Ho Chi Minh City, and one each in Hai Phong, Da Nang, Quang Ninh and Can Tho. SDLMS comprised three inter-related surveys: (1) a survey of all training institutions in the eight districts; (2) a tracer survey of those who graduated from these institutions 12 months earlier; and (3) a survey of a random sample of small (10-50 employees), medium (51-100) and large (more than 100) enterprises that operate in the same eight districts and may hire graduates of the training institutions and/or provide training for workers on the job. Data collection took place between May and July of 1996 and was carried out by GSO. RLMVTS was a qualitative study of employment and training in three rural districts (one each in the Red River Delta, Central Highlands, and Mekong Delta Regions). RLMVTS was carried out by MOLISA's Center for Population and Human Resources Studies (CPHRS), in collaboration with researchers from the French Research Institute for Development Cooperation (ORSTOM) and the University of Geneva.

Given the success of the VEFSS Working Groups and VEFSS Steering Committee in bridging the bureaucratic barriers that divide government agencies in Vietnam (as in many other countries), the World Bank hopes that the ad hoc VEFSS structure will remain intact at least through the end of the period of VEFSS dissemination and, to the extent that it may serve some purpose, into the future. As an example, the Working Group on Labor Market Linkages should continue to play an important role in coordinating activities for collecting and analyzing labor market information, including further tracer studies to assess the employment experience and earnings of graduates of VOTECH and higher education institutions. This option has been recommended and discussed with MOLISA, the lead agency for the working group, by the Hanoi based representative of Swiss Development Cooperation (SDC), which co-financed VEFSS and supports VOTECH in Vietnam.

VEFSS has been a collaborative effort between Government and several external partners. In addition to the World Bank's role in leading the study and making financing available, the completion of VEFSS reflects significant co-financing from SDC. In addition, the following agencies donated invaluable technical expertise in support of VEFSS: the East Asia Multidisciplinary Advisory Team (EASMAT) of the International Labour Office (ILO) based in Bangkok, Thailand; the Australian Department of Employment, Education, Training and Youth Affairs (DEETYA); the Australian Bureau of Statistics (ABS); and L'Institut Français de Recherche Scientifique pour le Dévelopement en Coopération (ORSTOM).

The core VEFSS team consisted of the following World Bank staff: *Peter Moock* (Principal Economist), team leader and principal author of the report; *Nicholas Prescott* (Senior Human Resources Economist), who focused on public finance issues; and *Harry Patrinos* (Human Resources Economist), who focused on labor market issues including the design of HEGTS and SDLMS. *Rapti Goonesekere* (World Bank Consultant) provided general research support and focused on the development of private sector education and training.

From the International Institute of Educational Planning in Paris, *Ta Ngoc Chau* (World Bank consultant) focused on student flows and other indicators of E&T performance, and he provided training on statistical methods for staff in MOET while on mission to Vietnam. *Trevor Riordan* from EASMAT, *Ivan Neville* from DEETYA, and *Richard Phillips* from ABS participated in at least one VEFSS mission each and contributed especially to planning the survey instruments and the analytic frameworks for SDLMS and HEGTS. *Christos Sakellariou* (World Bank consultant), lecturer in economics at the Nanyang Technological University in Singapore, contributed to the data processing and the analysis of both SDLMS and HEGTS. *Maureen Woodhall* from the University of Wales, *Nguyen X. Nguyen* and *Shobhana Sosale* (World Bank consultants) participated in missions fielded jointly by VEFSS and by the team responsible for preparation of a proposed World Bank-financed Higher Education Consolidation and Reform Project (HECRP) in Vietnam. Ms. Woodhall and Mr. Nguyen wrote background papers based on HEIFS, and they provided training on institutional cost analysis for MOET staff. Ms. Sosale worked on both HEIFS and HEGTS, and she wrote background papers on the higher education student loan scheme and on the financial operations of the public higher education institutions.

Jean-Luc Maurer and *Michel Carton* (SDC consultants from l'Institut Universitaire d'Etudes du Dévelopement at the University of Geneva) and *Jean-Yves Martin* and *Xavier Oudin* (ORSTOM researchers on extended assignments with the Center for Population and Human Resources Studies in Vietnam) worked on the design and the analysis of the rural labor markets study (RLMVTS). *Pham Thanh Nghi* (World Bank consultant), on leave from MOET's National Institute for Educational Development and currently a graduate student at the University of New England in Australia, contributed a background paper on policies and regulations for nonpublic education (Nghi 1996). *Paul Glewwe* (World Bank, Senior Economist) co-authored a background paper with Harry Patrinos comparing the performance of public and non-public education.

William McCleary (EA1 Lead Economist) and *Sven Burmester* (EA1HR Division Chief) in the World Bank provided excellent guidance and supervision for the study. *Elizabeth King, George Psacharopoulos,* and *James Socknat* were the designated Peer Reviewers, who commented on the study concept paper and on drafts of the report. *Bradley Babson, Concepcion Del Castillo, David Dollar, Thomas Eisemon, Marea Fatseas, Daniela Gressani, Keith Hinchliffe, Donna Haldane, Dean Jamison, Kathryn Johnston, Georges Capt, Jennifer Litvack, Ulrich Lütz, Victoria Kwakwa, Benoit Millot, Kyle Peters, Carol Priestley, Christopher Shaw, Jayasankar Shivakumar, John Shilling, David Steedman, Sachi Takeda, Christopher Thomas* and *Zafiris Tzannatos* provided valuable comments at different stages.

ANNEX C. RATES OF RETURN FOR WAGE WORKERS BASED ON ESTIMATIONS OF THE HUMAN CAPITAL EARNINGS FUNCTION

BASIC MODEL -- SCHOOLING ENTERED AS CONTINUOUS VARIABLE

The specification of the basic human capital earnings function (HCEF) is given in Equation (5.3) above. It is reproduced here as Equation (C.1):

$$(C.1) \qquad \ln Y_i = \alpha + \beta S_i + \gamma EXP_i + \phi EXP^2_i + \varepsilon_i$$

Earnings function results based on this model are presented in Table 5.1.1. When the earnings function is estimated for all workers in the VLSS sample, the estimate of the private rate of return to an additional year of schooling is about 5 percent (*column 1*, coefficient on *years of schooling*).

Table C.1.   Earnings Function Results Estimated for All Workers and Separately by Sex, Sector and Age

Variable	(1) All	(2) Males	(3) Females	(4) Public	(5) Private	(6) 0-5 years	(7) 6+ years
Constant	0.775	1.045	0.583	0.265	1.168	0.217	0.792
Years of schooling	0.048	0.034	0.068	0.062	0.039	0.144	0.044
	(8.4)	(4.5)	(7.6)	(6.3)	(4.0)	(5.9)	(7.5)
Years of experience	0.064	0.059	0.065	0.046	0.072	0.204	0.055
	(10.1)	(6.9)	(6.8)	(4.4)	(8.4)	(1.3)*	(6.5)
Experience squared	-0.001	-0.001	-0.001	-0.001	-0.001	0.006	-0.001
	(8.3)	(5.6)	(5.5)	(3.3)	(7.3)	(0.2)*	(5.9)
Ln of hours worked	0.726	0.722	0.697	0.878	0.617	0.489	0.759
	(11.7)	(9.1)	(7.1)	(10.5)	(6.7)	(2.6)	(11.7)
R-squared	0.112	0.095	0.137	0.145	0.085	0.138	0.103
Number of observations	2,259	1,355	904	950	1,309	328	1,931

: The dependent variable is the natural logarithm of monthly earnings; *t*-statistics are given in parentheses.

All coefficients are significant at the 5 percent level except where indicated by asterisks (*).

Source: VLSS 1992-93.

Men and Women

When earnings functions are estimated separately, however, for men and women (*columns 3 and 4*), one finds that men realize a lower rate of return to investments in education than do their female counterparts, even though men in Vietnam earn more at every education level than women. Women invest less when they go to school, because their opportunity costs (foregone earnings) are smaller, but they realize a higher return on their investment. Women earn 7 percent more for each additional year of schooling, whereas men earn just 3 percent more. A similar pattern was reported for China in the mid-1980s (Jamison and van der Gaag 1987).

Public and Private Sector Workers

Comparing workers in the public and private sectors, those in the public sector realize a higher rate of return on investments in education than do those in the private (*columns 5 and 6*). This is surprising. When this finding is pursued in a disaggregated analysis of returns to schooling at different levels (see Table C.3 below), one finds that the private sector rewards primary education (as compared with not having gone to school) and secondary education (as compared with primary education) about equally. The public sector, on the other hand, does not reward primary education at all, and it rewards secondary, VOTECH, and especially tertiary education quite handsomely -- perhaps more than warranted by differences in productivity.

Younger and Older Workers

A cross-sectional sample of workers and their earnings is most useful for analyzing earnings in a stable economy, where earnings differences do not change dramatically from one period to the next. Conversely, cross-sectional information could be misleading in a highly dynamic and rapidly changing situation such as exists in Vietnam. To get some sense of how new entrants to the labor market have fared relative to those who started working prior to the start of the economic reform program, the sample is divided into two groups -- those with less than six years of work experience and those with more experience than this. Younger workers, who entered directly into a free-market wage economy, are expected to be more affected by the recent reforms. Indeed, those with fewer years of labor market experience receive higher returns to schooling, 14 percent as compared with 4 percent for the more experienced workers (Table 5.1.1, *columns 6 and 7*). In China, too, the returns to schooling are found to be higher for younger workers.[1]

North and South

Evidence of low returns to schooling based on recent earnings information is not surprising. Ronnås' study (1992) of private enterprises in Vietnam suggests a negative correlation between education and earnings nationwide. This may reflect some anomalous regional differences in education and earnings levels. Educational attainment is higher in the North of Vietnam than in the South, but wage levels are higher in the South. Ronnås argues that the earnings differences can be explained by the higher ratio of capital to labor in the South. The VLSS data confirm the pattern of schooling and earnings reported by Ronnås (see Figure C.1). On average, workers in the North possessed 9.6 years of schooling, while those in the South only 6.9, but workers in the South earned 94 percent more than workers in the North in 1992-93 (VND 182,495 versus VND 94,174 per month).

---

[1] This finding is based on new earnings functions estimated by the VEFSS team using 1989 data for urban Chinese workers supplied to VEFSS by Yu Xie at the University of Michigan.

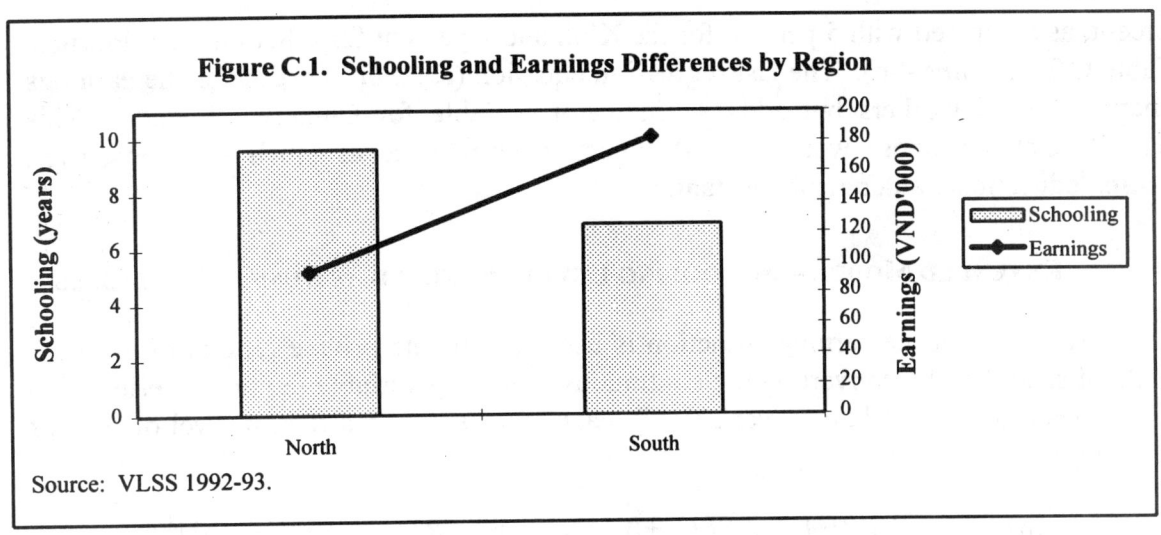

Figure C.1. Schooling and Earnings Differences by Region

Source: VLSS 1992-93.

Estimating earnings functions separately for workers in the North and the South shows rates of return to schooling that are similar -- about 8 percent (Table 5.1.2, *columns 2 and 3*). Experience, however, was rewarded more in the South. The earnings of young workers in the South rose nearly 8 percent a year. This increment declined gradually over time, disappearing altogether after about 40 years of work. In the North, the increments were only about half as large, and faded sooner.

Table C.2.   Earnings Function Results by Region and Ethnicity

Variable	North	South	Vietnamese (Kinh)	Chinese (Hoa)	Ethnic minorities other than Hoa	All workers
Constant	0.515	0.782	0.953	1.296	-0.286	0.83
Years of schooling	0.082	0.078	0.052	0.06	0.04	0.054
	(6.8)	(12.0)	(8.3)	(2.4)	(1.8)	(9.4)
Years of experience	0.041	0.078	0.063	0.023*	0.086	0.063
	(4.1)	(10.2)	(9.5)	(1.0)	(3.0)	(10.0)
Experience squared	-0.001	-0.001	-0.001	0.000*	-0.002	-0.001
	(3.0)	(8.5)	(7.6)	(0.2)	(2.8)	(8.1)
Ln of hours worked	0.639	0.698	0.661	0.896	0.912	0.69
	(6.7)	(9.4)	(10.2)	(3.5)	(3.8)	(11.3)
Chinese (0,1)						1.027
						(9.6)
R-squared	0.113	0.177	0.111	0.165	0.138	0.147
Number of observations	788	1,471	2,008	105	146	2,259

Note : The dependent variable is the natural logarithm of monthly earnings; t-statistics are given in parenthesis.

   All coefficients are significant at the 5 percent level except where indicated by asterisks(*).

Source: VLSS 1992-93.

Ethnicity

Although the Chinese (Hoa) had received slightly less education than the national average, they realized a slightly higher return on each year of education completed -- 6 percent, as compared with 5 percent for the Kinh and 4 percent for other ethnic minorities (Table C.2, *columns 4-6*). The last regression equation (*column 7*) estimates the earnings function for all workers but adds an indicator variable for Chinese ethnicity. This suggests that a Chinese worker could expect to earn twice as much as others, even holding educational attainment constant.

EXTENDED MODEL -- SCHOOLING LEVELS ENTERED AS DUMMY VARIABLES

A variant of the earnings function is used to estimate private returns to different levels of schooling by converting the continuous schooling variable (S) into a series of 0-1 variables (known as "dummy variables"), each representing a different level or type of schooling:[2]

$$(C.2) \qquad \ln Y_i = \alpha + \beta_p PRIM_i + \beta_s SEC_i + \beta_v VOC_i + \beta_t TERT_i + \gamma_1 EXP_i + \gamma_2 EXP^2_i + \varepsilon_i$$

After estimating the extended earnings function, the private rates of return (r_i) to different levels/types of schooling (i) are derived from equations (3) - (4):

$$(C.3) \qquad r_p \quad = \quad \beta_p / S_p,$$

$$(C.4) \qquad r_s \quad = \quad \beta_s / S_s,$$

$$(C.5) \qquad r_v \quad = \quad \beta_v / S_v$$

$$(C.6) \qquad r_t \quad = \quad \beta_t / S_t$$

where S_p, S_s, S_v and S_t are the number of years of earnings foregone, respectively, by a primary, secondary, VOTECH and tertiary education student, assumed here to be 1, 7, 5 and 4 years.

The HCEF estimates and the rates of return to different levels/types of education computed from the HCEF estimates are presented in Tables 5.1.3 and 5.1.4. The results are consistent with predictions, except that the primary education coefficient for male workers is not statistically significant. Primary education tended to be a good private investment, but especially if one was female or ended up working in the private sector. For workers in the public sector, it appears that those who had not completed primary education or had never attended school earned more than others who had entered the labor force after completing primary. The VLSS data set suggests that secondary

---

[2] The dummy variables for schooling in this study are created as sequential dummy variables. In other words, a household head who never completed primary education scores a 0 on all four variables. A head who completed primary scores a 1 on the primary variable and 0's on the other three. A head who completed secondary education scores 1's on the primary and secondary variables and 0's on the other two. A head who attended VOTECH scores 1's on the primary and VOTECH variables and 0's on the other two. A head who completed tertiary education scores 1's on all four dummy variables.

education and VOTECH were middling private investments, but tertiary was a good investment, nearly as good as primary.

Table C.3.   Results of Earnings Functions with Schooling Entered as Dummy Variables

Variable	(1) All	(2) Males	(3) Females	(4) Public	(5) Private
Constant	0.870	1.181	0.617	0.845	1.220
Primary	0.134	0.035*	0.214	-0.278	0.233
	(2.2)	(0.5)	(2.3)	(2.0)	(3.2)
Secondary	0.325	0.269	0.423	0.404	0.260
	(3.8)	(2.4)	(3.1)	(3.7)	(1.9)
VOTECH	0.207	0.240	0.259	0.276	---
	(2.8)	(2.3)	(2.4)	(3.4)	
Tertiary	0.437	0.414	0.488	0.429	---
	(3.8)	(2.8)	(2.7)	(3.5)	
Years of experience	0.064	0.057	0.066	0.053	0.072
	(9.9)	(6.6)	(6.7)	(5.1)	(8.3)
Experience squared	-0.001	-0.001	-0.001	-0.001	-0.001
	(8.4)	(5.5)	(5.8)	(4.2)	(7.3)
Ln of hours worked	0.750	0.732	0.751	0.888	0.618
	(12.1)	(9.3)	(7.5)	(10.8)	(6.8)
R-squared	0.124	0.111	0.142	0.179	0.087
Number of observations	2,259	1,355	904	950	1,309

Note : The dependent variable is the natural logarithm of monthly ernings; t-statistics are given in Parenthesis.
All coefficients are significant at the 5 percent level except where indicated by asterisks(*)

Source: VLSS 1992-93.

Table C.4. Rates of Return by Level of Education Based on Dummy Variable Results

Level of Education	All	Males	Females	Public	Private
Primary (vs less than primary)	13	...	21	Negative	23
Secondary (vs primary)	5	4	6	6	4
VOTECH (vs primary)	4	5	5	6	--
Tertiary (vs secondary)	11	10	12	11	--

...= Positive but not statistically significant.

--= Not estimated -- too few observations.

Source: VLSS 1992-93.

ANNEX D. MODEL OF ENROLLMENT PROJECTIONS AND FISCAL AFFORDABILITY

Table D.1: Macro/Fiscal Projections (base case)

	1994	1995	1996	1997	1998	1999	2000	2001	2002	2003	2004
Nominal aggregates (in VND billions)											
GDP	170,258	222,840	265,037	311,970	362,264	420,522	487,880	560,827	644,796	741,052	851,736
Government expenditure:											
current	29,992	38,774	40,816	55,531	60,860	70,648	81,964	94,219	107,036	120,791	136,278
capital	11,300	12,702	15,902	23,398	30,792	35,744	41,470	47,670	58,032	66,695	80,915
Interest payments:											
cash	2,915	2,962	4,506	4,506	4,506	4,506	4,506	4,506	4,506	4,506	4,506
accrual	4,275	2,962									
Private consumption	122,926	158,439	185,526	215,571	249,238	287,637	328,487	375,137	428,414	489,256	558,739
Real aggregates (in VND billions; at constant 1989 prices)											
GDP	39,982	43,799	47,967	52,522	57,537	63,009	68,964	75,500	82,660	90,488	99,051
GDP deflator	426	509	553	594	630	667	707	743	780	819	860
GDP growth (%)	9.5	9.5	9.5	9.5	9.5	9.5	9.5	9.5	9.5	9.5	43.6
Private consumption	28,867	31,141	33,577	36,293	39,585	43,098	46,786	50,790	55,137	59,855	64,977
Interest	1,004	582	-	-	-	-	-	-	-	-	-
Real aggregates (in VND billions; at constant 1994 prices)											
GDP	170,258	186,512	204,261	223,658	245,014	268,315	293,674	321,507	351,997	385,331	421,795
GDP deflator	100	119	130	139	148	157	166	174	183	192	202
Private consumption	122,926	132,610	142,983	154,548	168,569	183,528	199,234	216,283	234,792	254,885	276,698
Per capita con. (VND)	1,694,834	1,792,514	1,894,815	2,011,553	2,151,492	2,298,694	2,448,790	2,608,653	2,779,267	2,960,685	3,154,330
GDP shares (%)											
Private consumption	72.2	71.1	70.0	69.1	68.8	68.4					65.6
Government expenditure:											
current (exc. interest)	17.6	17.4	15.4	17.8	16.8	16.8	16.8	16.8	16.6	16.3	16.0
capital	6.6	5.7	6.0	7.5	8.5	8.5	8.5	8.5	9.0	9.0	9.5
Memo:											
Population (millions)	72.53	73.98	75.46	76.83	78.35	79.84	81.36	82.91	84.48	86.09	87.72
CRNI	2.2	2.0	2.0	1.9	1.9	1.9	1.9	1.9	1.9	1.9	1.9

Source: MOF and VEFSS Team

Table D.2: Functional Allocation of General Government Expenditure
(in billions of VND at current prices)

	1994	1995	1996	1997	1998	1999	2000	2001	2002	2003	2004
Current expenditure	32,907	41,736	45,321	60,036	65,366	75,153	86,469	98,725	111,542	125,297	140,783
Interest payments	2,915	2,962	4,506	4,506	4,506	4,506	4,506	4,506	4,506	4,506	4,506
Discretionary current	**29,992**	**38,774**	**40,816**	**55,531**	**60,860**	**70,648**	**81,964**	**94,219**	**107,036**	**120,791**	**136,278**
Administration	4,779	6,178	6,504	8,848	9,698	11,257	13,060	15,013	17,055	19,247	21,715
Economic services	3,085	3,988	4,198	5,712	6,260	7,267	8,431	9,691	11,010	12,425	14,018
energy	-	-	-	-	-	-	-	-	-	-	-
agriculture	-	-	-	-	-	-	-	-	-	-	-
irrigation	-	-	-	-	-	-	-	-	-	-	-
forestry	-	-	-	-	-	-	-	-	-	-	-
transportation	-	-	-	-	-	-	-	-	-	-	-
other	-	-	-	-	-	-	-	-	-	-	-
Social services	14,042	18,154	19,110	25,999	28,494	33,077	38,375	44,113	50,113	56,554	63,804
health	2,214	2,862	3,013	4,099	4,493	5,215	6,051	6,955	7,901	8,917	10,060
education & training	3,978	5,143	5,414	7,365	8,072	9,370	10,871	12,497	14,197	16,021	18,075
pensions & social relief	5,861	7,577	7,976	10,852	11,893	13,806	16,017	18,412	20,917	23,605	26,631
other social services	1,989	2,571	2,707	3,683	4,036	4,685	5,436	6,248	7,098	8,011	9,038
Other current	8,086	10,454	11,004	14,971	16,408	19,047	22,098	25,402	28,858	32,566	36,741
Capital expenditure	**11,300**	**12,702**	**15,902**	**23,398**	**30,792**	**35,744**	**41,470**	**47,670**	**58,032**	**66,695**	**80,915**
Education & training	1,033	1,162	1,454	2,140	2,816	3,269	3,793	4,360	5,307	6,099	7,400
Industry/construction	2,925	3,288	4,116	6,056	7,971	9,252	10,734	12,339	15,021	17,264	20,945
Agriculture and forestry	580	652	816	1,201	1,580	1,835	2,129	2,447	2,979	3,423	4,153
Irrigation	1,240	1,394	1,745	2,568	3,379	3,922	4,551	5,231	6,368	7,319	8,879
Transport	2,999	3,371	4,220	6,210	8,172	9,486	11,006	12,652	15,401	17,701	21,475
Commerce & services	35	39	49	72	95	111	128	148	180	207	251
Other capital	2,488	2,796	3,501	5,151	6,779	7,869	9,129	10,494	12,775	14,682	17,813
Consolidated expenditure	**44,207**	**54,438**	**61,224**	**83,434**	**96,158**	**110,898**	**127,939**	**146,395**	**169,573**	**191,992**	**221,698**
Discretionary expenditure	**41,292**	**51,476**	**56,718**	**78,928**	**91,653**	**106,392**	**123,434**	**141,889**	**165,068**	**187,486**	**217,193**

Source: MOF and VEFSS Team

Table D.3: Sector Shares of General Government Expenditure
(in percent)

	1994	1995	1996	1997	1998	1999	2000	2001	2002	2003	2004
As % of discretionary current expenditure:											
Current expenditure	109.72	107.64	111.04	108.11	107.40	106.38	105.50	104.78	104.21	103.73	103.31
Interest payments	9.72	7.64	11.04	8.11	7.40	6.38	5.50	4.78	4.21	3.73	3.31
Discretionary current	100.00	100.00	100.00	100.00	100.00	100.00	100.00	100.00	100.00	100.00	100.00
Administration	15.93	15.93	15.93	15.93	15.93	15.93	15.93	15.93	15.93	15.93	15.93
Economic services	10.29	10.29	10.29	10.29	10.29	10.29	10.29	10.29	10.29	10.29	10.29
energy	0.00	0.00	0.00	0.00	0.00	0.00	0.00	0.00	0.00	0.00	0.00
agriculture	0.00	0.00	0.00	0.00	0.00	0.00	0.00	0.00	0.00	0.00	0.00
irrigation	0.00	0.00	0.00	0.00	0.00	0.00	0.00	0.00	0.00	0.00	0.00
forestry	0.00	0.00	0.00	0.00	0.00	0.00	0.00	0.00	0.00	0.00	0.00
transportation	0.00	0.00	0.00	0.00	0.00	0.00	0.00	0.00	0.00	0.00	0.00
other	0.00	0.00	0.00	0.00	0.00	0.00	0.00	0.00	0.00	0.00	0.00
Social services	46.82	46.82	46.82	46.82	46.82	46.82	46.82	46.82	46.82	46.82	46.82
health	7.38	7.38	7.38	7.38	7.38	7.38	7.38	7.38	7.38	7.38	7.38
education & training	13.26	13.26	13.26	13.26	13.26	13.26	13.26	13.26	13.26	13.26	13.26
pensions & social relief	19.54	19.54	19.54	19.54	19.54	19.54	19.54	19.54	19.54	19.54	19.54
other social services	6.63	6.63	6.63	6.63	6.63	6.63	6.63	6.63	6.63	6.63	6.63
Other current	26.96	26.96	26.96	26.96	26.96	26.96	26.96	26.96	26.96	26.96	26.96
Discretionary current	37.68	37.68	37.68	37.68	37.68	37.68	37.68	37.68	37.68	37.68	37.68
Interest	3.45	3.45	3.45	3.45	3.45	3.45	3.45	3.45	3.45	3.45	3.45
As percent of capital expenditure:											
Capital expenditure	100.00	100.00	100.00	100.00	100.00	100.00	100.00	100.00	100.00	100.00	100.00
Education and Training	9.15	9.15	9.15	9.15	9.15	9.15	9.15	9.15	9.15	9.15	9.15
Industry	25.88	25.88	25.88	25.88	25.88	25.88	25.88	25.88	25.88	25.88	25.88
Agriculture	5.13	5.13	5.13	5.13	5.13	5.13	5.13	5.13	5.13	5.13	5.13
Irrigation	10.97	10.97	10.97	10.97	10.97	10.97	10.97	10.97	10.97	10.97	10.97
Transport	26.54	26.54	26.54	26.54	26.54	26.54	26.54	26.54	26.54	26.54	26.54
Commerce & services	0.31	0.31	0.31	0.31	0.31	0.31	0.31	0.31	0.31	0.31	0.31
Other capital											

Source: MOF and VEFSS Team

Table D.4: Program Shares on Expenditure on Education and Training
(in percent)

	1994	1995	1996	1997	1998	1999	2000	2001	2002	2003	2004
Current expenditure	100.00	100.00	100.00	100.00	100.00	100.00	100.00	100.00	100.00	100.00	100.00
Education	77.39	77.39	77.39	77.39	77.39	77.39	77.39	77.39	77.39	77.39	77.39
pre-school	4.91	4.91	4.91	4.91	4.91	4.91	4.91	4.91	4.91	4.91	4.91
primary	32.41	32.41	32.41	32.41	32.41	32.41	32.41	32.41	32.41	32.41	32.41
lower secondary	19.15	19.15	19.15	19.15	19.15	19.15	19.15	19.15	19.15	19.15	19.15
upper secondary	7.86	7.86	7.86	7.86	7.86	7.86	7.86	7.86	7.86	7.86	7.86
other	13.05	13.05	13.05	13.05	13.05	13.05	13.05	13.05	13.05	13.05	13.05
Training	22.61	22.61	22.61	22.61	22.61	22.61	22.61	22.61	22.61	22.61	22.61
vocational	3.36	3.36	3.36	3.36	3.36	3.36	3.36	3.36	3.36	3.36	3.36
technical	5.43	5.43	5.43	5.43	5.43	5.43	5.43	5.43	5.43	5.43	5.43
university/college	10.11	10.11	10.11	10.11	10.11	10.11	10.11	10.11	10.11	10.11	10.11
postgraduate	0.69	0.69	0.69	0.69	0.69	0.69	0.69	0.69	0.69	0.69	0.69
other	3.02	3.02	3.02	3.02	3.02	3.02	3.02	3.02	3.02	3.02	3.02
Capital expenditure	100.00	100.00	100.00	100.00	100.00	100.00	100.00	100.00	100.00	100.00	100.00
Education	53.78	53.78	53.78	53.78	53.78	53.78	53.78	53.78	53.78	53.78	53.78
pre-school	3.09	3.09	3.09	3.09	3.09	3.09	3.09	3.09	3.09	3.09	3.09
primary	18.86	18.86	18.86	18.86	18.86	18.86	18.86	18.86	18.86	18.86	18.86
lower secondary	11.96	11.96	11.96	11.96	11.96	11.96	11.96	11.96	11.96	11.96	11.96
upper secondary	11.56	11.56	11.56	11.56	11.56	11.56	11.56	11.56	11.56	11.56	11.56
other	8.30	8.30	8.30	8.30	8.30	8.30	8.30	8.30	8.30	8.30	8.30
Training	46.22	46.22	46.22	46.22	46.22	46.22	46.22	46.22	46.22	46.22	46.22
vocational	11.25	11.25	11.25	11.25	11.25	11.25	11.25	11.25	11.25	11.25	11.25
technical	9.07	9.07	9.07	9.07	9.07	9.07	9.07	9.07	9.07	9.07	9.07
university/college	18.28	18.28	18.28	18.28	18.28	18.28	18.28	18.28	18.28	18.28	18.28
postgraduate	0.76	0.76	0.76	0.76	0.76	0.76	0.76	0.76	0.76	0.76	0.76
other	6.86	6.86	6.86	6.86	6.86	6.86	6.86	6.86	6.86	6.86	6.86
Consolidated expenditure	100.00	100.00	100.00	100.00	100.00	100.00	100.00	100.00	100.00	100.00	100.00
Education	72.52	72.52	72.52	72.52	72.52	72.52	72.52	72.52	72.52	72.52	72.52
pre-school	4.54	4.54	4.54	4.54	4.54	4.54	4.54	4.54	4.54	4.54	4.54
primary	29.61	29.61	29.61	29.61	29.61	29.61	29.61	29.61	29.61	29.61	29.61
lower secondary	17.67	17.67	17.67	17.67	17.67	17.67	17.67	17.67	17.67	17.67	17.67
upper secondary	8.63	8.63	8.63	8.63	8.63	8.63	8.63	8.63	8.63	8.63	8.63

other	12.07	12.07	12.07	12.07	12.07	12.07	12.07	12.07	12.07
Training	27.48	27.48	27.48	27.48	27.48	27.48	27.48	27.48	27.48
vocational	4.99	4.99	4.99	4.99	4.99	4.99	4.99	4.99	4.99
technical	6.18	6.18	6.18	6.18	6.18	6.18	6.18	6.18	6.18
university/college	11.80	11.80	11.80	11.80	11.80	11.80	11.80	11.80	11.80
postgraduate	0.70	0.70	0.70	0.70	0.70	0.70	0.70	0.70	0.70
other	3.81	3.81	3.81	3.81	3.81	3.81	3.81	3.81	3.81

Source: MOF and VEFSS Team

Table D.5: Functional Allocation of Expenditure on Education and Training
(in millions of VND at current prices)

	1994	1995	1996	1997	1998	1999	2000	2001	2002	2003	2004
Current expenditure	3,977,673	5,142,825	5,413,605	7,365,330	8,072,235	9,370,383	10,871,304	12,496,763	14,196,777	16,021,222	18,075,251
Education	3,078,425	3,980,167	4,189,730	5,700,221	6,247,314	7,251,984	8,413,586	9,671,571	10,987,257	12,399,242	13,988,909
pre-school	195,306	252,516	265,811	361,642	396,351	460,091	533,787	613,598	697,070	786,651	887,505
primary	1,289,167	1,666,794	1,754,554	2,387,109	2,616,218	3,036,949	3,523,398	4,050,211	4,601,187	5,192,491	5,858,203
lower secondary	761,916	985,099	1,036,966	1,410,815	1,546,222	1,794,880	2,082,378	2,393,732	2,719,367	3,068,836	3,462,281
upper secondary	312,825	404,459	425,754	579,248	634,843	736,936	854,976	982,811	1,116,509	1,259,993	1,421,532
other	519,211	671,300	706,645	961,406	1,053,680	1,223,129	1,419,046	1,631,219	1,853,124	2,091,272	2,359,387
Training	899,248	1,162,658	1,223,875	1,665,109	1,824,922	2,118,399	2,457,718	2,825,192	3,209,521	3,621,980	4,086,342
vocational	133,673	172,829	181,929	247,518	271,274	314,900	365,339	419,964	477,094	538,406	607,434
technical	215,891	279,130	293,827	399,758	438,126	508,584	590,048	678,271	770,540	869,563	981,047
university/college	402,244	520,071	547,453	744,822	816,308	947,584	1,099,366	1,263,741	1,435,656	1,620,153	1,827,868
postgraduate	27,474	35,522	37,392	50,873	55,755	64,722	75,089	86,316	98,058	110,659	124,847
other	119,966	155,107	163,273	222,137	243,457	282,609	327,877	376,900	428,173	483,198	545,147
Capital expenditure	1,033,430	1,161,638	1,454,321	2,139,817	2,816,091	3,268,965	3,792,578	4,359,638	5,307,225	6,099,494	7,399,992
Education	555,733	624,677	782,070	1,150,699	1,514,369	1,757,905	2,039,481	2,344,421	2,853,991	3,280,038	3,979,389
pre-school	31,952	35,916	44,965	66,160	87,069	101,071	117,260	134,793	164,091	188,587	228,796
primary	194,863	219,038	274,226	403,483	531,001	616,394	715,127	822,051	1,000,727	1,150,117	1,395,338
lower secondary	123,624	138,961	173,973	255,976	336,875	391,050	453,687	521,521	634,876	729,652	885,224
upper secondary	119,514	134,341	168,189	247,465	325,675	378,049	438,604	504,183	613,769	705,394	855,793
other	85,780	96,422	120,716	177,616	233,750	271,341	314,803	361,872	440,527	506,289	614,237
Training	477,697	536,960	672,252	989,118	1,301,722	1,511,060	1,753,097	2,015,217	2,453,234	2,819,456	3,420,603
vocational	116,295	130,723	163,659	240,800	316,903	367,867	426,790	490,603	597,238	686,394	832,743
technical	93,726	105,354	131,898	194,069	255,403	296,476	343,964	395,393	481,334	553,188	671,136
university/college	188,936	212,375	265,885	391,210	514,850	597,646	693,375	797,047	970,289	1,115,135	1,352,897
postgraduate	7,821	8,791	11,006	16,194	21,312	24,740	28,702	32,994	40,165	46,161	56,003
other	70,919	79,717	99,803	146,845	193,254	224,332	260,265	299,180	364,208	418,577	507,823
Consolidated expenditure	5,011,103	6,304,463	6,867,927	9,505,147	10,888,327	12,639,348	14,663,883	16,856,402	19,504,002	22,120,716	25,475,243
Education	3,634,158	4,604,844	4,971,800	6,850,920	7,761,683	9,009,889	10,453,067	12,015,992	13,841,248	15,679,281	17,968,297
pre-school	227,258	288,432	310,776	427,802	483,420	561,162	651,048	748,391	861,161	975,238	1,116,301
primary	1,484,030	1,885,831	2,028,780	2,790,592	3,147,219	3,653,343	4,238,525	4,872,262	5,601,914	6,342,608	7,253,542
lower secondary	885,540	1,124,060	1,210,939	1,666,791	1,883,097	2,185,930	2,536,065	2,915,254	3,354,243	3,798,487	4,347,505
upper secondary	432,339	538,800	593,943	826,713	960,518	1,114,985	1,293,580	1,486,994	1,730,278	1,965,386	2,277,326

other	604,991	767,722	827,361	1,139,022	1,287,430	1,494,470	1,733,849	1,993,092	2,293,651	2,597,561	2,973,624
Training	1,376,945	1,699,619	1,896,126	2,654,227	3,126,643	3,629,459	4,210,815	4,840,409	5,662,754	6,441,436	7,506,945
vocational	249,968	303,551	345,588	488,318	588,177	682,766	792,129	910,567	1,074,332	1,224,801	1,440,177
technical	309,617	384,484	425,726	593,827	693,529	805,060	934,012	1,073,664	1,251,874	1,422,751	1,652,183
university/college	591,180	732,446	813,338	1,136,033	1,331,158	1,545,230	1,792,741	2,060,788	2,405,945	2,735,288	3,180,765
postgraduate	35,295	44,313	48,398	67,067	77,068	89,461	103,791	119,310	138,223	156,820	180,850
other	190,885	234,824	263,076	368,982	436,711	506,942	588,142	676,080	792,380	901,775	1,052,970

Source: MOF and VEFSS Team

Table D.6: Projected Public Sector Budget Constraint for Education and Training

(in VND millions; at constant 1994 prices)

	1994	1995	1996	1997	1998	1999	2000	2001	2002	2003	2004
Current expenditure	3,977,673	4,304,432	4,172,205	5,280,361	5,459,575	5,978,803	6,543,861	7,164,050	7,750,074	8,330,690	8,951,199
Education	3,078,425	3,331,312	3,228,978	4,086,609	4,225,308	4,627,152	5,064,465	5,544,445	5,997,985	6,447,338	6,927,567
pre-school	195,306	211,350	204,858	259,269	268,068	293,563	321,307	351,759	380,533	409,042	439,509
primary	1,289,167	1,395,070	1,352,215	1,711,369	1,769,453	1,937,735	2,120,871	2,321,874	2,511,805	2,699,983	2,901,091
lower secondary	761,916	824,506	799,178	1,011,444	1,045,772	1,145,229	1,253,465	1,372,261	1,484,513	1,595,728	1,714,586
upper secondary	312,825	338,523	328,124	415,275	429,370	470,204	514,643	563,418	609,506	655,169	703,969
other	519,211	561,863	544,604	689,253	712,646	780,421	854,179	935,133	1,011,628	1,087,416	1,168,412
Training	899,248	973,120	943,227	1,193,752	1,234,267	1,351,651	1,479,396	1,619,605	1,752,089	1,883,351	2,023,632
vocational	133,673	144,654	140,210	177,451	183,474	200,923	219,912	240,754	260,448	279,960	300,812
technical	215,891	233,626	226,449	286,595	296,322	324,504	355,173	388,834	420,641	452,154	485,833
university/college	402,244	435,288	421,916	533,979	552,102	604,609	661,751	724,468	783,730	842,445	905,194
postgraduate	27,474	29,731	28,818	36,472	37,710	41,296	45,199	49,482	53,530	57,541	61,826
other	119,966	129,821	125,833	159,255	164,660	180,320	197,362	216,067	233,741	251,252	269,967
Capital expenditure	1,033,430	972,265	1,120,829	1,534,081	1,904,635	2,085,774	2,282,901	2,499,260	2,897,234	3,171,605	3,664,613
Education	555,733	522,841	602,732	824,961	1,024,229	1,121,637	1,227,643	1,343,992	1,558,004	1,705,549	1,970,667
pre-school	31,952	30,061	34,654	47,431	58,888	64,489	70,584	77,273	89,578	98,061	113,304
primary	194,863	183,330	211,343	289,265	359,137	393,292	430,462	471,259	546,301	598,036	690,997
lower secondary	123,624	116,307	134,079	183,514	227,842	249,511	273,092	298,974	346,581	379,403	438,379
upper secondary	119,514	112,440	129,622	177,413	220,267	241,215	264,013	289,034	335,059	366,789	423,805
other	85,780	80,703	93,035	127,337	158,094	173,130	189,492	207,451	240,485	263,260	304,182
Training	477,697	449,424	518,097	709,120	880,406	964,137	1,055,258	1,155,269	1,339,229	1,466,056	1,693,946
vocational	116,295	109,412	126,130	172,635	214,334	234,718	256,902	281,249	326,034	356,910	412,390
technical	93,726	88,179	101,653	139,132	172,739	189,167	207,046	226,668	262,762	287,646	332,359
university/college	188,936	177,754	204,915	280,467	348,213	381,330	417,369	456,925	529,684	579,846	669,980
postgraduate	7,821	7,358	8,482	11,610	14,414	15,785	17,277	18,914	21,926	24,003	27,734
other	70,919	66,722	76,917	105,276	130,705	143,136	156,664	171,511	198,822	217,651	251,484
Consolidated expenditure	5,011,103	5,276,697	5,293,034	6,814,442	7,364,210	8,064,576	8,826,762	9,663,310	10,647,308	11,502,295	12,615,812
Education	3,634,158	3,854,153	3,831,711	4,911,570	5,249,536	5,748,788	6,292,108	6,888,437	7,555,989	8,152,887	8,898,234
pre-school	227,258	241,411	239,512	306,700	326,957	358,051	391,891	429,032	470,111	507,103	552,813
primary	1,484,030	1,578,399	1,563,558	2,000,635	2,128,590	2,331,027	2,551,333	2,793,133	3,058,106	3,298,019	3,592,088
lower secondary	885,540	940,813	933,257	1,194,958	1,273,614	1,394,739	1,526,557	1,671,235	1,831,094	1,975,131	2,152,965
upper secondary	432,339	450,963	457,746	592,688	649,637	711,420	778,656	852,453	944,565	1,021,958	1,127,774

other	604,991	642,566	637,638	816,589	870,740	953,551	1,043,671	1,142,585	1,252,113	1,350,676	1,472,594
Training	1,376,945	1,422,543	1,461,323	1,902,872	2,114,674	2,315,788	2,534,654	2,774,873	3,091,319	3,349,407	3,717,578
vocational	249,968	254,066	266,341	350,086	397,808	435,641	476,814	522,003	586,482	636,870	713,202
technical	309,617	321,805	328,102	425,727	469,061	513,671	562,218	615,502	683,403	739,800	818,191
university/college	591,180	613,041	626,831	814,446	900,315	985,939	1,079,120	1,181,393	1,313,414	1,422,291	1,575,174
postgraduate	35,295	37,089	37,300	48,082	52,124	57,081	62,476	68,397	75,456	81,543	89,560
other	190,885	196,543	202,750	264,531	295,365	323,456	354,026	387,578	432,563	468,903	521,450

Source: MOF and VEFSS Team

Table D.7: Real Public Expenditure per Capita on Education and Training
(in VND; at constant 1994 prices)

	1994	1995	1996	1997	1998	1999	2000	2001	2002	2003	2004
Current expenditure	**54,842**	**58,184**	**55,290**	**68,728**	**69,682**	**74,885**	**80,431**	**86,408**	**91,739**	**96,767**	**102,043**
Education	42,443	45,030	42,791	53,190	53,929	57,955	62,248	66,873	70,999	74,891	78,974
pre-school	2,693	2,857	2,715	3,375	3,421	3,677	3,949	4,243	4,504	4,751	5,010
primary	17,774	18,857	17,920	22,275	22,584	24,270	26,068	28,005	29,733	31,362	33,072
lower secondary	10,505	11,145	10,591	13,165	13,347	14,344	15,406	16,551	17,572	18,536	19,546
upper secondary	4,313	4,576	4,348	5,405	5,480	5,889	6,326	6,796	7,215	7,610	8,025
other	7,159	7,595	7,217	8,971	9,096	9,775	10,499	11,279	11,975	12,631	13,320
Training	12,398	13,154	12,500	15,538	15,753	16,929	18,183	19,534	20,740	21,877	23,069
vocational	1,843	1,955	1,858	2,310	2,342	2,517	2,703	2,904	3,083	3,252	3,429
technical	2,977	3,158	3,001	3,730	3,782	4,064	4,365	4,690	4,979	5,252	5,538
university/college	5,546	5,884	5,591	6,950	7,047	7,573	8,134	8,738	9,277	9,786	10,319
postgraduate	379	402	382	475	481	517	556	597	634	668	705
other	1,654	1,755	1,668	2,073	2,102	2,259	2,426	2,606	2,767	2,918	3,078
Capital expenditure	**14,248**	**13,142**	**14,853**	**19,967**	**24,309**	**26,124**	**28,059**	**30,144**	**34,295**	**36,841**	**41,776**
Education	7,662	7,067	7,987	10,737	13,072	14,049	15,089	16,210	18,442	19,811	22,465
pre-school	441	406	459	617	752	808	868	932	1,060	1,139	1,292
primary	2,687	2,478	2,801	3,765	4,584	4,926	5,291	5,684	6,467	6,947	7,877
lower secondary	1,704	1,572	1,777	2,389	2,908	3,125	3,357	3,606	4,103	4,407	4,997
upper secondary	1,648	1,520	1,718	2,309	2,811	3,021	3,245	3,486	3,966	4,261	4,831
other	1,183	1,091	1,233	1,657	2,018	2,168	2,329	2,502	2,847	3,058	3,468
Training	6,586	6,075	6,866	9,230	11,237	12,076	12,970	13,934	15,853	17,029	19,311
vocational	1,603	1,479	1,671	2,247	2,736	2,940	3,158	3,392	3,859	4,146	4,701
technical	1,292	1,192	1,347	1,811	2,205	2,369	2,545	2,734	3,110	3,341	3,789
university/college	2,605	2,403	2,716	3,650	4,444	4,776	5,130	5,511	6,270	6,735	7,638
postgraduate	108	99	112	151	184	198	212	228	260	279	316
other	978	902	1,019	1,370	1,668	1,793	1,926	2,069	2,353	2,528	2,867
Consolidated expenditure	**69,090**	**71,326**	**70,144**	**88,695**	**93,991**	**101,009**	**108,490**	**116,552**	**126,033**	**133,608**	**143,819**
Education	50,106	52,097	50,778	63,928	67,001	72,004	77,337	83,083	89,441	94,702	101,439
pre-school	3,133	3,263	3,174	3,992	4,173	4,485	4,817	5,175	5,565	5,890	6,302
primary	20,461	21,335	20,720	26,040	27,168	29,196	31,359	33,689	36,199	38,309	40,949
lower secondary	12,209	12,717	12,368	15,553	16,255	17,469	18,763	20,157	21,675	22,943	24,544
upper secondary	5,961	6,096	6,066	7,714	8,291	8,911	9,571	10,282	11,181	11,871	12,857

other	8,341	8,686	8,450	10,629	11,113	11,943	12,828	13,781	14,821	15,689	16,787
Training	18,984	19,229	19,366	24,767	26,990	29,005	31,154	33,468	36,592	38,906	42,380
vocational	3,446	3,434	3,530	4,557	5,077	5,456	5,861	6,296	6,942	7,398	8,130
technical	4,269	4,350	4,348	5,541	5,987	6,434	6,910	7,424	8,090	8,593	9,327
university/college	8,151	8,287	8,307	10,601	11,491	12,349	13,264	14,249	15,547	16,521	17,957
postgraduate	487	501	494	626	665	715	768	825	893	947	1,021
other	2,632	2,657	2,687	3,443	3,770	4,051	4,351	4,675	5,120	5,447	5,944

Source: MOF and VEFSS Team

Table D.8: GDP Shares of Public Expenditure on Education and Training

(at constant 1994 prices)

	1994	1995	1996	1997	1998	1999	2000	2001	2002	2003	2004
Current expenditure	**2.34**	**2.31**	**2.04**	**2.36**	**2.23**	**2.23**	**2.23**	**2.23**	**2.20**	**2.16**	**2.12**
Education	1.81	1.79	1.58	1.83	1.72	1.72	1.72	1.72	1.70	1.67	1.64
pre-school	0.11	0.11	0.10	0.12	0.11	0.11	0.11	0.11	0.11	0.11	0.10
primary	0.76	0.75	0.66	0.77	0.72	0.72	0.72	0.72	0.71	0.70	0.69
lower secondary	0.45	0.44	0.39	0.45	0.43	0.43	0.43	0.43	0.42	0.41	0.41
upper secondary	0.18	0.18	0.16	0.19	0.18	0.18	0.18	0.18	0.17	0.17	0.17
other	0.30	0.30	0.27	0.31	0.29	0.29	0.29	0.29	0.29	0.28	0.28
Training	0.53	0.52	0.46	0.53	0.50	0.50	0.50	0.50	0.50	0.49	0.48
vocational	0.08	0.08	0.07	0.08	0.07	0.07	0.07	0.07	0.07	0.07	0.07
technical	0.13	0.13	0.11	0.13	0.12	0.12	0.12	0.12	0.12	0.12	0.12
university/college	0.24	0.23	0.21	0.24	0.23	0.23	0.23	0.23	0.22	0.22	0.21
postgraduate	0.02	0.02	0.01	0.02	0.02	0.02	0.02	0.02	0.02	0.01	0.01
other	0.07	0.07	0.06	0.07	0.07	0.07	0.07	0.07	0.07	0.07	0.06
Capital expenditure	**0.61**	**0.52**	**0.55**	**0.69**	**0.78**	**0.78**	**0.78**	**0.78**	**0.82**	**0.82**	**0.87**
Education	0.33	0.28	0.30	0.37	0.42	0.42	0.42	0.42	0.44	0.44	0.47
pre-school	0.02	0.02	0.02	0.02	0.02	0.02	0.02	0.02	0.03	0.03	0.03
primary	0.11	0.10	0.10	0.13	0.15	0.15	0.15	0.15	0.16	0.16	0.16
lower secondary	0.07	0.06	0.07	0.08	0.09	0.09	0.09	0.09	0.10	0.10	0.10
upper secondary	0.07	0.06	0.06	0.08	0.09	0.09	0.09	0.09	0.10	0.10	0.10
other	0.05	0.04	0.05	0.06	0.06	0.06	0.06	0.06	0.07	0.07	0.07
Training	0.28	0.24	0.25	0.32	0.36	0.36	0.36	0.36	0.38	0.38	0.40
vocational	0.07	0.06	0.06	0.08	0.09	0.09	0.09	0.09	0.09	0.09	0.10
technical	0.06	0.05	0.05	0.06	0.07	0.07	0.07	0.07	0.07	0.07	0.08
university/college	0.11	0.10	0.10	0.13	0.14	0.14	0.14	0.14	0.15	0.15	0.16
postgraduate	0.00	0.00	0.00	0.01	0.01	0.01	0.01	0.01	0.01	0.01	0.01
other	0.04	0.04	0.04	0.05	0.05	0.05	0.05	0.05	0.06	0.06	0.06
Consolidated expenditure	**2.94**	**2.83**	**2.59**	**3.05**	**3.01**	**3.01**	**3.01**	**3.01**	**3.02**	**2.99**	**2.99**
Education	2.13	2.07	1.88	2.20	2.14	2.14	2.14	2.14	2.15	2.12	2.11
pre-school	0.13	0.13	0.12	0.14	0.13	0.13	0.13	0.13	0.13	0.13	0.13
primary	0.87	0.85	0.77	0.89	0.87	0.87	0.87	0.87	0.87	0.86	0.85
lower secondary	0.52	0.50	0.46	0.53	0.52	0.52	0.52	0.52	0.52	0.51	0.51
upper secondary	0.25	0.24	0.22	0.26	0.27	0.27	0.27	0.27	0.27	0.27	0.27

other	0.36	0.34	0.31	0.37	0.36	0.36	0.36	0.36	0.36	0.35	0.35
Training	0.81	0.76	0.72	0.85	0.86	0.86	0.86	0.86	0.88	0.87	0.88
vocational	0.15	0.14	0.13	0.16	0.16	0.16	0.16	0.17	0.17	0.17	0.17
technical	0.18	0.17	0.16	0.19	0.19	0.19	0.19	0.19	0.19	0.19	0.19
university/college	0.35	0.33	0.31	0.36	0.37	0.37	0.37	0.37	0.37	0.37	0.37
postgraduate	0.02	0.02	0.02	0.02	0.02	0.02	0.02	0.02	0.02	0.02	0.02
other	0.11	0.11	0.10	0.12	0.12	0.12	0.12	0.12	0.12	0.12	0.12

Source: MOF and VEFSS Team

Table D.9: School Age Population
(number of children)

	1994	1995	1996	1997	1998	1999	2000	2001	2002	2003	2004
Education											
nursery (0-2)	5,909,600	6,108,100	6,056,965	6,006,257	5,955,974	5,906,112	5,857,700	5,762,045	5,662,130	5,563,947	5,467,467
kindergarten (3-5)	5,609,500	5,709,900	5,760,330	5,811,205	5,862,530	5,914,308	5,967,700	5,907,596	5,836,471	5,751,440	5,657,476
pre-school (0-5)	11,519,100	11,519,100	11,579,560	11,640,337	11,701,433	11,762,849	11,825,400	11,669,641	11,498,601	11,315,387	11,124,943
primary (6-10)	9,117,000	9,154,200	9,251,470	9,349,773	9,449,121	9,549,524	9,653,700	9,747,340	9,794,073	9,794,871	9,750,521
lower secondary (11-14)	6,849,000	7,035,300	7,082,055	7,129,120	7,176,498	7,224,191	7,273,000	7,334,067	7,425,713	7,537,956	7,649,889
upper secondary (15-17)	4,619,500	4,766,900	4,879,945	4,995,671	5,114,141	5,235,421	5,367,000	5,389,688	5,395,672	5,404,863	5,432,370
Training											
vocational (15-17)	4,619,500	4,766,900	4,879,945	4,995,671	5,114,141	5,235,421	5,367,000	5,389,688	5,395,672	5,404,863	5,432,370
technical (15-17)	4,619,500	4,766,900	4,879,945	4,995,671	5,114,141	5,235,421	5,367,000	5,389,688	5,395,672	5,404,863	5,432,370
university/college (18-21)	5,707,900	5,835,900	5,981,896	6,131,545	6,284,937	6,442,167	6,613,500	6,804,646	6,959,568	7,067,347	7,127,134
postgraduate											
other											

Source: MOF and VEFSS Team

Table D.10: Enrollment Rate Policy Targets

(gross enrollments as per cent of school age population)

	1994	1995	1996	1997	1998	1999	2000	2001	2002	2003	2004
Baseline scenario											
Education											
pre-school	18.69	18.69	18.69	18.69	18.69	18.69	18.69	18.69	18.69	18.69	18.69
primary	109.14	109.14	109.14	109.14	109.14	109.14	109.14	109.14	109.14	109.14	109.14
lower secondary	49.30	49.30	49.30	49.30	49.30	49.30	49.30	49.30	49.30	49.30	49.30
upper secondary	16.91	16.91	16.91	16.91	16.91	16.91	16.91	16.91	16.91	16.91	16.91
Training											
vocational	8.07	8.07	8.07	8.07	8.07	8.07	8.07	8.07	8.07	8.07	8.07
technical	3.78	3.78	3.78	3.78	3.78	3.78	3.78	3.78	3.78	3.78	3.78
university/college	4.86	4.86	4.86	4.86	4.86	4.86	4.86	4.86	4.86	4.86	4.86
Plan Scenario											
Education											
pre-school	18.69	21.15	24.68	26.49	27.65	28.50	29.72	31.57	33.59	35.79	38.16
primary	109.14	112.66	117.32	119.46	120.74	121.63	122.16	122.84	124.13	126.02	128.54
lower secondary	49.30	55.43	61.10	63.32	64.59	68.54	76.34	84.89	94.01	103.85	114.75
upper secondary	16.91	19.46	21.29	21.62	21.99	22.17	22.33	22.95	23.67	24.39	25.05
Training											
vocational	8.07	8.93	9.97	10.89	11.61	12.45	13.34	14.59	16.01	17.56	19.18
technical	3.78	3.74	3.73	3.72	3.70	3.68	3.65	3.69	3.74	3.80	3.84
university/college	4.86	6.10	6.29	6.65	6.80	6.90	6.78	6.64	6.54	6.49	6.49

Source: MOF and VEFSS Team

Table D.11: Gross Enrollment Scenarios

(number of students)

	1994	1995	1996	1997	1998	1999	2000	2001	2002	2003	2004
Baseline scenario											
Education											
pre-school	2,153,071	2,153,071	2,164,372	2,175,732	2,187,151	2,198,631	2,210,322	2,181,209	2,149,239	2,114,994	2,079,398
primary	9,950,475	9,991,076	10,097,238	10,204,528	10,312,958	10,422,541	10,536,240	10,638,441	10,689,446	10,690,317	10,641,912
lower secondary	3,376,712	3,468,562	3,491,613	3,514,817	3,538,176	3,561,690	3,585,754	3,615,861	3,661,045	3,716,383	3,771,568
upper secondary	781,121	806,045	825,160	844,729	864,761	885,268	907,517	911,354	912,366	913,920	918,571
Training											
vocational	372,781	384,676	393,798	403,137	412,697	422,484	433,102	434,933	435,416	436,158	438,377
technical	174,568	180,138	184,410	188,783	193,260	197,843	202,816	203,673	203,899	204,246	205,286
university/college	277,488	283,711	290,808	298,083	305,540	313,184	321,513	330,806	338,337	343,577	346,484
Plan Scenario											
Education											
pre-school	2,153,071	2,436,061	2,858,200	3,083,800	3,235,000	3,352,600	3,514,675	3,684,584	3,862,708	4,049,443	4,245,205
primary	9,950,475	10,313,138	10,854,000	11,169,600	11,409,000	11,614,800	11,792,886	11,973,702	12,157,290	12,343,693	12,532,955
lower secondary	3,376,712	3,899,682	4,327,400	4,514,400	4,635,600	4,951,200	5,552,013	6,225,732	6,981,205	7,828,353	8,778,299
upper secondary	781,121	927,800	1,039,000	1,080,000	1,124,400	1,160,800	1,198,278	1,236,966	1,276,903	1,318,129	1,360,686
Training											
vocational	372,781	425,823	486,416	543,923	593,682	652,016	716,129	786,545	863,885	948,830	1,042,128
technical	174,568	178,264	182,039	185,798	189,338	192,579	195,671	198,812	202,004	205,247	208,542
university/college	277,488	356,222	376,440	407,880	427,380	444,800	448,311	451,850	455,417	459,011	462,635

Source: MOF and VEFSS Team

Table D.12: Financing Instruments: Public Provision Ratio

(public sector share of gross enrollments in percent)

	1994	1995	1996	1997	1998	1999	2000	2001	2002	2003	2004
Baseline scenario											
Education											
pre-school	75	75	75	75	75	75	75	75	75	75	75
primary	99.8	99.8	99.8	99.8	99.8	99.8	99.8	99.8	99.8	99.8	99.8
lower secondary	96	96	96	96	96	96	96	96	96	96	96
upper secondary	83	83	83	83	83	83	83	83	83	83	83
Training											
vocational	75	75	75	75	75	75	75	75	75	75	75
technical	75	75	75	75	75	75	75	75	75	75	75
university/college	82	82	82	82	82	82	82	82	82	82	82
Plan scenario											
Education											
pre-school	75	75	75	75	75	75	75	75	75	75	75
primary	99.8	99.8	99.8	99.8	99.8	99.8	99.8	99.8	99.8	99.8	99.8
lower secondary	96	96	96	96	96	96	96	96	96	96	96
upper secondary	83	83	83	83	83	83	83	83	83	83	83
Training											
vocational	75	75	75	75	75	75	75	75	75	75	75
technical	75	75	75	75	75	75	75	75	75	75	75
university/college	82	82	82	82	82	82	82	82	82	82	82

Source: MOF and VEFSS Team

Table D.13: Public Sector Enrollment Scenarios
(number of students)

	1994	1995	1996	1997	1998	1999	2000	2001	2002	2003	2004
Baseline scenario											
Education											
pre-school	1,614,803	1,614,803	1,623,279	1,631,799	1,640,364	1,648,973	1,657,742	1,635,907	1,611,930	1,586,246	1,559,548
primary	9,930,574	9,971,094	10,077,043	10,184,119	10,292,332	10,401,696	10,515,168	10,617,164	10,668,067	10,668,936	10,620,629
lower secondary	3,241,644	3,329,820	3,351,949	3,374,225	3,396,649	3,419,222	3,442,323	3,471,227	3,514,603	3,567,728	3,620,706
upper secondary	648,330	669,017	684,883	701,125	717,752	734,773	753,239	756,424	757,263	758,553	762,414
Training											
vocational	279,586	288,507	295,349	302,353	309,523	316,863	324,827	326,200	326,562	327,118	328,783
technical	130,926	135,104	138,308	141,587	144,945	148,382	152,112	152,755	152,924	153,185	153,964
university/college	227,540	232,643	238,463	244,428	250,543	256,811	263,641	271,261	277,437	281,733	284,117
Plan scenario											
Education											
pre-school	1,614,803	1,827,046	2,143,650	2,312,850	2,426,250	2,514,450	2,636,006	2,763,438	2,897,031	3,037,082	3,183,904
primary	9,930,574	10,292,512	10,832,292	11,147,261	11,386,182	11,591,570	11,769,300	11,949,755	12,132,975	12,319,006	12,507,889
lower secondary	3,241,644	3,743,695	4,154,304	4,333,824	4,450,176	4,753,152	5,329,932	5,976,703	6,701,957	7,515,219	8,427,167
upper secondary	648,330	770,074	862,370	896,400	933,252	963,464	994,571	1,026,682	1,059,829	1,094,047	1,129,369
Training											
vocational	279,586	319,367	364,812	407,942	445,262	489,012	537,097	589,909	647,914	711,623	781,596
technical	130,926	133,698	136,529	139,349	142,004	144,434	146,753	149,109	151,503	153,935	156,407
university/college	227,540	292,102	308,681	334,462	350,452	364,736	367,615	370,517	373,442	376,389	379,361

Source: MOF and VEFSS Team

Table D.14: Private Sector Enrollment Scenarios

(number of students)

	1994	1995	1996	1997	1998	1999	2000	2001	2002	2003	2004
Baseline scenario											
Education											
pre-school	538,268	538,268	541,093	543,933	546,788	549,658	552,581	545,302	537,310	528,749	519,849
primary	19,901	19,982	20,194	20,409	20,626	20,845	21,072	21,277	21,379	21,381	21,284
lower secondary	135,068	138,742	139,665	140,593	141,527	142,468	143,430	144,634	146,442	148,655	150,863
upper secondary	132,791	137,028	140,277	143,604	147,009	150,496	154,278	154,930	155,102	155,366	156,157
Training											
vocational	93,195	96,169	98,450	100,784	103,174	105,621	108,276	108,733	108,854	109,039	109,594
technical	43,642	45,035	46,103	47,196	48,315	49,461	50,704	50,918	50,975	51,062	51,321
university/college	49,948	51,068	52,345	53,655	54,997	56,373	57,872	59,545	60,901	61,844	62,367
Plan scenario											
Education											
pre-school	538,268	609,015	714,550	770,950	808,750	838,150	878,669	921,146	965,677	1,012,361	1,061,301
primary	19,901	20,626	21,708	22,339	22,818	23,230	23,586	23,947	24,315	24,687	25,066
lower secondary	135,068	155,987	173,096	180,576	185,424	198,048	222,081	249,029	279,248	313,134	351,132
upper secondary	132,791	157,726	176,630	183,600	191,148	197,336	203,707	210,284	217,074	224,082	231,317
Training											
vocational	93,195	106,456	121,604	135,981	148,421	163,004	179,032	196,636	215,971	237,208	260,532
technical	43,642	44,566	45,510	46,450	47,335	48,145	48,918	49,703	50,501	51,312	52,136
university/college	49,948	64,120	67,759	73,418	76,928	80,064	80,696	81,333	81,975	82,622	83,274

Source: MOF and VEFSS Team

Table D.15: Financing Instruments: Public Subsidy

(public subsidy is percent of economic cost per student)

	1994	1995	1996	1997	1998	1999	2000	2001	2002	2003	2004
Baseline scenario											
Education											
pre-school	71.45	71.45	71.45	71.45	71.45	71.45	71.45	71.45	71.45	71.45	71.45
primary	55.64	55.64	55.64	55.64	55.64	55.64	55.64	55.64	55.64	55.64	55.64
lower secondary	51.32	51.32	51.32	51.32	51.32	51.32	51.32	51.32	51.32	51.32	51.32
upper secondary	48.50	48.50	48.50	48.50	48.50	48.50	48.50	48.50	48.50	48.50	48.50
Training											
vocational	37.97	37.97	37.97	37.97	37.97	37.97	37.97	37.97	37.97	37.97	37.97
technical	67.86	67.86	67.86	67.86	67.86	67.86	67.86	67.86	67.86	67.86	67.86
university/college											
Plan scenario											
Education											
pre-school	71.45	71.45	71.45	71.45	71.45	71.45	71.45	71.45	71.45	71.45	71.45
primary	55.64	55.64	55.64	55.64	55.64	55.64	55.64	55.64	55.64	55.64	55.64
lower secondary	51.32	51.32	51.32	51.32	51.32	51.32	51.32	51.32	51.32	51.32	51.32
upper secondary	48.50	48.50	48.50	48.50	48.50	48.50	48.50	48.50	48.50	48.50	48.50
Training											
vocational	37.97	37.97	37.97	37.97	37.97	37.97	37.97	37.97	37.97	37.97	37.97
technical	67.86	67.86	67.86	67.86	67.86	67.86	67.86	67.86	67.86	67.86	67.86
university/college	69.36	69.36	69.36	69.36	69.36	69.36	69.36	69.36	69.36	69.36	69.36

Source: MOF and VEFSS Team

Table D.16: Unit Fiscal Costs

(at constant 1994 prices; in VND)

	1994	1995	1996	1997	1998	1999	2000	2001	2002	2003	2004
Education											
pre-school	120,947	120,947	120,947	120,947	120,947	120,947	120,947	120,947	120,947	120,947	120,947
primary	129,818	129,818	129,818	129,818	129,818	129,818	129,818	129,818	129,818	129,818	129,818
lower secondary	235,040	235,040	235,040	235,040	235,040	235,040	235,040	235,040	235,040	235,040	235,040
upper secondary	482,509	482,509	482,509	482,509	482,509	482,509	482,509	482,509	482,509	482,509	482,509
Training											
vocational	478,111	478,111	478,111	478,111	478,111	478,111	478,111	478,111	478,111	478,111	478,111
technical	1,648,954	1,648,954	1,648,954	1,648,954	1,648,954	1,648,954	1,648,954	1,648,954	1,648,954	1,648,954	1,648,954
university/college	1,767,793	1,767,793	1,767,793	1,767,793	1,767,793	1,767,793	1,767,793	1,767,793	1,767,793	1,767,793	1,767,793

Source: MOF and VEFSS Team

Table D.17: Unit Economic Costs
(at constant 1994 prices; in VND)

	1994	1995	1996	1997	1998	1999	2000	2001	2002	2003	2004
Education											
pre-school	**48,321**	48,321	48,321	48,321	48,321	48,321	48,321	48,321	48,321	48,321	48,321
primary	**103,517**	103,517	103,517	103,517	103,517	103,517	103,517	103,517	103,517	103,517	103,517
lower secondary	**222,978**	222,978	222,978	222,978	222,978	222,978	222,978	222,978	222,978	222,978	222,978
upper secondary	**512,422**	512,422	512,422	512,422	512,422	512,422	512,422	512,422	512,422	512,422	512,422
Training											
vocational	**781,000**	781,000	781,000	781,000	781,000	781,000	781,000	781,000	781,000	781,000	781,000
technical	**781,000**	781,000	781,000	781,000	781,000	781,000	781,000	781,000	781,000	781,000	781,000
university/college	**781,000**	781,000	781,000	781,000	781,000	781,000	781,000	781,000	781,000	781,000	781,000

Source: MOF and VEFSS Team

Table D.18: Unit Economic Costs

(at constant 1994 prices; in VND)

	1994	1995	1996	1997	1998	1999	2000	2001	2002	2003	2004
Education											
pre-school	169,268	169,268	169,268	169,268	169,268	169,268	169,268	169,268	169,268	169,268	169,268
primary	233,335	233,335	233,335	233,335	233,335	233,335	233,335	233,335	233,335	233,335	233,335
lower secondary	458,018	458,018	458,018	458,018	458,018	458,018	458,018	458,018	458,018	458,018	458,018
upper secondary	994,931	994,931	994,931	994,931	994,931	994,931	994,931	994,931	994,931	994,931	994,931
Training											
vocational	1,259,111	1,259,111	1,259,111	1,259,111	1,259,111	1,259,111	1,259,111	1,259,111	1,259,111	1,259,111	1,259,111
technical	2,429,954	2,429,954	2,429,954	2,429,954	2,429,954	2,429,954	2,429,954	2,429,954	2,429,954	2,429,954	2,429,954
university/college	2,548,793	2,548,793	2,548,793	2,548,793	2,548,793	2,548,793	2,548,793	2,548,793	2,548,793	2,548,793	2,548,793

Source: MOF and VEFSS Team

Table D.19: Projected Public Expenditure on Education and Training
(at 1994 prices; in VND millions)

	1994	1995	1996	1997	1998	1999	2000	2001	2002	2003	2004
Baseline scenario											
Education	3,078,425	3,157,044	3,167,420	3,340,072	3,391,843	3,488,375	3,592,264	3,692,148	3,782,951	3,868,855	3,954,666
pre-school	195,306	195,306	196,331	197,362	198,397	199,439	200,499	197,858	194,958	191,852	188,623
primary	1,289,167	1,294,427	1,308,181	1,322,082	1,336,130	1,350,327	1,365,058	1,378,299	1,384,907	1,385,020	1,378,748
lower secondary	761,916	782,641	787,842	793,078	798,348	803,654	809,084	815,877	826,072	838,559	851,011
upper secondary	312,825	322,807	330,462	338,299	346,321	354,534	363,444	364,981	365,386	366,009	367,871
other	519,211	561,863	544,604	689,253	712,646	780,421	854,179	935,133	1,011,628	1,087,416	1,168,412
Training	899,248	931,534	945,476	1,005,855	1,032,272	1,071,776	1,114,752	1,152,928	1,186,020	1,215,833	1,245,128
vocational	133,673	137,938	141,209	144,558	147,986	151,496	155,303	155,960	156,133	156,399	157,195
technical	215,891	222,780	228,063	233,471	239,008	244,676	250,825	251,886	252,165	252,595	253,880
university/college	402,244	411,264	421,553	432,099	442,909	453,989	466,063	479,533	490,451	498,046	502,259
postgraduate	27,474	29,731	28,818	36,472	37,710	41,296	45,199	49,482	53,530	57,541	61,826
other	119,966	129,821	125,833	159,255	164,660	180,320	197,362	216,067	233,741	251,252	269,967
E&T Total	3,977,673	4,088,578	4,112,896	4,345,927	4,424,115	4,560,151	4,707,016	4,845,076	4,968,971	5,084,688	5,199,793
Plan scenario											
Education	3,078,425	3,370,478	3,602,627	3,867,243	3,980,497	4,171,392	4,433,500	4,720,803	5,023,699	5,348,236	5,702,897
pre-school	195,306	220,976	259,269	279,733	293,448	304,116	318,818	334,230	350,388	367,327	385,084
primary	1,289,167	1,336,153	1,406,226	1,447,115	1,478,131	1,504,794	1,527,867	1,551,293	1,575,078	1,599,228	1,623,749
lower secondary	761,916	879,918	976,428	1,018,622	1,045,970	1,117,181	1,252,748	1,404,764	1,575,228	1,766,377	1,980,722
upper secondary	312,825	371,567	416,101	432,521	450,302	464,880	479,889	495,383	511,377	527,887	544,930
other	519,211	561,863	544,604	689,253	712,646	780,421	854,179	935,133	1,011,628	1,087,416	1,168,412
Training	899,248	1,049,083	1,099,886	1,211,807	1,268,937	1,338,361	1,391,209	1,448,462	1,507,036	1,568,238	1,634,021
vocational	133,673	152,693	174,421	195,042	212,884	233,802	256,792	282,042	309,775	340,234	373,690
technical	215,891	220,462	225,131	229,779	234,157	238,165	241,989	245,874	249,822	253,832	257,907
university/college	402,244	516,376	545,684	591,259	619,526	644,778	649,867	654,998	660,168	665,378	670,631
postgraduate	27,474	29,731	28,818	36,472	37,710	41,296	45,199	49,482	53,530	57,541	61,826
other	119,966	129,821	125,833	159,255	164,660	180,320	197,362	216,067	233,741	251,252	269,967
E&T Total	3,977,673	4,419,561	4,702,513	5,079,050	5,249,434	5,509,753	5,824,709	6,169,266	6,530,734	6,916,473	7,336,919

Source: MOF and VEFSS Team

Table D.20: Projected Private Expenditure on Public Provision

(at 1994 prices; in VND billions)

	1994	1995	1996	1997	1998	1999	2000	2001	2002	2003	2004
Baseline scenario											
Education											
pre-school	78,029	78,029	78,438	78,850	79,264	79,680	80,104	79,049	77,890	76,649	75,359
primary	1,027,983	1,032,178	1,043,145	1,054,229	1,065,431	1,076,752	1,088,499	1,099,057	1,104,326	1,104,416	1,099,416
lower secondary	722,815	742,477	747,411	752,378	757,378	762,411	767,562	774,007	783,679	795,525	807,338
upper secondary	332,219	342,819	350,949	359,272	367,792	376,514	385,976	387,608	388,038	388,699	390,678
Training											
vocational	218,356	225,324	230,667	236,137	241,737	247,470	253,690	254,762	255,045	255,479	256,780
technical	102,253	105,516	108,018	110,580	113,202	115,887	118,799	119,301	119,434	119,637	120,246
university/college	177,709	181,694	186,239	190,899	195,674	200,569	205,904	211,855	216,678	220,034	221,895
Plan scenario											
Education											
pre-school	78,029	88,285	103,583	111,759	117,239	121,501	127,374	133,532	139,987	146,755	153,849
primary	1,027,983	1,065,450	1,121,326	1,153,931	1,178,663	1,199,925	1,218,323	1,237,003	1,255,969	1,275,227	1,294,779
lower secondary	722,815	834,762	926,318	966,347	992,291	1,059,848	1,188,458	1,332,673	1,494,389	1,675,728	1,879,073
upper secondary	332,219	394,603	441,897	459,335	478,219	493,700	509,640	526,094	543,080	560,614	578,714
Training											
vocational	218,356	249,426	284,918	318,603	347,749	381,918	419,473	460,719	506,021	555,777	610,426
technical	102,253	104,418	106,629	108,831	110,905	112,803	114,614	116,454	118,324	120,223	122,153
university/college	177,709	228,132	241,080	261,215	273,703	284,859	287,107	289,374	291,658	293,960	296,281

Source: MOF and VEFSS Team

Table D.21: Projected Private Expenditure on Private Provision

(at 1994 prices; in VND billions)

	1994	1995	1996	1997	1998	1999	2000	2001	2002	2003	2004
Baseline scenario											
Education											
pre-school	91,112	91,112	91,590	92,071	92,554	93,040	93,534	92,302	90,949	89,500	87,994
primary	4,644	4,663	4,712	4,762	4,813	4,864	4,917	4,965	4,988	4,989	4,966
lower secondary	61,864	63,547	63,969	64,394	64,822	65,253	65,694	66,245	67,073	68,087	69,098
upper secondary	132,117	136,333	139,566	142,876	146,264	149,733	153,496	154,145	154,316	154,579	155,365
Training											
vocational	117,343	121,087	123,959	126,899	129,908	132,989	136,331	136,907	137,059	137,293	137,991
technical	106,048	109,432	112,027	114,684	117,403	120,188	123,208	123,729	123,866	124,077	124,709
university/college	127,307	130,162	133,418	136,756	140,177	143,684	147,505	151,768	155,223	157,627	158,961
Plan scenario											
Education											
pre-school	91,112	103,087	120,951	130,497	136,896	141,872	148,731	155,921	163,458	171,361	179,645
primary	4,644	4,813	5,065	5,213	5,324	5,420	5,503	5,588	5,673	5,760	5,849
lower secondary	61,864	71,445	79,281	82,707	84,928	90,710	101,717	114,060	127,901	143,421	160,825
upper secondary	132,117	156,926	175,735	182,669	190,179	196,336	202,675	209,218	215,973	222,946	230,144
Training											
vocational	117,343	134,040	153,113	171,215	186,878	205,240	225,421	247,587	271,932	298,671	328,039
technical	106,048	108,293	110,587	112,870	115,021	116,990	118,868	120,776	122,715	124,685	126,687
university/college	127,307	163,429	172,704	187,128	196,075	204,067	205,677	207,301	208,937	210,586	212,249

Source: MOF and VEFSS Team

Table D.22: Fiscal Affordability

(projected public expenditure as percent of budget constraint)

	1994	1995	1996	1997	1998	1999	2000	2001	2002	2003	2004
Baseline scenario											
Education											
pre-school	100.00	92.41	95.84	76.12	74.01	67.94	62.40	56.25	51.23	46.90	42.92
primary	100.00	92.79	96.74	77.25	75.51	69.69	64.36	59.36	55.14	51.30	47.53
lower secondary	100.00	94.92	98.58	78.41	76.34	70.17	64.55	59.45	55.65	52.55	49.63
upper secondary	100.00	95.36	100.71	81.46	80.66	75.40	70.62	64.78	59.95	55.86	52.26
other	100.00	100.00	100.00	100.00	100.00	100.00	100.00	100.00	100.00	100.00	100.00
Training											
vocational	100.00	95.36	100.71	81.46	80.66	75.40	70.62	64.78	59.95	55.86	52.26
technical	100.00	95.36	100.71	81.46	80.66	75.40	70.62	64.78	59.95	55.86	52.26
university/college	100.00	94.48	99.91	80.92	80.22	75.09	70.43	66.19	62.58	59.12	55.49
postgraduate	100.00	100.00	100.00	100.00	100.00	100.00	100.00	100.00	100.00	100.00	100.00
other	100.00	100.00	100.00	100.00	100.00	100.00	100.00	100.00	100.00	100.00	100.00
E&T Total	100.00	94.99	98.58	82.30	81.03	76.27	71.93	67.63	64.12	61.04	58.09
Plan scenario											
Education											
pre-school	100.00	104.55	126.56	107.89	109.47	103.59	99.23	95.02	92.08	89.80	87.62
primary	100.00	95.78	103.99	84.56	83.54	77.66	72.04	66.81	62.71	59.23	55.97
lower secondary	100.00	106.72	122.18	100.71	100.02	97.55	99.94	102.37	106.11	110.69	115.52
upper secondary	100.00	109.76	126.81	104.15	104.88	98.87	93.25	87.92	83.90	80.57	77.41
other	100.00	100.00	100.00	100.00	100.00	100.00	100.00	100.00	100.00	100.00	100.00
Training											
vocational	100.00	105.56	124.40	109.91	116.03	116.36	116.77	117.15	118.94	121.53	124.23
technical	100.00	94.37	99.42	80.18	79.02	73.39	68.13	63.23	59.39	56.14	53.09
university/college	100.00	118.63	129.33	110.73	112.21	106.64	98.20	90.41	84.23	78.98	74.09
postgraduate	100.00	100.00	100.00	100.00	100.00	100.00	100.00	100.00	100.00	100.00	100.00
other	100.00	100.00	100.00	100.00	100.00	100.00	100.00	100.00	100.00	100.00	100.00
E&T Total	100.00	102.67	112.71	96.19	96.15	92.15	89.01	86.11	84.27	83.02	81.97

Source: MOF and VEFSS Team

REFERENCES

GENERAL

Anh, T., J. Knodel, Le Huong and Tran Thi Thanh Thuy. 1995. "Education in Vietnam: Trends and Differentials." Research Report No. 96-359. Population Studies Center, University of Michigan. December.

ADB (Asian Development Bank). 1994. *General Secondary Education in the Socialist Republic of Vietnam.* Manila. October.

____. 1995. *Socialist Republic of Vietnam, Secondary Education Development Project.* Draft Final Report. Manila. February.

Agrawal, N., D. Lindauer and Walton, M. 1996. "Involving Workers in East Asian Growth." (Draft). Regional perspectives on *World Development Report 1995.* The World Bank, East Asia and Pacific Region, Country Department 3, Washington, D.C.

Benavot, A. and D. Kamens. 1989. "The Curricular Content of Primary Education in Developing Countries." Policy, Planning and Research Working Paper 237. The World Bank, Population and Human Resources Department, Washington, D.C.

Bernard, D.C. and Le Thac Can. 1995. "Vietnam System of Education." In T. Neville Postlethwaite, ed., *International Encyclopedia of National Systems of Education.* Oxford: Pergamon.

Byron, R. and E.Q. Manolato. 1990. "Returns to Education in China." *Economic Development and Cultural Change* 38 (4): 783-796.

Chau, T.N. 1996. "Vietnam: Performance of the Educational System." Background paper for the Vietnam Education Finance Sector study (VEFSS). International Institute of Education Planning, Paris.

Cheng, P.W.-H. 1995. *Education Finance in Taipei, China.* Manila, ADB.

Dang Ba Lam. 1996. *Education and Training in Vietnam and its Development Orientations up to 2010.* Hanoi.

Elley, W. 1992. *How in the World Do Students Read?* International Association for the Evaluation of Educational Achievement (IEA), The Hague.

Fong, M. 1994. "Poverty and Ethnic Minorities in Vietnam." ESP Discussion Paper Series 49. World Bank, Education and Social Policy Department, Washington, D.C.

Gallup, J. 1995. "The Economic Value of Children in Vietnam." Paper presented at a Seminar on Aging, Development, and Population, North Conference Facility, Institutes of Economics and Sociology, Hanoi, December 15.

Gerver, T. 1995. *The Third Wave of Privatization: Privatization of Social Services in Developing Countries - Higher Education, First Steps.* Washington, D.C.

Glewwe, P. and H.A. Patrinos. 1996. "The Role of the Private Sector in Education in Vietnam: Evidence from the Vietnam Living Standards Survey, 1992-93." Background paper for the Vietnam Education Finance Sector study (VEFSS). The World Bank, Policy Research Department and Human Development Department, Washington, D.C.

Glewwe, P. and H. Jacoby. 1996. "School Enrollment and Completion in Vietnam: An Investigation of Recent Trends." In David Dollar, Paul Glewwe, and Jenny Litvack, eds., *Household Welfare and Vietnam's Transition to the Market Economy* (forthcoming).

Gregory, R.G. and Xin Meng. 1995. "Wage Determination and Occupational Attainment in the Rural Industrial Sector of China." *Journal of Comparative Economics* 21: 353-374.

Haveman, R.H. and B.L. Wolfe. 1984. "Schooling and Economic well-being: The Role of Nonmarket Effects." *Journal of Human Resources* 19: 377-407.

Hiebert, M. 1993. *The Far Eastern Economic Review.* "Wage Revolution: Vietnam Makes Salaries Reflect Responsibilities." September 28.

International Labour Organization (ILO). 1994. *Vietnam: Labour and Social Issues in a Transition Economy.* ILO East Asia Multidisciplinary Advisory Team (ILO/EASMAT), ILO Regional Office for Asia and the Pacific Region, Bangkok.

Jamison, D. and J. van der Gaag. 1987. "Education and Earnings in the People's Republic of China." *Economics of Education Review* 6 (2): 161-166.

Johnstone, J.N. 1982. "Three useful but often forgotten education system indicators." In *Socio-economic Planning Sciences* 16 (4). London.

Kaneko, M. 1995. *Financing Education in Japan.* ADB, Manila.

Korea Education Development Institute (KEDI). 1994. *Educational Indicators in Korea.* Seoul.

Lapointe, A., N. Mead and J. Askew. 1992. *Learning Science.* Educational Testing Service (ETS), Princeton.

Lindauer, D. and J. Haughton. 1996. "Economic Growth and the Labor Market." In D. Dapice, J. Haughton, and D. Perkins, eds., *In Search of the Dragon's Trail: Economic Reform in Vietnam.* Cambridge: Harvard University Press (forthcoming).

Lockheed, M., D. Jamison and L. Lau. 1980. "Farmer Education and Farm Efficiency: A Survey." *Economic Development and Cultural Change* 29: 37-76.

Lockheed, M., A. Verspoor et al. 1991. *Improving Primary Education in Developing Countries.* World Bank Publication. Oxford: Oxford University Press.

Low, L. 1995. *Education Financing in HPAEs: Singapore Case.* ADB, Manila.

McGurn, W. 1996. *The Far Eastern Economic Review.* "English in Asia: Money Talks." March 21.

McKay, R. 1995. *Performance Indicators for Higher Education Resource Allocation.* The World Bank, Washington, D.C.

Meng, X. 1995. "The Role of Education in Wage Determination in China's Rural Industrial Sector." *Education Economics* 3(3): 235-248.

Mincer, J. 1974. *Schooling, Experience and Earnings.* New York: National Bureau of Economic Research.

Mingat, A. 1995. "Towards Improving Our Understanding of High-performing Asian Economies in the Education Sector." IREDU; CNRS and University of Dijon..

Moock, P.R. 1994. "Agricultural Productivity and Education." In *International Encyclopedia of Education,* Second Edition, 1:244-54. Oxford: Pergamon Press.

Norlund, I. 1993. "The Creation of a Labour Market in Vietnam: Legal Framework and Practices." In C.A. Thayer and D.G. Marr, eds., *Vietnam and the Rule of Law* (Political and Social Change Monograph 19). Australian National University, Research School of Pacific Studies, Department of Political and Social Change, Canberra.

Orazem, P. and M. Vodopivec. 1995. "Winners and Losers in Transition: Returns to Education, Experience, and Gender in Slovenia." *World Bank Economic Review* 9(2): 201-230.

Paik, S.-J. 1995. *Education Financing in Korea: Its Development, Current Issues and Policy Directions.* ADB, Manila.

Psacharopoulos, G. 1981. "Returns to Education: An Updated International Comparison." *Comparative Education* 17(3): 321-41.

_____. 1994. "Returns to Investment in Education: A Global Update." *World Development* 22(9): 1325-1343.

_____. 1996. "RR Manual: A Program to Estimate the Rate of Return to Investment in Education." The World Bank, Human Development Department, Washington, D.C.

Robitaille, D. and R. Garden. 1988. *The IEA Study of Mathematics.* Oxford: Pergamon Press.

Ronnås, P. 1992. "Employment Generation Through Private Entrepreneurship in Vietnam." Geneva: SIDA/ILO-ARTEP.

Ronnås, P. and O. Sjöberg. 1995. "Economic Reform, Employment and Labour Market Policy in Vietnam." Labour Market Paper 9, Employment Department, International Labour Office, Geneva.

Rorris, A. and K. Evans. 1994. "Towards Universalized Primary Education in Vietnam." UNICEF, Hanoi.

Schleischer, A. and J. Yip. 1994. *Indicators of Between-Schools Differences in Reading Achievement.* IEA, The Hague.

Schultz, T.W. 1961. "Investments in Human Capital." *American Economic Review* 51: 1-17. March.

Socialist Republic of Vietnam. 1994a. General Statistical Office. *Guideline for the Implementation of Censuses and Sample Surveys in Education.* Hanoi.

_____. 1994b. State Planning Committee and General Statistical Office. *Vietnam Living Standards Survey: 1992-1993.* Hanoi.

_____. 1995a. Chamber of Commerce and Industry, and Ministry of Education and Training. *EDUKASIA 95: Market Brief.* Hanoi.

_____. 1995b. Ministry of Education and Training. *Developing and Improving the Quality and Efficiency of Non-Public Education.* Hanoi.

_____. 1995c. State Planning Committee. *Public Investment Programme.* Hanoi. September.

_____. 1995d. General Statistical Office. *Questionnaires of Multi-objective Household Surveys.* Hanoi.

_____. 1995e. Report of the Government of Vietnam to Sectoral Aid Coordination Meeting on Education. Hanoi.

_____. 1995f. Ministry of Education and Training. *Statistical Data on Education and Training 1981-1990.* Educational Management Information Office. Hanoi.

_____. 1995g. Ministry of Education and Training. *Statistical Data on Education and Training 1945-1995.* Educational Management Information Office. Hanoi.

_____. 1995h. General Statistical Office. *Statistical Yearbook 1994.* Statistical Publishing House. Hanoi.

_____. 1995i. Ministry of Education and Training and The World Bank. *Vietnam Higher Education Institutional Finance Survey.* Hanoi.

_____. 1996a. Ministry of Education and Training, National Institute for Educational Development, with Shobhana Sosale. "Financial Operations and Unit Costs of Higher Education in Vietnam: A Descriptive Analysis of the Vietnam Survey of Higher Education Institutions, 1995-96." Background paper for VEFSS and proposed higher education operation in Vietnam. Hanoi.

_____. 1996b. Ministry of Education and Training, National Institute for Educational Development, with Nguyen X. Nguyen. "Internal Efficiency of Higher Education in Vietnam: An Analysis of Economies of Scale and Economies of Scope, 1993-95." Background paper for VEFSS and proposed higher education operation in Vietnam. Hanoi.

____. 1996c. Ministry of Education and Training, National Institute for Educational Development, with M. Woodhall. "Managing Resources and Finances of Higher Education." Background paper for VEFSS and proposed higher education operation in Vietnam. Hanoi.

____. 1996d. Ministry of Labor, Invalids and Social Affairs with C. Sakellariou. "Vietnam Higher Education Tracer Study: Discussion of Analytical Results." Background Paper for VEFSS Higher Education Graduate Tracer Study. Hanoi.

____. 1996e. Government Statistical Office and Asian Development Bank. *Vietnam Social Sector Survey.* Hanoi.

Sosale, S. and M. Woodhall. 1996. "Higher Education Student Loan Scheme." Background paper for VEFSS and proposed higher education operation in Vietnam. Hanoi.

Stroup, R. and M.B. Hargrove. 1969. "Earnings and Education in Rural South Vietnam." *Journal of Human Resources* 4 (2): 215-225.

The Saigon Times. 1995. "Doi Moi's Challenge." October 7-13.

The Economist. 1996. "The Search for the Asian Manager." March 9.

Tan, J.-P. and A. Mingat. 1992. *Education in Asia: A Comparative Study on the Cost and Financing.* The World Bank, Regional and Sectoral Studies, Washington, D.C.

Toan, Vu Van et al. 1994. "Issues of Using Labour Force in Rural Areas of Vietnam." In Vietnam Living Standards Survey Topical Papers using Vietnam Living Standards Survey (Project VIE/90/007). Hanoi.

United Nations Development Programme (UNDP), UNESCO, UNICEF and World Bank. 1990. *Final Report - World Conference on Education for All: Meeting Basic Learning Needs."* World Conference on Education for All. 5 -9 March. Jomtien, Thailand.

United Nations Development Programme (UNDP). 1995. *Development Co-operation Report for Vietnam.* 1994 Report. Hanoi.

United Nations Educational, Scientific and Cultural Organization (UNESCO)/UNDP. 1992a.. "Education Sector Review and Human Resources Sector Analysis."

____. 1992b. "Vietnam Education and Human Resources Sector Analysis, Synthesis Report." Hanoi.

____. 1992c. "Vietnam Education and Human Resources Sector Analysis, Final Report." Hanoi.

United Nations. 1995. *Poverty Elimination in Vietnam.* Hanoi.

Van, Dang Nghiem, Chu Thai Son, and Luu Hung. 1993. *Ethnic Minorities in Vietnam.* Hanoi: The Gioi Publishers.

VEFSS. 1996a. Report of VEFSS Working Group on Education Statistics. Ministry of Education and Training. Hanoi.

____. 1996b. Report of VEFSS Working Group on Labor Market Linkages. Ministry of Labor, Invalids and Social Affairs. Hanoi.

____. 1996c. Report of VEFSS Working Group on Private Sector Development. Ministry of Education and Training. Hanoi.

____. 1996d. Report of VEFSS Working Group on Public Finance. Ministry of Finance. Hanoi.

Vu, Tu Lap and C. Taillard. (1994). *An Atlas of Vietnam.* Reclus.

Wolfe, B.L. 1995. "External Benefits of Education." In M. Carnoy, ed., "*International Encyclopedia of Economics of Education* (Second Edition). Oxford: Pergamon Press.

World Bank. 1993a. *The East Asian Miracle: Economic Growth and Public Policy.* New York: Oxford University Press.

____. 1993b. *Vietnam: Transition to the Market: An Economic Report* (Report No. 11902-VN). East Asia and the Pacific Region, Country Department 1, Washington, D.C.

____. 1994. *"Higher Education: The Lessons of Experience.* Washington, D.C.

____. 1995a. *Priorities and Strategies for Education: A World Bank Review.* Washington, D.C.

____. 1995b. *Vietnam: Economic Report on Industrialization and Industrial Policy* (Report No. 14645-VN). East Asia and the Pacific Region, Country Department 1, Washington, D.C.

____. 1995c. *Vietnam: Poverty Assessment and Strategy* (Report No. 13442-VN). East Asia and the Pacific Region, Country Department 1, Washington, D.C.

____. 1995d. *World Development Indicators 1996.* New York: Oxford University Press.

____. 1995e. *World Development Report 1995.* New York: Oxford University Press.

____. 1996. *Vietnam: Fiscal Decentralization and the Delivery of Rural Services* (Draft Report No. 15745 VN). East Asia and the Pacific Region, Country Department 1, Washington, D.C.

Xie, Yu and E. Hannum. 1996. "Regional Variations in Earnings Inequality in Reform-era Urban China." *American Journal of Sociology* 101(4): 950-992.

LEGAL REGULATIONS GOVERNING EDUCATION AND TRAINING IN VIETNAM

Resolution of the Sixth CPV Congress, Hanoi, 1986.

Resolution of the 4th Plenum of the Party Central Committee (7th Tenure), organized in February 1992, on the "Continuation of Education and Training."

Decision 255/CT, dated August 31, 1991, of the Council of Ministers on the Reorganization and Rearrangement of Schools in the National Education System.

Circular 53/TT, dated December 17, 1991, of MOET on Guidelines of Restructuring Pre-school, General and Professional Education.

Decree 90/CP, dated November 24, 1993 of the Government on the Structure of the National Education System, the System of Degrees and Certificates for Education and Training in Vietnam.

Government Instruction No. 347/KTTH, January 21, 1995.

Joint Ministerial Circular on Guidance for Tuition Fees for Public Basic Education, Ministry of Education and Training and Ministry of Finance, No. 14/TT-LB, September 4, 1993.

Decision 1245/QD, dated September 11, 1991 of the Minister of MOET on the Regulations   Governing Operations of Family Crèches and Kindergartens; Private Crèches and Kindergartens.

Decision 1447/QD dated June 2, 1994 of the Minister of MOET on the Regulations Governing Operations of Early Childhood Schools and Classes.

Decision 1932/QD dated August 20, 1991 of the Minister of MOET on the Regulations Governing Operations of Semi-public Schools.

Decision 1931/QD dated August 20, 1991 of the Minister of MOET on the Regulations Governing Operations of People-founded Schools.

Draft Regulations Governing Operations of People-founded Vocational Schools.

Decision 1670/QD dated November 26, 1989 on the Provisional Regulations Governing Operations and Management of Private Vocational Classes.

Decision 697/QD dated March 20, 1991 of the Minister of MOET on the Regulations Governing Operations of Private Vocational Schools.

Decision 04/QD dated January 3, 1994 of the Minister of MOET on Provisional Regulations Governing Semi-public Universities.

Decision 196/QD dated January 21, 1994 of the Minister of MOET on Provisional Regulations Governing People-founded Universities.

Distributors of World Bank Publications

Prices and credit terms vary from country to country. Consult your local distributor before placing an order.

ARGENTINA
Oficina del Libro Internacional
Av. Cordoba 1877
1120 Buenos Aires
Tel: (54 1) 815-8354
Fax: (54 1) 815-8156

AUSTRALIA, FIJI, PAPUA NEW GUINEA, SOLOMON ISLANDS, VANUATU, AND WESTERN SAMOA
D.A. Information Services
648 Whitehorse Road
Mitcham 3132
Victoria
Tel: (61) 3 9210 7777
Fax: (61) 3 9210 7788
E-mail: service@dadirect.com.au
URL: http://www.dadirect.com.au

AUSTRIA
Gerold and Co.
Weihburggasse 26
A-1011 Wien
Tel: (43 1) 512-47-31-0
Fax: (43 1) 512-47-31-29
URL: http://www.gerold.co/at.online

BANGLADESH
Micro Industries Development
Assistance Society (MIDAS)
House 5, Road 16
Dhanmondi R/Area
Dhaka 1209
Tel: (880 2) 326427
Fax: (880 2) 811188

BELGIUM
Jean De Lannoy
Av. du Roi 202
1060 Brussels
Tel: (32 2) 538-5169
Fax: (32 2) 538-0841

BRAZIL
Publicacões Tecnicas Internacionais Ltda.
Rua Peixoto Gomide, 209
01409 Sao Paulo, SP.
Tel: (55 11) 259-6644
Fax: (55 11) 258-6990
E-mail: postmaster@pti.uol.br
URL: http://www.uol.br

CANADA
Renouf Publishing Co. Ltd.
5369 Canotek Road
Ottawa, Ontario K1J 9J3
Tel: (613) 745-2665
Fax: (613) 745-7660
E-mail: order.dept@renoufbooks.com
URL: http://www.renoufbooks.com

CHINA
China Financial & Economic
Publishing House
8, Da Fo Si Dong Jie
Beijing
Tel: (86 10) 6333-8257
Fax: (86 10) 6401-7365

Infoenlace Ltda.
Carrera 6 No. 51-21
Apartado Aereo 34270
Santafé de Bogotá, D.C.
Tel: (57 1) 285-2798
Fax: (57 1) 285-2798

COTE D'IVOIRE
Center d'Edition et de Diffusion Africaines (CEDA)
04 B.P. 541
Abidjan 04
Tel: (225) 24 6510; 24 6511
Fax: (225) 25 0567

CYPRUS
Center for Applied Research
Cyprus College
6, Diogenes Street, Engomi
P.O. Box 2006
Nicosia
Tel: (357 2) 44-1730
Fax: (357 2) 46-2051

CZECH REPUBLIC
National Information Center
prodejna, Konviktska 5
CS - 113 57 Prague 1
Tel: (42 2) 2422-9433
Fax: (42 2) 2422-1484
URL: http://www.nis.cz/

DENMARK
SamfundsLitteratur
Rosenoerns Allé 11
DK-1970 Frederiksberg C
Tel: (45 31) 351942
Fax: (45 31) 357822

ECUADOR
Libri Mundi
Libreria Internacional
P.O. Box 17-01-3029
Juan Leon Mera 851
Quito
Tel: (593 2) 521-606; (593 2) 544-185
Fax: (593 2) 504-209
E-mail: librimu1@librimundi.com.ec
E-mail: librimu2@librimundi.com.ec

EGYPT, ARAB REPUBLIC OF
Al Ahram Distribution Agency
Al Galaa Street
Cairo
Tel: (20 2) 578-6083
Fax: (20 2) 578-6833

The Middle East Observer
41, Sherif Street
Cairo
Tel: (20 2) 393-9732
Fax: (20 2) 393-9732

FINLAND
Akateeminen Kirjakauppa
P.O. Box 128
FIN-00101 Helsinki
Tel: (358 0) 121 4418
Fax: (358 0) 121-4435
E-mail: akatilaus@stockmann.fi
URL: http://www.akateeminen.com/

FRANCE
World Bank Publications
66, avenue d'Iéna
75116 Paris
Tel: (33 1) 40-69-30-56/57
Fax: (33 1) 40-69-30-68

UNO-Verlag
Poppelsdorfer Allee 55
53115 Bonn
Tel: (49 228) 949020
Fax: (49 228) 217492
URL: http://www.uno-verlag.de
E-mail: unoverlag@aol.com

GREECE
Papasotiriou S.A.
35, Stoumara Str.
106 82 Athens
Tel: (30 1) 364-1826
Fax: (30 1) 364-8254

HAITI
Culture Diffusion
5, Rue Capois
C.P. 257
Port-au-Prince
Tel: (509) 23 9260
Fax: (509) 23 4858

HONG KONG, MACAO
Asia 2000 Ltd.
Sales & Circulation Department
Seabird House, unit 1101-02
22-28 Wyndham Street, Central
Hong Kong
Tel: (852) 2530-1409
Fax: (852) 2526-1107
E-mail: sales@asia2000.com.hk
URL: http://www.asia2000.com.hk

HUNGARY
Euro Info Service
Margitszgeti Europa Haz
H-1138 Budapest
Tel: (36 1) 111 6061
Fax: (36 1) 302 5035
E-mail: euroinfo@mail.matav.hu

INDIA
Allied Publishers Ltd.
751 Mount Road
Madras - 600 002
Tel: (91 44) 852-3938
Fax: (91 44) 852-0649

INDONESIA
Pt. Indira Limited
Jalan Borobudur 20
P.O. Box 181
Jakarta 10320
Tel: (62 21) 390-4290
Fax: (62 21) 390-4289

IRAN
Ketab Sara Co. Publishers
Khaled Eslamboli Ave., 6th Street
Delafrooz Alley No. 8
P.O. Box 15745-733
Tehran 15117
Tel: (98 21) 8717819; 8716104
Fax: (98 21) 8712479
E-mail: ketab-sara@neda.net.ir

Kowkab Publishers
P.O. Box 19575-511
Tehran
Tel: (98 21) 258-3723
Fax: (98 21) 258-3723

IRELAND
Government Supplies Agency
Oifig an tSoláthair
4-5 Harcourt Road
Dublin 2
Tel: (353 1) 661-3111
Fax: (353 1) 475-2670

Yozmot Literature Ltd.
P.O. Box 56055
3 Yohanan Hasandar Street
Tel Aviv 61560
Tel: (972 3) 5285-397
Fax: (972 3) 5285-397

R.O.Y. International
PO Box 13056
Tel Aviv 61130
Tel: (972 3) 5461423
Fax: (972 3) 5461442
E-mail: royil@netvision.net.il

Palestinian Authority/Middle East
Index Information Services
P.O.B. 19502 Jerusalem
Tel: (972 2) 6271219
Fax: (972 2) 6271634

ITALY
Licosa Commissionaria Sansoni SPA
Via Duca Di Calabria, 1/1
Casella Postale 552
50125 Firenze
Tel: (55) 645-415
Fax: (55) 641-257
E-mail: licosa@ftbcc.it
URL: http://www.ftbcc.it/licosa

JAMAICA
Ian Randle Publishers Ltd.
206 Old Hope Road, Kingston 6
Tel: 876-927-2085
Fax: 876-977-0243
E-mail: irpl@colis.com

JAPAN
Eastern Book Service
3-13 Hongo 3-chome, Bunkyo-ku
Tokyo 113
Tel: (81 3) 3818-0861
Fax: (81 3) 3818-0864
E-mail: orders@svt-ebs.co.jp
URL: http://www.bekkoame.or.jp/~svt-ebs

KENYA
Africa Book Service (E.A.) Ltd.
Quaran House, Mfangano Street
P.O. Box 45245
Nairobi
Tel: (254 2) 223 641
Fax: (254 2) 330 272

KOREA, REPUBLIC OF
Daejon Trading Co. Ltd.
P.O. Box 34, Youida, 706 Seoun Bldg
44-6 Youido-Dong, Yeongchengpo-Ku
Seoul
Tel: (82 2) 785-1631/4
Fax: (82 2) 784-0315

MALAYSIA
University of Malaya Cooperative
Bookshop, Limited
P.O. Box 1127
Jalan Pantai Baru
59700 Kuala Lumpur
Tel: (60 3) 756-5000
Fax: (60 3) 755-4424

MEXICO
INFOTEC
Av. San Fernando No. 37
Col. Toriello Guerra
14050 Mexico, D.F.
Tel: (52 5) 624-2800
Fax: (52 5) 624-2822
E-mail: infotec@rtn.net.mx
URL: http://rtn.net.mx

Everest Media International Services (P) Ltd.
GPO Box 5443
Kathmandu
Tel: (977 1) 472 152
Fax: (977 1) 224 431

NETHERLANDS
De Lindeboom/InOr-Publikaties
P.O. Box 202, 7480 AE Haaksbergen
Tel: (31 53) 574-0004
Fax: (31 53) 572-9296
E-mail: lindeboo@worldonline.nl
URL: http://www.worldonline.nl/~lindeboo

NEW ZEALAND
EBSCO NZ Ltd.
Private Mail Bag 99914
New Market
Auckland
Tel: (64 9) 524-8119
Fax: (64 9) 524-8067

NIGERIA
University Press Limited
Three Crowns Building Jericho
Private Mail Bag 5095
Ibadan
Tel: (234 22) 41-1356
Fax: (234 22) 41-2056

NORWAY
NIC Info A/S
Book Department, Postboks 6512 Etterstad
N-0606 Oslo
Tel: (47 22) 97-4500
Fax: (47 22) 97-4545

PAKISTAN
Mirza Book Agency
65, Shahrah-e-Quaid-e-Azam
Lahore 54000
Tel: (92 42) 735 3601
Fax: (92 42) 576 3714

Oxford University Press
5 Bangalore Town
Sharae Faisal
PO Box 13033
Karachi-75350
Tel: (92 21) 446307
Fax: (92 21) 4547640
E-mail: ouppak@TheOffice.net

Pak Book Corporation
Aziz Chambers 21, Queen's Road
Lahore
Tel: (92 42) 636 3222; 636 0885
Fax: (92 42) 636 2328
E-mail: pbc@brain.net.pk

PERU
Editorial Desarrollo SA
Apartado 3824, Lima 1
Tel: (51 14) 285380
Fax: (51 14) 286628

PHILIPPINES
International Booksource Center Inc.
1127-A Antipolo St. Barangay, Venezuela
Makati City
Tel: (63 2) 896 6501; 6505; 6507
Fax: (63 2) 896 1741

POLAND
International Publishing Service
Ul. Piekna 31/37
00-677 Warzawa
Tel: (48 2) 628-6089
Fax: (48 2) 621-7255
E-mail: books%ips@ikp.atm.com.pl
URL: http://www.ipscg.waw.pl/ips/export/

Livraria Portugal
Apartado 2681, Rua Do Carmo 70-74
1200 Lisbon
Tel: (1) 347-4982
Fax: (1) 347-0264

ROMANIA
Compani De Librarii Bucuresti S.A.
Str. Lipscani no. 26, sector 3
Bucharest
Tel: (40 1) 613 9645
Fax: (40 1) 312 4000

RUSSIAN FEDERATION
Isdatelstvo <Ves Mir>
9a, Lolpachniy Pereulok
Moscow 101831
Tel: (7 095) 917 87 49
Fax: (7 095) 917 92 59

SINGAPORE, TAIWAN, MYANMAR, BRUNEI
Asahgate Publishing Asia Pacific Pte. Ltd.
41 Kallang Pudding Road #04-03
Golden Wheel Building
Singapore 349316
Tel: (65) 741-5166
Fax: (65) 742-9356
E-mail: ashgate@asianconnect.com

SLOVENIA
Gospodarski Vestnik Publishing Group
Dunajska cesta 5
1000 Ljubljana
Tel: (386 61) 133 83 47; 132 12 30
Fax: (386 61) 133 80 30
E-mail: repansekj@gvestnik.si

SOUTH AFRICA, BOTSWANA
For single titles:
Oxford University Press Southern Africa
Vasco Boulevard, Goodwood
P.O. Box 12119, N1 City 7463
Cape Town
Tel: (27 21) 595 4400
Fax: (27 21) 595 4430
E-mail: oxford@oup.co.za

For subscription orders:
International Subscription Service
P.O. Box 41095
Craighall
Johannesburg 2024
Tel: (27 11) 880-1448
Fax: (27 11) 880-6248
E-mail: iss@is.co.za

SPAIN
Mundi-Prensa Libros, S.A.
Castello 37
28001 Madrid
Tel: (34 1) 431-3399
Fax: (34 1) 575-3998
E-mail: libreria@mundiprensa.es
URL: http://www.mundiprensa.es/

Mundi-Prensa Barcelona
Consell de Cent, 391
08009 Barcelona
Tel: (34 3) 488-3492
Fax: (34 3) 487-7659
E-mail: barcelona@mundiprensa.es

SRI LANKA, THE MALDIVES
Lake House Bookshop
100, Sir Chittampalam Gardiner Mawatha
Colombo 2
Tel: (94 1) 32105
Fax: (94 1) 432104
E-mail: LHL@sri.lanka.net

Wennergren-Williams AB
P.O. Box 1305
S-171 25 Solna
Tel: (46 8) 705-97-50
Fax: (46 8) 27-00-71
E-mail: mail@wwi.se

SWITZERLAND
Librairie Payot Service Institutionnel
Côtes-de-Montbenon 30
1002 Lausanne
Tel: (41 21) 341-3229
Fax: (41 21) 341-3235

ADECO Van Diemen EditionsTechniques
Ch. de Lacuez 41
CH1807 Blonay
Tel: (41 21) 943 2673
Fax: (41 21) 943 3605

THAILAND
Central Books Distribution
306 Silom Road
Bangkok 10500
Tel: (66 2) 235-5400
Fax: (66 2) 237-8321

TRINIDAD & TOBAGO, AND THE CARRIBBEAN
Systematics Studies Unit
9 Watts Street
Curepe
Trinidad, West Indies
Tel: (809) 662-5654
Fax: (809) 662-5654
E-mail: tobe@trinidad.net

UGANDA
Gustro Ltd.
PO Box 9997, Madhvani Building
Plot 16/4 Jinja Rd.
Kampala
Tel: (256 41) 251 467
Fax: (256 41) 251 468
E-mail: gus@swiftuganda.com

UNITED KINGDOM
Microinfo Ltd.
P.O. Box 3, Alton, Hampshire GU34 2PG
England
Tel: (44 1420) 86848
Fax: (44 1420) 89889
E-mail: wbank@ukminfo.demon.co.uk
URL: http://www.microinfo.co.uk

VENEZUELA
Tecni-Ciencia Libros, S.A.
Centro Cuidad Comercial Tamanco
Nivel C2, Caracas
Tel: (58 2) 959 5547; 5035; 0016
Fax: (58 2) 959 5636

ZAMBIA
University Bookshop, University of Zambia
Great East Road Campus
P.O. Box 32379
Lusaka
Tel: (260 1) 252 576
Fax: (260 1) 253 952

ZIMBABWE
Longman Zimbabwe (Pvt.)Ltd.
Tourle Road, Ardbennie
Southerton
Harare
Tel: (263 4) 6216617
Fax: (263 4) 621670